HOPPING HOME BACKWARDS
Body Intelligence and Movement Play

Published by JABADAO Centre for Movement Studies
Branch House 18 Branch Road Armley Leeds LS12 3AQ
Phone: 0113 231 0650 Fax: 0113 263 5863
email: info@jabadao.org Internet: www.jabadao.org

This book was made possible by a grant from the National Lottery through the Arts Council of England.

HOPPING HOME BACKWARDS

Body Intelligence and Movement Play

Penny Greenland

Penny Greenland is Director of JABADAO Centre for Movement Studies. She was educated in Ipswich and took a degree in Drama (and dance) at Hull University before working as a dancer, actor, teacher and director in community and education settings. In 1985 she founded JABADAO to search for 'a new role for dancers in our society'. She lives in Suffolk with her partner, who is a community musician, her two children and an improbable number of animals. She was awarded an MBE in the 2001 New Years Honour list.

Acknowledgements

Many people have influenced and supported the writing of this book.

Over the years I have worked with many movement specialists who have shared their ideas and approaches, both in practical workshops and in late night conversations. I have also read everything I can lay my hands on about movement, the body and learning thus gathering more ideas from people I have never met. I am a magpie: in pursuit of different ways of bringing the body back into everyday life I have taken precious jewels of ideas and tucked them into my own nest. So it is important to acknowledge all those people whose ideas are woven into this Movement Play.

Thanks to:
  Sandy Crichton: for being a thoroughly wonderful colleague, challenging and supporting in
      just the right ways ... and for coming up with a lot of the practical ideas in the last section
  Kedzie Penfield: for teaching me so much about movement
  Tina Stromsted: for teaching me about Authentic Movement and providing such clarity
      through the 'I Saw ... I Felt ... I Imagined' structure
  Bette Lamont: for teaching me about Developmental Movement

And books don't get written without a lot of support from people around. It's a family affair ...

Thanks to:
  Pat Pickavance, Linda Neary and Wendy Leveson, the women from JABADAO for their
      constant support and encouragement
  Phil Vaughan, from JABADAO, for his tireless commitment to making it look right
  My children, Abi and Rowan, who have brought my attention to things I would never have
      noticed without them
  My parents, Dickie and Audrey Greenland, for managing to equip me with enough courage
      and tenacity to muddle through
  Ian Heywood, my partner, for his friendship throughout and for putting up with me
      monopolising the kitchen table for so long

  And to Nick Greenland, my brother, for helping me turn all these words and ideas into
      something coherent.

Introduction

This book has three aims.

Firstly, to make movement more visible as a primary means through which human beings learn. Just as that vase on our sideboard becomes invisible through familiarity, and it takes a visitor to the house to help us notice and appreciate it again, so this book is intended to nudge you into noticing movement afresh.

Secondly, to suggest a new way of addressing movement in Early Years settings, one that focuses on the development of 'body intelligence' - the ability to acquire knowledge and understanding by direct participation with sensation, feeling, movement and image.

Thirdly, to persuade those of you who are anxious about working in movement that it is something you are already doing in your everyday dealings with children, and to offer practical help so that you can use movement more, and to better effect.

It is a book that you can use in many ways. If you like ideas, or you need persuading about the significance of movement in learning, section one is for you. If you want to set up movement activities tomorrow, but need some more practical activities to do with children, turn to section three. If you want to develop a consistent approach to movement in the curriculum, section two explores a framework for learning.

The ideas in this book are designed to support the ways in which you organise movement play with children. Since the author cannot know the children you work with, or the conditions you work in, it is your responsibility to assess what is, and what is not, appropriate in your particular circumstances.

About this book

SECTION ONE
Body Intelligence and Movement Play

takes a theoretical look at the importance of movement in early years learning and suggests that 'body intelligence' (learning by direct perception through the senses) is a necessary accompaniment to learning through the intellect.

SECTION TWO
Organising Movement Play

offers practical ways in which anyone can support Movement Play with young children and suggests a framework for extending learning.

SECTION THREE
Practical Activities

provides ideas for things to do with babies and children up to eight years old.

Back to the Body ...

In some chapters you will find sections called Back to the Body. These are designed to enable you to explore the ideas contained within the book in your own body (sensation, feelings, movement, visual image and inner sound) as well as through your rational intellect. The extent to which you feel comfortable in doing this may well depend on where you are reading this book. If you're on an Inter City 125 you may feel compromised. If you are in the privacy of your own home it may be easier. Perhaps you will read them and wait before you feel like giving them a go. However, I urge you to dip into them at some stage, even if you are not, and never have been, a 'mover'. Don't worry if they make little sense the first time. If you find you really don't like the suggestions just notice your dislike, move on, and perhaps come back to them at a later stage.

The Back to the Body sections are intended for you, the adult reader. They are not suggestions for ways to work with children - you'll find those at the back.

Contents

SECTION I

Body Intelligence
and
Movement Play

1

The significance of movement

Human beings are essentially playful, physical beings

who need to live in their whole bodies,

not just their heads.

When I arrived at the school gate to pick up my two young children they pleaded with me to let some friends come round to play. They had it all planned - who they would ask, what they would play, and what I would make them for tea. Somehow I ended up with five children, ranging from four to eleven, skipping, leaping, bounding and dawdling home with me. I rapidly became the human equivalent of a sheepdog - rounding up the stragglers, calling the front runners back and paying particular attention to Jack, the four year old, to prevent him from being run over. No matter what attractive alternative I suggested, he couldn't be dissuaded from hopping home ... backwards ... with his eyes shut.

Whilst the others, released from a day of sitting down, shifted rapidly between running, jumping, shuffling and swinging round lamp posts, he remained single-mindedly focused on his peculiar backwards progression. In the beginning he was in grave danger of falling off the pavement into the path of on-coming traffic, but by the half way mark he seemed to realise the importance of staying away from the kerb. He remained, however, entirely oblivious of other innocent pavement users, threatening to leap backwards into them if I didn't grab him and stick him to the spot, still bouncing up and down, while they dashed uneasily past. Once or twice he cracked his eyes open a little in order to lunge for my sleeve to steady himself, then he used the support of my (rapidly weakening) frame to perform an extra large backwards bound. I was, needless to say, completely exhausted when we finally arrived back home.

There was nothing very unusual about this murderous journey. Jack was doing what all young children do - exploring his world through movement. This kind of spontaneous exploration is as natural to a young child as breathing. It is also the kind of behaviour that we adults often squash - which isn't surprising since we seldom have the energy to withstand so much activity. But perhaps there is another more fundamental reason we squash it. If we really believed that children learnt valuable things through spontaneous movement play surely we would find ways of supporting it more readily. After all, most activities with young children are pretty exhausting. Teaching them to read isn't always easy, but we persevere because we know that reading will be vitally important all through their lives and anything less than our best effort would be unfair.

When those of us who are now teachers, nursery workers and childminders were children, most of us were rewarded for sitting still - 'sitting nicely' - and told off for wriggling, jiggling and exploring our capacity to move freely and spontaneously. We heard many versions of 'walk properly and save your hopping for the playground' or 'stop being silly'. We came to understand that movement play was what we did as a break from learning, a necessary release that would allow us to do more sitting still and more serious learning once we returned to the classroom. Gradually, during our young lives, we learnt that spontaneous movement play had limited worth in the eyes of the adults around us and that stillness and physical containment were infinitely preferable. In this way, for many of us, spontaneous exploration in movement has become inextricably linked with 'being silly' and with feeling embarrassed. Without clear reasons for behaving differently, we are likely to pass this on to the children we care for - even if we don't mean to.

As Jack hopped home, it would certainly have been easier for me to say 'Stop being silly, Jack. Walk properly!' I would have arrived home less tired and I could have avoided the disapproving stares of the other pavement-users. But there are compelling reasons for supporting, rather then shutting down, this kind of behaviour. However, these reasons are currently hidden in isolated pockets of esoteric research which use complicated psychological or physiological vocabulary and highly technical movement observation data. They seem to have little to do with ordinary playgroup workers, childminders, teachers, nursery workers, mums and dads.

This book is intended to present some of the same ideas and theories in a very ordinary way, because they refer to a very ordinary part of our lives. It draws on the substantial body of knowledge developed by neurologists, movement analysts, movement and dance therapists, body workers and dancers from across the world. It also draws on the experience and stories of many ordinary people who use movement in ordinary ways. Jack's journey is a starting point for looking at the layers of experience and learning that interweave as a person engages in spontaneous movement play; a place to begin the search for reasons to support behaviour we currently squash.

Jack chose to hop backwards. We could equally well look at other choices made by other children: Sally spinning slowly in the front room; Ali rocking backwards and forwards as he sits on the carpet at Nursery; Kate sliding on her back along the kitchen floor; or Winston rolling down the hill in the park. Are these children taking time out from meaningful experience or is there serious purpose in this kind of movement play? If there is, what might it be? In trying to answer this question - in unpacking the kinds of experience that these children might be engaging with - I don't want to suggest they are consciously trying to learn something. They may be oblivious, or only dimly aware, of the greater part of their sensations, feelings and movements. But are they learning important things within this unconscious behaviour? If the behaviour became conscious, could they learn more or better?

Pleasure and enjoyment

Before we analyse the layers of experience that Jack may have been engaged in that day, guessing at which aspect of his life and learning was uppermost, it is important to remember that he might simply have been driven by the desire to have fun - to enjoy his physicality, revel in a flood of physical sensations. And there's nothing wrong with that.

Practising a specific physical skill

Perhaps Jack wants to practice hopping because he has just discovered how to, and he'd like to get better at it. Perhaps he is good on his right leg and wants to practice on his left. Perhaps his friends have been boasting about their hopping and he wants to catch up. Perhaps he is very aware of what he is doing and glad of the sustained and supported opportunity to practice. If all goes well, maybe next time I take him home he will be practising skipping backwards, or galloping sideways, or ... I can hardly wait.

Developing general physical knowledge

Maybe Jack is involved in a wider physical exploration. Perhaps hopping home backwards makes new demands on his ability to balance and coordinate, requiring him to find new ways of organising his muscles and bones, nerves, organs, fluids and thought processes. And as he searches for these new ways, perhaps he learns what he can and can't do, what is easy, what is difficult; what requires my help, what he can achieve on his own. He may be engaged in a kind of physical problem-solving for which hopping is just one possible starting point among many.

Developing kinesthetic awareness

Maybe Jack is developing his ability to pick up the signals from his body. Perhaps, by focusing on the sensations he has, he is learning to receive more detailed and differentiated information from his nervous system. Perhaps he begins by noticing something of the whole experience of hopping, then focuses in on parts of that whole - the sensation in his feet as they travel backwards rather than forwards, the slight pull up the back of his legs, the tilt of his pelvis, or the pushing of his thigh bones into his hip sockets as he takes each hop. Perhaps he is building up his ability to take his attention, at will, to different parts of his bodily-felt experience.

Back to the Body...

As you read this, using your intellectual skills to reflect upon movement and the body, stop for a moment and dip into movement instead. Shut your eyes, just as Jack did, take your attention to your body and gradually begin to notice what is there - the sensations, feelings (emotions), tiny movements, or urges to move, that lap and over-lap at the edges of your awareness. Let your attention wander through the many different things you might notice - get interested and spend time in your body. Don't rush. Reject any desire to make things happen. This is a matter of being, not doing - and the transition from doing to being, from intellect to body, must take its own time. Throughout this book there will be opportunities to dip into bodily-felt experience and the same thing always applies. Let the body take its own time. Don't worry about interruptions from the intellect (What's for tea? Have I done the shopping? What am I doing? Is anyone watching? What's the point? and so on). They're bound to be there; let them roll around with everything else that you experience and try not to let them get the upper hand.

When you've had enough, reverse the process and make the transition back to your intellect. This may take a minute or two depending on how deeply you moved into the kinesthetic state. To some people this is a bit like waking up, it takes each of us a different amount of time.

A thought in his head (reasoning)

Jack may have a rational thought, a mental process, a question that he is exploring with the help of his body. Perhaps he is thinking about what his teacher said to him as they stood at the painting table earlier, and using the movement to focus his attention. Perhaps he is wondering how long it is possible to stay in the air with a single hop, or how high it is possible to rise. Perhaps he is gathering more information from his body to augment a rational process of discovery.

A thought in his body (direct perception)

Or perhaps the thought, or question, comes from his body. Perhaps the hop *is* the thought. We are familiar with mental thoughts that arrive by way of words or pictures and seem to locate themselves in our heads. But 'body thoughts' that arrive by way of wriggles and jiggles, postures and gestures, sensations and feelings, are less recognisable. Perhaps Jack's hopping is a body thought - an idea or discovery that forms in sensation, feeling and movement.

A definition

The Oxford English Dictionary defines thought as 'an idea or piece of reasoning produced by thinking' and 'sober reflection or consideration'. Thinking is 'using thought or rational judgment'. I define body thought as 'an idea or discovery produced by focused sensing, feeling and moving'. Body thinking is not another sort of reasoning; it is a process of discovering knowledge by means of direct perception through the senses.

It is Friday morning and I am watching an experienced movement practitioner preparing to lead a day on movement observation with a group of ten fiercely intelligent women, all hungry for knowledge. She sets up her tapes, her teaching materials, and retreats to the corner of the room to 'check in'. At the start of a day about movement and the body, she starts by listening in to her own body-thoughts.

There is nothing mystical about this; she is at work. This is an ordinary part of her preparation. She has her eyes shut and she is concentrating hard. She begins to move. Her arms and hands are involved in small flickings and staccato wriggles. The little movements have no particular pattern at the moment. On her face (eyes shut) there is a look of inquiry. She is listening intently to the movement and wondering what it will become. Her eyes screw up in a gesture of concentration. She is following the movement, not directing it. Finally, a clear gesture becomes evident. Her hands rise and fall in opposition to one another. She opens her eyes and watches as her hands tip and tilt.

'Ah!', she says. 'Look at this. Up and down. Up and down. Perhaps we're in for some conflict today'.

As it happens it is a bit of a roller coaster. No open conflict but a lots of grumbles, plenty of hilarity and several challenges to her leadership.

This experienced movement worker has developed learning strategies that enable her to make use of her body thoughts alongside her rational thoughts. She has a heightened ability to make use of sense and sensibility, bodily-felt experience, as part of problem solving and learning. Perhaps Jack, at his young age, is building up his ability to make use of his sensibility so that one day, given the tools, he too might be able to make focused use of it.

Sensibility: openness to sensory stimuli. From the Middle English sensibilitas ... sensible. Oxford English Dictionary.

Back to the body...

Listen in to your body (eyes open or shut, whichever is easier) and trawl through the sensations, feelings and tiny movements you find there. See what calls for your attention. Do you sense the desire to move any part of you? If you do, let the movement grow of its own accord; avoid thinking out what to do. You don't have to know what is going to happen next, or why it is happening. This is a body thought. Follow it. Take a ride on the flow of movement that occurs. Let your rational thoughts be occupied by noticing what is happening, not by directing operations. Small children often do this quite naturally. Since it has grown unfamiliar to most adults, a dim and distant memory, it may take a while before you have any sense of following the movement. You may feel as if your head is continually directing.

A sound in his inner hearing

Perhaps, as he hops, Jack can hear some sound in his inner hearing; perhaps each hop heightens that sound, or changes it. Perhaps it is an unfolding conversation remembered from the day, or something entirely new. Perhaps he is listening to the traffic as it passes, or the sound of my feet, or my voice (as it rises and falls with anxiety and increasing exhaustion). Perhaps he is learning to match intonation with meaning. Inside his body there may be a whole world of sound that is all his own.

(Although this isn't strictly a bodily-felt experience - not sensation, feeling or movement - it is an important part of his inner world that is available when he listens in. I include it, therefore, as one of the possible experiences prompted by movement play.)

Visual imagination

Perhaps Jack is oblivious of all but the pictures in his mind's eye. Perhaps he doesn't have to wait until he gets home to put on a video; perhaps he has a personalised screen behind his eyes that shows his own movies - patterns in light and dark, images from his imagination. Perhaps he sees colours, red when he lands and green as he hops through the air. Perhaps the thud of his landing shoots a picture of a dog into his mind; it is impossible to know without asking, and Jack may not be able to articulate what is going on for him yet. For some people, adults as well as children, this is a very strong accompaniment to movement. It is as if the movement sparks off and supports the working of their internal visual imagination. Like sound, it is an important aspect of experience prompted by attention to bodily-felt experience.

Joey (5) was sitting on the sofa with his fists pressed into his eyes. Every so often he pushed them a little harder into his eye sockets and turned them back and forth. Squeaks and squawks were escaping from his mouth. 'If I wait and watch', he said, 'the green swipes across the whole screen and then it turns red. Then if I twist my hands the American army marches across.'

Back to the Body...

When you were a child did you ever put your fists in your eye sockets and rub them around until you got vivid bursts of colour and vibrant, bursting firework patterns in front of your eyes? Maybe this exercise is a little like that ... only you don't need the fists. Shut your eyes and gently ease into movement. If you are sitting, perhaps you might roll your head comfortably around. Or start with your shoulders. If you are happy to be on the floor, find some movement that feels right lying down. It doesn't have to be big or strenuous. As you slide into the movement, away from the flood of thoughts in your intellect, become aware of any pictures or images that form in your mind's eye. Keep moving - don't get so caught up with trying to find the pictures that you freeze. Keep your attention with the movement and let (rather than make) the pictures arrive. Some people experience the bursts of colour and pattern I mentioned earlier. Others have a more distant, yet no less present, flow of pictures - like a waking dream. Some have little or no connection between movement and their visual imagination because their connections lie elsewhere.

Learning about how the world works

Let's suppose that Jack's backwards hopping prompts a memory of something he has seen earlier in the day - his cat backing nervously away from his rabbit, a state of affairs that made his mother laugh and one that he couldn't make sense of at the time. Becoming the cat, and finding out what it might feel like to go backwards, is one way he can try to understand what happened. Through direct perception he is able to fill a gap in his understanding which reason alone cannot help him with.

Back to the body...

Watch colleagues, friends or strangers as they talk about a problem or an issue. Watch the postures and gestures that accompany their words; see if you can spot where their bodies are offering information that complements and extends their verbal reasoning. Sometimes you can see bodies get there 'first' and words catch up a bit later. Sometimes bodies seem to have a point of view which is then contradicted by words; the classic example is someone who nods their head but says 'no'. See if you can spot an example like this, where you feel that a body says one thing and the intellect another.

Using his movement memory

Jack may be remembering the last time he hopped and comparing it to this experience. Perhaps it gives him different pictures and feelings this time. Perhaps he tries to work his way back to the exact same feelings he had before. Perhaps he is developing his ability to compare and contrast, using his own direct experience as the stuff of his inquiry.

Understanding emotions

Walking backwards with your eyes shut has built in dangers, especially near a busy road. Despite my feeling that Jack is completely oblivious of the potential danger, maybe this is the whole point. Perhaps Jack is getting to know the sensations that pass through his body as he takes these risks - anxiety, fear, discomfort, exhilaration, independence. Perhaps he is taking himself to an edge to see what it's like.

Back to the body...

Sit in a chair which has no arms. Sit squarely on it, balanced and steady. Shut your eyes and notice the sensations, feelings and movement impulses. Now lean over to one side and keep leaning towards the point where you are bound to fall off the chair. Focus carefully on all the different stages as you get closer to the point of overbalancing. Heighten your awareness of the sensations, the feelings, the movement, the visual images, the thoughts as you move closer to that point. Which bit of this little journey do you like? Not like? Look forward to? Skip over? Do you let yourself fall ... or not? Do it again and again seeing what changes each time, what patterns emerge. Do it even when you are bored. What does that feel like?

Developmental movement patterns

Hopping is one of twenty six significant developmental patterns, identified by the Gesell Institute, that occur as a natural part of development between conception and the age of about eight or nine. Their function is to promote the process of neurological organisation through which 'an organism, subject to environmental forces, achieves the potential in its genetic endowment' (*Edward B Le Winn*. Human Neurological Organisation)

Given the narrow frame of reference in our culture we tend to think of movement development being solely about our future ability to move with ease and co-ordination. We help a baby of a few months to strengthen its limbs so that it will crawl; we encourage a baby of eight months to crawl so it will walk soon; we support a baby that can take a few steps so that it will go quickly and confidently on to walking, running, hopping and skipping. As soon as a baby arrives at one stage, we hurry them onto the next. However, in addition to these important physical developments, the movement patterns also prepare the brain and the nervous system for many other kinds of learning. Babies and young children need to take their time in each stage to ensure good foundations for many aspects of future learning.

The patterns, some based in sensory stimulation and some in simple repetitive movements, are not complicated. They are things that you will have seen over and over again - seemingly random movements of head, arms and legs as babies lie on their backs or their tummies; crawling on their bellies; crawling on all fours. Through these patterns babies develop many functions: smooth neck rotation and smooth tracking of the eyes (that will enable them to read easily along a line in a book); eyes that converge on the same point (without which words might move on the page or the world around might appear rather hazy and unpredictable); and an accurate sense of pain, heat, cold, hunger (without which it is hard to empathise with others, or take enough care of yourself). These patterns even affect the mechanisms by which children develop control of rage and other big emotions.

The step by step development of the nervous system, prompted both by sensory experiences and early movement patterns, is a vital foundation for learning. Without full neurological organisation a child cannot learn certain things, no matter how sympathetically they are presented. It doesn't matter how much work we do to develop curriculums and different ways of delivering them, if children cannot process what we offer. It is as if the developmental movement patterns create the roadways that will enable us to travel to a variety of places in future. Without the roads we cannot get there (or, at best, the journey will be bumpy).

In the past, things 'neurological' have been left to health experts in the belief that there is nothing a non-medical person can do. Developmental movement specialists work with a detailed understanding of each of the twenty six patterns, working with people who have significant gaps in their development. However, within learning settings, it is important to use a broad understanding of the patterns to support what children do naturally. Without this understanding we are often left dealing with symptoms rather than causes. Where a child has difficulty reading, we address the problem by offering more reading practice. Where a child has difficulty taking care of themselves and others, displaying various forms of 'challenging behaviour' and 'attention deficit', we offer a great deal of discipline, some behaviour modification work and, in desperation, drugs.

In other words, we address the symptoms not the cause.

But we can make a significant difference by working with the developmental movement patterns - the body's own 'software' that programmes the brain for future functioning. There is excellent evidence to show that going back to missed movement patterns can fill many of the gaps. It is much better, of course, if the gaps don't occur in the first place. The implications for Early Years settings are considerable.

Neurological organisation is a natural phenomenon that doesn't have to be taught, but it does need to be supported. Most of us miss some parts of the patterns. Life isn't perfect and many factors get in our way - a cold or scratchy floor just when we need to creep along on our bellies; being held by loving arms when we need to be down on the floor; being put in baby walkers, baby bouncers, car seats and bouncing chairs when we need to be crawling; sitting still at nursery and school when we need to be running, rolling, spinning and hopping; and some of us are even restricted by the instruction to keep tiny designer clothes and shoes clean. All these things affect our ability to complete the patterns. Increasingly in Western culture, the need to make babies fit in with adult lives disrupts the natural progress of these patterns. Almost all of us will have missed enough of the patterns to reduce some part of our potential, but for most of us it won't be a significant problem. We can live with the fact that we read a bit slowly; we're probably even rather pleased that our pain threshold is quite high. For some, however, the gaps will have a significant effect on the whole of their lives.

Animals, if they miss or skimp on a developmental stage, return to it at a later point in their life, and play and play and play until they have made up the lost ground. Human beings don't, partly because we don't understand the need and partly because of our drive to go forwards, not backwards. It is common practice that if a child can walk adults discourage them from crawling again. 'You're a big girl now - you don't have to crawl'. We resist the spiralling, self-directed learning path that might enable a child to make up lost ground. Where there is a specific problem (hyperactivity, behaviour disorders, memory problems, speech, balance problems, reading difficulties, difficulty in sleeping and many other issues) taking a child back through missed or disorganised developmental stages can have a significant effect. In the United States, Temple Fay, Glen Doman, Carl Delacarto and Florence Scott (amongst others) have developed a body of knowledge which illuminates the ways in which these patterns influence our learning. (See 'A Missing Piece of the Jigsaw', *JABADAO Publications*, for further information.)

So perhaps Jack, quite unconsciously, is getting on with the business of programming his brain for future functioning as he hops home backwards.

Sharing his experience

When I next saw Jack's mother I mentioned this journey home. She laughed and commiserated with me. Apparently, when he got home he showed her something of what he had been doing. 'Look at me Mummy! Look at me!' and he performed a bit of his backwards hopping with his eyes shut (thus necessitating more sheepdog behaviour from her). This short piece of movement was rich in meaning for Jack. In repeating something of it for his mum he was making a leap from inward exploration to sharing his experience with someone else. He was involved in representing his experience, giving it a form so that it could be both his own and separate from him.

Jack's mum said he was obsessed with hopping, and also with travelling backwards in all kinds of ways - walking, slithering, jumping and crawling. Whatever Jack was exploring that day was certainly important to him. His intense concentration and unswerving attention made that perfectly obvious. His focus may have been on the physical experience, the feeling experience, the imaginative experience, his emotions, his thoughts or the sense of himself as a whole. It could also have been on something unimaginable to me, no less important for my inability to conceive of it.

Maturing and Learning

When we support young children's development we are concerned with two things: maturing and learning. Maturing is the natural process of development that is set in motion from the moment of conception, neurological development being just one aspect. We don't have to teach children to mature, but we must make sure we know enough to ensure support for the natural process as it occurs.

Children's learning is also a natural process - they learn whether we interfere or not - but we *extend* their learning by helping them to develop specific understanding, dispositions, attitudes and skills (to use the jargon) and by encouraging them to develop learning strategies that will bring these things together in practical and useful ways throughout their lives.

Movement Play, the new approach to physical education for early years settings outlined in this book, addresses both of these processes - by supporting the developmental movement patterns (creating the roadways) and by helping a child to notice, value and make use of the information that comes from inside their body (journey along particular roads). But before we can address either of these we need to realise how much we get in children's way, how much we (unconsciously) undermine learning in the body.

A baby will complete the significant developmental movement patterns if they have the right conditions. A child of two or three is generally happy to move spontaneously when invited; to play in movement, to communicate through movement games and to explore their world through their senses. A child of eight in our culture is probably happy to play in movement privately, but will be filled with discomfort if an adult watches. Very few adults even remember that this kind of spontaneous exploration, this embodiment of their experience, is possible. The process of disembodiment is not a natural one, but a cultural one; we disembody our children through the signs and messages we give off and through the environments we create. We educate our children to cut off from their bodies, to live in their heads, to reject their innate capacity for a whole-hearted physical existence.

The remainder of this book, therefore, is about ways in which we can reclaim an ordinary human potential that has been lost along the way - our ability to learn through movement, to solve problems using information from our bodies (as well as our intellects) and our capacity to live in our whole bodies (not just our heads). The opportunity to complete the developmental movement patterns is vital. Direct perception is as deep a source of knowing and understanding as our capacity for intellectual reasoning. It is a child's entitlement to be body literate as well as verbally literate, and our job to help them. The starting point is to make more conscious many of the body processes that we have relegated to the back of our minds.

Footnote

This book is about the body as a source for learning through direct perception. But it is not the only source. My own experience is of working with movement and the body. A visual artist may work in very similar ways through colour, painting, making and marking. A musician may use sound, rhythm and melody. An actor may use improvisation, voice work and visualisation. Movement Play is just one way of encouraging children to visit their inner, non-verbal experience and to make use of it as part of a range of resources to cope with what life will throw at them in the future.

2

Body Intelligence

'I want to ... be all that I am capable of becoming.'

Katherine Mansfield

I have been impossibly busy for weeks, hanging on to the stuff of ordinary life by the skin of my teeth. There are overflowing cupboards and piles of ironing trail in my wake, but I am sticking doggedly to my task. Each day I get 'faster and stiffer', as my friend would say, but I stay focused. Then, one morning, in a bit of a pickle about how I will get through this patch, I remember to consult my body. 'OK body! What have you got to say? How do you propose that we get through the next few days?'

I stand in the kitchen and wait ... I let my attention sink down into my body, sink into the darkness ... and I wait.

Pop! My eyes close and I am spinning, spinning fast enough to mean that my arms fly out to the sides with the centrifugal force. Very soon I am impossibly dizzy, but I don't open my eyes. I am dizzy in the dark.

Intellect says, 'OK ... so we're in a flat spin ... I know that. But what can we do about it?'.

Body keeps on spinning.

Intellect says, 'Stop! Find out how to stop. That's what we need to do. Find out how we can go from spinning and stiff, to open and relaxed'.

Body goes on turning, turning.

Then (taking intellect by surprise) slows and stops, rocking from side to side quite vigorously, feet bumping down onto the floor. Bump, bump, bump ... the feel of the floor under my feet ... bump, bump, bump.

Head says, 'OK ... now ... find out how to stop'.
Body goes on rocking ... feet go on bumping. Nothing changes.
Then my head falls to one side and slips backwards, hanging uncomfortably down.
Intellect says, 'Ah ha! Cut off at the neck - a desire to slip into the unconscious state. I know the theory. So that's where we're going ... what we need is a good sleep, more dreams, less attention to reality'.

Body keeps on rocking, head hangs. Rocking ... rocking ... rocking.

'O come on!', says intellect. 'Come on! We'll be at it all day at this rate ... OK, I get the message. Body takes time. Intellect always wants instant answer. Go on then ...'

Body keeps on rocking ... rocking.
Feet go bump ... bump. Neck strains and pulls.
I feel so relieved to be moving.

Then suddenly I take a huge breath in and out. Of course! I haven't really breathed for days. Intellect says, 'O yes!'.
And I breathe and breathe for a bit. Breathe and breathe ...
Then Pop! My jaw falls open. It must have been clamped for weeks. It feels so good to let it hang. Saliva collecting in my throat.

Lolling ... bumping ... hanging ...
'O dear!', says intellect. 'Now we're not spinning, but we're lolling about with our jaw

hanging open. It feels great but it won't get the work done. How can we create a balance between frantic spinning, and lolling about with our mouth open?'

Body lolls some more. Lolls and lolls. Lolls ... lolls ... lolls.

'So ...?', says intellect searching for meaning. 'What we need is time, eh? But we haven't got any!'

The bumping is gentler now. The rocking steadier. My head comes round to the front and hangs.
'Lift your head', says intellect. 'Come on. We're getting there ...'
Swaying ... breathing ... jaw loose ... head lifting ... breathing.
'Will this lead to walking?', says intellect brightly.
Breathing ... swaying ... sighing ... smiling.

Heels lift with each step. Knees begin to bend. Shoulders twist around and I am off, flop-stepping round in a circle. 'Ah ha! It's back to a circle, but going slower. Not spinning. We've made real progress. Now, if we could just find out how to go in something other than a circle, we'd really be getting somewhere.'

Circling ... circling. Jaw falls open ... head reaches round and the circling stops. I am meandering around the room with flip-flopping feet ... easy ... easy ... neck unwinding ... jaw on the move ... breathing great breaths. I come to rest at my chair, flop into it and sway saggily from side to side. This is a sway from long ago ... a sway I know of old. A sway of comfort and relief. A sway. I have a sway in me, where before there was none ... I am on the move.

'Well', says intellect, 'that feels good.'
And all morning I sit at the computer swaying ... typing ... swaying ... typing. Easing out a little. Working and breathing.
And I feel good.

One of the disadvantages of being part of a culture that emphasises the intellect and rational thought is that we have become distanced from the lived experience of our bodies, and no longer recognise the learning processes that stem from the body itself. In order to redress this imbalance we need to start by exploring what it is like to *be* a body rather than to *have* a body. The best way of doing this, of course, is in our body. How do we learn French? By speaking French. How do we develop a better backhand? By practising backhands - not by reading about them in books. However, since we are re-examining body processes in the midst of a culture dominated by the intellect, it is important to do so in reasoned ways, as well as in movement. 'Thinking about things' has a credibility in our culture that 'moving things' doesn't.

As we embark upon thinking-about-moving it is important to note, however, that the very act of reading about the body maintains the distance, upholds this dominant culture. 'We do not know very much about our body until we move it ... knowledge of our body is to a great extent dependent upon our actions.' (*Deane Juhan* Job's Body: A Handbook for Bodyworkers)

The last chapter outlined many ways in which Jack may have been engaging with, and learning in, the lived experience of his body. In the story above, 'the intellect' moved over and made space for 'the body' to address a specific problem. In this chapter I want to call this basic human capacity 'body intelligence' - not in order to make a scientifically provable claim for a new way of understanding human learning, but in order to make visible something quite ordinary that has got lost. In some ways this is jumping on a bandwagon. 'Emotional intelligence' has been much talked about recently; the phrase has given us a simple way of drawing a line round a particular subject area in order to take a fresh look at it. I hope the phrase 'body intelligence' will help us to do something similar around the subject of our bodies and learning. I think of it as a kind of flag flapping brightly over a particular territory, drawing attention to the ground below. This chapter, therefore, will offer a definition of 'body intelligence' and consider some of the ways that body thinking is different from intellectual thinking.

A definition

Before I attempt a definition, I want to borrow from Howard Gardner, the writer of many books on education, creativity and the nature of intelligence who suggests that intelligence is merely 'a convenient way of labelling some phenomena that may well (but may well not) exist'. So too, 'body intelligence'.

Gardner describes intelligence as the 'collection of ways that human beings use to resolve problems or difficulties, create an effective product, or create problems and then solve them thus enabling the acquisition of new knowledge'. Body intelligence is one of these ways. It is the capacity we have to acquire knowledge and come to understanding by direct participation with sensation, feeling and movement, and to make this knowledge and understanding useful.

Ultimately, it isn't separate from other ways we think; our body intelligence weaves in and out of, and is continuous with, all our other intelligences. But since this capacity is largely ignored, it is important to separate it out, in order to get to know it afresh and to recognise that it has equal significance in human learning.

> Rowan (5) asks me to watch him in the tall, thin, spindly elm tree at the edge of the garden. He has been practising for half an hour he says, and now he can get right to the top and down again. He runs ahead to prepare.
>
> By the time I arrive he is nearly at the top of the tree and I feel very anxious. It is a poor specimen with twiggy branches no more that an inch in diameter - surely they can't take his weight. 'Are you ready?', he calls and seeing me in place below, starts to swing from branch to branch along a well-rehearsed route. Some of the branches are outside his reach, so he swings, lets go with both hands, falls a little, and catches the next one - for all the world like a small monkey. As he descends he builds a rhythm: swing, fall, grasp, look for the next branch. And then again: swing, fall, grasp, look for the next branch. 'I'm perfectly safe', he says when he sees my face. 'My body knows how to do it. I won't fall.'

Single intelligence or multiple intelligences?

A century ago, psychologists trying to define intelligence and devise tests to measure it, believed that intelligence was a single, general capacity for conceptualising and problem solving. In the sixties a number of psychologists began to doubt this and suggested that intelligence has many aspects. However, they differed about the way these fitted together. Some separated out general, verbal and numerical intelligence, holding them to be more important; others suggested that all the aspects are equal and intertwined.

More recently, Howard Gardner has identified seven separate intelligences: linguistic, musical, logical-mathematical, visual-spatial, bodily-kinesthetic and two personal intelligences (internal: access to one's own feeling life, and external: the ability to make distinctions, and influence things, in the external environment). His analysis and separation of these intelligences is based on many forms of scientific evidence and he offers them not as hard and fast facts but as as 'fictions - at most, useful fictions - for discussing processes and abilities that (like all life) are continuous with one another'.

When I first began using the term 'body intelligence' I discovered that educationalists who were familiar with Howard Gardner's theories leapt to the conclusion that I was talking about the single intelligence that he calls 'bodily-kinesthetic' - the capacity for using the body in highly refined ways for both functional and expressive purposes. But 'body intelligence' is involved in all aspects of our capacity for intelligent action; it isn't another term for just one of them.

'As she talked, her motions were quite intense and linear except for a fleeting moment when one of her hands quickly tossed a sweater she was carrying into the air, throwing it in a nonchalant manner off to the side. When I encouraged her to notice this unexpected tossing of the sweater and to focus awareness on the quality of her movement, she seemed shy but curious to find out what the motion was about. She picked up the sweater again and seemed to enjoy flippantly tossing it into the air. After she did this a number of times, I asked her to stand up and try the same movement but this time without the sweater.

She stood up and experimented with quick, indirect flicking movements as she threw her arms, legs, head and finally her whole body in unexpected spurts in many directions around the room. She laughed, thoroughly enjoying the sense of abandon and freedom. But suddenly she stopped and said sheepishly, 'I don't know what I'm doing. It feels great but could it be helpful?'. I suggested she follow this mysterious dance just a bit longer and let its meaning reveal itself to her.

I joined the dance as we threw ourselves in quick lunges and spurts around the room. As we moved I asked her to make a face to go along with the quality of movements and possibly add sounds as well. Her eyes opened wide as she made strong blowing sounds with her mouth. I then asked her to 'see' what she was doing, or tell a story about it. She said she saw and felt the image of a great wind goddess who was following the winds of fate! She continued to unfold the story of the wind goddess as she tumbled and turned in an unexpected and thrilling way.

When she finally landed on the ground, smiling, she said she realised that this was the quality she needed in dealing with her everyday problems; not so much organising, analysing or planning life but instead - living it spontaneously!'

Contact Quarterly. *Amy Mindell.*

In making this new fiction I am concerned to show that we learn things in our body, through direct perception; that by engaging with our bodily-felt experience we can learn things we couldn't otherwise learn and know things we couldn't otherwise know. The body is a site for learning that is separate from the intellect, providing us with a parallel source of information and understanding. To make full use of its capacity we must first learn to let our intellect stand back and observe, rather than direct. Body thought must be allowed its equal existence, alongside intellectual thought. When the two strands have equal weight we can move on and ask how this kind of thinking can supplement, interweave or become continuous with intellectual thought.

A car stops beside us as we walk along the pavement. A man leans out and says, 'Can you tell me how to get to Felixstowe from here?'. This isn't easy. It might be just across the river as the crow flies, but it's miles round by the road and I'm not good at directions. I go rigid and consult the non-existent map in my head. 'It's left at the crossroads', I say limply, pointing right. (My gesture is correct ... my words are wrong.) 'I mean right', I correct myself. 'Then you go under the ... the ...' (I've lost the words but my body makes a helpful suggestion; my left arm forms an arch and my right hand darts backwards and forward underneath it.) '... under the ... the bridge', I say, finding the words. 'Then it's a long straight road with ...' (At this point I am bending my knees up and down rather oddly.) '... with a nasty humpback bridge. Then ...' (My right index finger and thumb make a circle which I wave around in front of me.) '... then ... what next ... um ... yes, there's a large roundabout with trees in the middle.' (My right hand swerves to the right.) 'Take the right turn which will be signed to the Town Centre and you're there.' I slap both thighs triumphantly.

'Do you realise that you did a sort of absurd ballet throughout that', says my companion uncomfortably as the car pulls away ...

An aside: on separating mind and body

In separating the learning processes that happen in our body from those that happen in our intellect it might at first seem as if I am prolonging an unhelpful mind-body split. I believe the problem is that in our culture we confuse 'mind' with 'intellect'. Mind is defined in the Concise Oxford English Dictionary as 'the seat of awareness, thought, volition and feeling'. Surely this is not just an intellectual process, but a bodily-felt one as well?

I want to separate intellect from body in order first to emphasise the different capacities of each, but ultimately to bring them back together again as a single, continuous source of experience and learning. The mind is the unifying factor: a river fed by two tributaries, drawing both on our capacity for rational thought and our capacity for discovery by direct perception through the senses. If we are going to plan learning environments that build lively minds, we must give equal weight to both developing the intellect and listening to the body. Movement Play is the area of the curriculum in which to focus rigorously on the development of direct perception, not in order to dismiss the intellect, but to reaffirm the experience of the body as an equal and intertwined way of learning. We will do this only if we focus afresh on the lived experience of the body, get to know its richness and complexity, and discover the contribution it makes to an intelligent living of our lives. Our anatomical development underpins the impossibility of making a division.

'Skin and brain develop from exactly the same primitive cells. Depending upon how you look at it, the skin is the outer surface of the brain, or the brain is the deepest layer of the skin. Surface and innermost core spring from the same mother tissue, and throughout the life of the organism they function as a single unit, divisible only by dissection or analytical abstraction. Every touch initiates a variety of mental responses,

and nowhere along the line can I draw a sharp distinction between a periphery which purely responds as opposed to a central nervous system which purely thinks.'

Job's Body. *Deane Juhan.*

Emma's mum said, 'Would you like to go to the park, to the swings?'. Emma paused in her activity. She became still, tilting her head on one side and stared upwards in what you might read as a thinking pose. Then she started to hop and shuffle about the room, three hops on the back foot and three on the front, tilting her body backwards and forwards as she went, her hands jiggling by her ears. 'Emma! Stand still and think about what I asked you!'

Could it be that she was thinking? That she thought about it in two ways - in her intellect and in her body.

THINKING IN OUR BODY

If we want to enable children to use their body intelligence we must help them to understand the ways in which they can acquire knowledge, and come to understanding, by direct participation with sensation, feeling, movement and image. We must make the processes involved in body thinking conscious, so that children can use them at will, and with confidence.

We cannot simply use the methods we have developed to support learning through the intellect; we must find new ways that match the pace, rhythm and 'ways' of the body. This means getting to know what is particular about body thinking.

Recognising body thoughts

To have access to our body thoughts we need first to notice them - and then to recognise them. Body thoughts occur in sensation, feeling, movement and image, not areas of our experience that we generally equate with thought and thinking. They become thoughts (rather than a generalised flow of background experience) when we recognise the ways in which they contribute to our understanding of ourselves - our needs, our history, our desires - and we learn to explore them in their own terms. Then, they give us greater access to our own internal lives and a larger pool of information from which to resolve problems and respond to the outside environment.

Identify the bump, bump, bump of feet on the floor as a body thought, and the bump becomes a discovery, a piece of information, to add to many others. We don't have to rationalise: 'the bump means that ... '. We can accept the bump in its own terms and explore it further - in movement and sensation, not in reason.

The process of body thinking

Body thinking is the exploration of an initial body idea through further participation with sensation, movement, feeling and image. If the 'thought' is the bump of the feet on the kitchen floor, the 'thinking' is following that bump to see where it will go: the changing sensation of the soles of the feet on the floor, the changing shape of the rise and fall of the heels, the shift of awareness from heels to knees, the image of a red line rising through the shin bone. This is a circular process of stimulation ... sensation ... movement, which in turn provides further stimulation ... sensation ... movement. Thus the body thinking deepens.

Then the next body thought might slide in - the sudden huge breath that is the next discovery, the next body thought to be followed. The thinking then shifts to the sensation of the muscles as they yield to the intake of breath, the drop of the shoulders that accompanies it and the changing nature of the bump of the feet underneath.

Movement as the basis for body thinking

Movement is the basis of body thinking. If we lie completely motionless we may begin to lose our body image - the sense of our body. Do you remember, as a child, playing that game (or perhaps you still play it) of focusing on the sense that your arms are as long as a mile, or that your head is a million miles from your toes, your fingers as round as balloons, your legs as thin as sticks? This can be triggered by separating sensing from moving. Movement allows us to assimilate the information we receive through our nervous system more accurately than sensing alone. (Which is one of the reasons why many children you know wriggle a lot ... they are supporting their

developing ability to feel themselves in their body, being a body.) It is through a variety of friction, stretching and impact that we build, rebuild and revisit our sense of tactile reality - and movement is the key to them all.

If we want to pursue body thoughts that arise in sensation, or feeling, or image, it is through movement that we can inquire more deeply. As a sensation rises in our awareness, we do not freeze our body, and ask, 'What is this like? Why is it there?'. We move into the sensation, around the sensation, and it is the movement that asks the questions, probes and pries, and gradually reveals the understanding. So too, if we want to find out more about a particular emotion through our body intelligence - we do not freeze our body and ask, 'What is this feeling like?'. We move with the emotion as a focus: the emotion informs our movement and our movement, in turn, informs the emotion. Each affects the other and we discover new information in direct participation with the issue, rather than through reason.

Body thinking is not a linear process. We do not come to a fixed understanding as we might hope to through reasoning. As we move to find out more, we create new sensory information which changes the thing we were exploring. Engaging with body thinking, therefore, means that we are alive to the moment to moment changes that occur within our bodily-felt experience.

Many years ago I was invited to work with a group of people who were studying a variety of therapeutic interventions, whilst also being involved in their own therapeutic process. My job was to introduce movement as a therapeutic tool.

One woman was having an especially difficult time with herself. After a tense tea-break I thought we'd do something quite light and introduced a playful structure for everyone to try. As they moved, I talked - making suggestions for things they might try. In the midst of my suggestions I said in a dancerly way, 'Keep moving ... try not to get stuck ...' and quick as a flash came a deadly voice from the back of the room, 'I've been stuck for years ... and you expect me to change just like that!'.

Later that afternoon, with some trepidation, I offered another structure - find your way into a movement, search out the opposite, then find the journey between. They moved for about an hour. As they spoke about their experiences afterwards, this woman looked somewhat lighter, less weighed down. 'I like that structure', she said, 'I discovered that I'm not as stuck as I thought I was ... there's movement always happening even if I haven't been aware of it ...'

MAKING BODY THINKING USEFUL

Jack used movement unconsciously, to think things out on his way home. I, in my kitchen, used movement consciously, to see if I could find another way of addressing a particular issue. If we are going to make use of our body intelligence to address everyday issues and problems, we need to know how to use it at will - how to switch our focus from intellect to body, or how to let the two work together. We need to be able to listen to bodily-felt experience; to concentrate in ways that will maximise our ability to access body-thoughts; to develop our awareness of sensation in order to nurture those body thoughts, and learn ways to make sense of, and integrate, the body thinking we do into our lives.

Listening to bodily-felt experience

Maureen (30 something) is glowing. She finds it difficult to string a sentence together and keeps stopping to both sigh and laugh. She is trying to explain to the group what she has just experienced. 'It's as if my body is one of those massive ... antennae trained on outer space waiting for ... for signals from ... aliens.' She has been moving with her attention focused on her ability to pick things up kinesthetically, in her body. She pauses and rubs her arm gently, as we used to wipe dust from LP records lest it dulled their quality. 'It's amazing ... I can get so much.' A little while later when the glow has subsided she says, 'But I can't go out there in this state' (indicating the outside world with a busy road and rushing traffic), 'I'd be on overload in seconds'.

This woman's focus has changed so thoroughly from intellect to body that stringing words together has become difficult. She has swapped an intellectual way of being, for a body way. This was her first 'go' at using her 'kinesthetic awareness' and she really allowed herself to indulge in it; her whole attention was caught up with the minute sensations that she noticed almost for the first time. As she gets more practised she will probably move more easily between the two modes, although it always takes time to adjust after a period of deep body listening - since it draws on such a different part of us.

We process a vast amount of information in our bodies, some of it with awareness and some of it without. At any moment we have sensation, feeling, movement, visual images, inner sound and intellectual activity all providing information. In order to make this information useful, we need to take our attention to it, scan, differentiate, prioritise and focus on particular parts. Something of this process happens all the time in our body.

As I sit here writing, grasping for the thoughts and words, I have to be able to remain upright on the chair without putting too much effort into organising my body. I have to adjust my position without taking up too much of my attention. I have to 'let go' of the sensation of the chair against my thighs (slightly hard and uncomfortable) so that I can focus on the writing. (Come to think of it, the cushion has slipped. I'll adjust it then let my attention return to the writing.) Now I need to key-in words on the computer without putting all my attention into the signals of sensation in my fingers. If I couldn't heighten or suppress these simultaneous messages as appropriate, I would be completely overloaded and unable to carry out my desired task. To make use of body intelligence we need to develop the skill of listening, differentiating and prioritising these different aspects of our experience.

(It is this very skill that children so often labelled 'Attention Deficit' seem to lack. Perhaps they are incapable of suppressing one stimulus in favour of another; everything catches their attention - the book in front of them, the label in their jumper, the person coming into the room, the tickle in their socks, the elastic in their pants, the gerbil in the corner, the impulse to jump up and down. Rather than attention deficit, perhaps this is attention overload. No lack of attention here, but a lack of focus. An impossible inner clamour. Working directly with the body, learning the steps that will allow them to filter incoming stimuli, and make choices about how they respond, may help these children to overcome some of their difficulties.)

Back to the body ...

Shut your eyes and imagine you are going up an unfamiliar staircase in the dark, trying to make sure that you don't fall. Focus carefully on the sensations in your body as you imagine using feet and hands as eyes. Pay particularl attention to that feeling of prediction that goes on the second before your foot touches each stair ... as your hand reaches for the wall ... as you try to work out whether this is the top stair, or whether there is another. Notice what it feels like to open up your kinesthetic awareness to this degree. When you have finished roaming around the sensations, feelings and inner experience be sure you pay attention to shutting it down again and returning to your usual ways of sensing and seeing.

Back to the body ...

Now take your attention to your own body. Shut your eyes. Settle in. Notice the things that take your attention. Remember the feeling of alertness you created to make your way up the imaginary stairs. Take time. Let your new alertness roam around all the different sensations, feelings, movements and images you find. Follow your desires as you do so ... move into the sensations, follow your body's interests. Let the degree of sensing you do wax and wane as you need to. Take it easy. Listen. Then reverse the process and let your intellectual thoughts and desires rise in your awareness, have more control over what you do. Restore yourself gently to an open-eyed, quiet alertness to the outside world letting sensation and feeling diminish in your awareness.

Body concentration

When I am teaching movement work with adults it still alarms me that so often, when given the opportunity, participants dive straight for the floor, lie down and close their eyes, and, at most, twitch a little or roll about a bit. I still panic that I have lost them, that they have drifted off, they are not listening to me and are bored. But they are, in fact, concentrating intently on their body experience. I know, because at the end of a piece of moving when they feedback what was going on for them, they are absolutely full of information and insight. They have been concentrating and working very hard.

An important step towards making use of our thoughts - body or intellect - is our ability to concentrate. Concentrating in order to learn through direct perception is wholly different from the kind of concentration we need for reasoning. It requires a heightening of kinesthetic awareness - which is often accompanied by shutting the eyes and 'switching off'. Body concentration often looks like the kind of drifting and dreaming that many of us were told off for at school.

The children are doing activity songs. 'Five little sausages in the pan ... all of a sudden one went BANG!' There is a high level of involvement and delight in the room. Morgan, however, is doing something different. He is slumped back against the leg of the table behind him staring into space. One hand is poised just below his chin and his index finger is bobbing. He is certainly not concentrating on the activity organised by the teacher, but he is concentrating. His concentration lies with his body experience, known only to himself - perhaps on sensation, feeling or movement, or perhaps on visual image or inner sound. His teacher may need to bring him back to their shared activity, but Morgan also needs time to concentrate in this way at some other point in his day. This drifting and dreaming is as significant a part of his learning as anything else we offer.

Supporting body concentration may be challenging for adults who have been schooled to think of concentration as sitting up straight, sitting still, making eye contact. We must rediscover the quality (and depth) of the drifting, dreaming process.

Back to the body...
Think back over any of the movement exercises you have done so far as you have been reading. What would an outsider have seen if they had walked in as you were doing them? Remember the quality of your concentration as you did them; how was this reflected in the way you moved?

Back to the body...
Think back to a time you have seen a young child total engaged 'in a world of their own' and try to remember what their body was doing. Remember times when you have seen children totally absorbed in their wriggles and jiggles to the exclusion of everything else. Try and remember as much as you can about what it looked like. Move, doodle, draw or write to support your remembering.

Back to the body...
Let yourself get absorbed by a wriggle or a jiggle, a writhe or a rocking motion - whatever feels right at

the moment. Notice as much as you can about the sensations, feelings, visual images, memories and stories that might accompany this movement. Doodle, draw or write about it if you want to. Notice the quality of your concentration.

Starting to think (in movement)

Movement is the body's way of thinking; it is important therefore to develop ways of switching this thinking on and off. We can get our thought processes going in different ways: we can give ourselves intellectual prompts, but we can also use movement to activate our direct perception. For some this might be playing with the shapes their body makes and how they feel. For others, it might be focusing on the space around the body, and ways of moving through it. Others still might prompt their thinking process by exploring the quality of their movements. And some might begin a thinking process by playing with the way the body moves - actions, postures and gestures.

Starting to think (in sensation)

But movement doesn't have to be the starting point. The organisation and reproduction of movement doesn't stem, as you might expect, from the motor cortex part of the brain. Our movements are directed by the sensory cortex. When we decide to perform an action we first recall a 'sensory engram' created through past repetitions of that particular movement. We remember (in sensation) what it felt like, then our motor systems reproduce the remembered sequence of sensation laid down in that engram. When we get on a bicycle we don't remember the movements, we remember the sensations that lie 'underneath' the movement. Recreating the sensations causes the movement to occur.

We need to pay equal attention to sensation as well as movement, therefore, if we want to work in depth and detail with the body as a source of learning. Enabling our bodies to dance with internal sensation is every bit as important as learning to read and write. We practice the skills that give us access to our intellectual thought processes. We must also practice tuning into sensation as a route to using our body thinking processes.

Oliver (4) is sitting at the craft table staring into space with his middle undulating backwards and forwards. Every so often he gives a little jerk forward, followed by complete stillness. Sometimes he slumps, then sits taut again and resumes the undulating ... jerk ... stillness sequence. He is not involved in the gluing activity that is happily engaging the other children at the table. After a while he suddenly announces 'I fell off!' to no-one in particular. When I ask him what he fell off he says simply, 'The monkey bars ... I fell off the monkey bars'. It emerges that Oliver was practising how to negotiate the rungs, to keep up with his friend. When we talk about what he learned he says, 'It's here that you do it', and pats his tummy.

Back to the body ...

Shut your eyes and drift back until you can find a strong memory of a physical activity when you were a child. (Take care of yourself; choose the memories you want to work with, not those you don't.) Perhaps being on a swing in the park. Sink into the physical memory until you are able to build the feeling sense of it - the body memory of the sensations that are still held in your muscles, bones, nerves, organs, fluids. Even though you can do this sitting still, don't freeze. Let small movements play through your body as they will. When you have finished you may want to move in a different way, or doodle, draw, write or think back over it as a way of completing it.

Back to the body...

Think back to when you learned to ride a bike. As you replay it in your body memory see if you can remember any of the sensations that underpin the physical task of learning to keep the bike upright. Build up awareness of the sensations in your body that accompany the fantasy task. Then let small movements build up around the memory of the sensations. Doodle, draw, write or move any information you uncover.

Back to the body...

Plan to carry our some simple task, like picking up the newspaper and opening it. Before you do pick it up, practise in your body. Shut your eyes and, in your mind's eye, think through the actions you will have to take. Work through the image in a logical way, then let it settle into your body. Take yourself through the projected activity focusing purely on sensations; then on the movements your body will do (you might like to focus on different systems within your body - bones, muscles, nerves, fluids, organs). Notice any visual images that accompany either exercise. Allow yourself to float between reality and fantasy if this is appropriate; if fantasy ropes lift your arm towards the newspaper, let them help you. Don't feel that it has to be exactly the same each time. Let it move on, change, develop as you go. Finish by carrying out the practical task and gathering any thoughts in movement, doodling, drawing or words if you wish.

Back to the body...

Now repeat the exercise, only this time make the task drawing letters from the alphabet. Involve your whole body in the sensations that accompany the shape making task, not just your hand. Notice the colours that go with letters. All the same, or each different? Notice any preferences; any images that pop into your head or body; any particular wriggles, jiggles and movements that grow from the letters. If you have a safe enough space, and feel comfortable, you might be able to let this internal movement grow into whole body physical movement. After you have moved the shapes, try doodling/drawing the letters or images that you have discovered from each, on large sheets of paper. Pastels or paint are best (rather than felt tips or crayons) since they offer more possibility for texture.

Body memory

Sensation is not only the source of information in the present moment, it is also the source of our body memory. In the intellectual realm, we learn to make good use of memory so that we can store, retrieve and act upon knowledge gained through intellectual means - learn from experience. To develop the capacity to make use of body intelligence we must develop parallel skills that will allow us to make active use of body memory.

Everything that has happened to us throughout our lives is stored in our body - in sensation. Things that we repeat often are stored as 'sensory engrams'; mostly these develop without our conscious effort.

> *Spouse (53) came back across the garden from the office where he had been faxing things to a colleague. 'I couldn't remember the fax number', he said cheerfully, 'but my hand could!'*

Sometimes we work hard to create a sensory engram - practising a piano piece until we can play it

'without thinking about it', for example. At other times, our body memory is triggered accidentally, by sensation and movement.

> *On a training day for community development workers, as we were all engaged in different kinds of moving, one woman found herself doing a kind of arm-swing that leapt out from all the other movements. She repeated it several times, trying to find out what it was about this particular movement that held her interest. Then suddenly it struck her. 'I'm flooded with memories of learning my tables', she said, and laughed. 'Why on earth should that be? Every time I do that swing I'm pitched right back to being about seven - the sights the sounds, the smells, the feelings. Isn't that weird!'*

If we develop the ability to retrieve sensation-memories and movement-memories at will, we can learn from the accumulation of bodily-felt experience that we build up throughout our lives. We can also learn to revisit pieces of experience using sensation or movement as the doorway - the retrieval mechanism.

> *My son (9), fresh from football training, was sitting in the car groaning and gasping in what I thought was an outrageously theatrical fashion. 'I've got cramp in my toe', he squealed. 'Ahhhhhhh!' 'O for goodness sake,' I snapped. 'It's not that bad.' 'It is', he growled between gritted teeth. 'You don't know.'*
>
> *'I've had cramp loads of times', I snapped again. 'Well then, you've forgotten what it's like', he said darkly.*
>
> *I was stung. Forgotten? I consulted my body, retrieving what I could remember about cramp. From a long way away a most definite sensation formed in the middle of my left foot. O yes! It's that business where you feel as if the bones in your toes are going to cross and lock, and never untangle again! (I'd been thinking of that sort of achy cramp that I get in my upper arms sometimes.)*
>
> *'Sorry ...', I said. 'I remember ... it's horrible ...'*

Just as we learn to retrieve words, so we can learn to retrieve sensation in order to make comparisons, build a more detailed understanding of felt experience and make mature, informed felt-responses. Knowing how we feel is a vital part of developing self-confidence and (to use a quaintly old fashioned word) self-possession. We can only feel self-possessed if we truly own the thing in which we live - our body.

Back to the body ...

Can you remember a time when a particular sensation has evoked a vivid memory of something that happened to you in the past? Somebody brushes your arm and you find yourself inexplicably thinking of the dinner-line at your primary school. If you have an example, play with it a little. Shut your eyes, listen in to your body and dwell with the sensation, finding out as much as you can about it in your body. Let the memories float around. If the sensation is supported by movement, let yourself move. When you've finished, you might like to doodle or draw something of the memory, or write, or think.

Body-thoughts, interpreting them and creating meaning

As I was writing I vaguely noticed an annoying noise in my right ear; immediately a part of me felt grumpy in case it took my attention away from writing but I managed to ignore it. Then I stopped for lunch and as I listened to the boys shrieking their approval of last night's 'Match of the Day' while they crammed in sausage sandwiches, I found myself gently bashing my ear as if it might clear the noise and help me to hear them better. Then the noise receded until later when I was loading the dishwasher and there it was again. I suddenly remembered to ask myself 'What's this noise about? If it is a message from my body (rather than merely an annoying irrelevance) what might it be saying?'. And instantly I knew. Up to now in writing this book, over days and weeks and months and years, I have completely forgotten to mention sound as one of the channels of information in our bodies. Not surprising; it is always the one I'm shy about. (So any references to sound that you have already read I had to insert retrospectively.) As soon as I stopped trying to ignore the feeling, denying the information it had to offer, it became a useful idea and broadened my ability to carry out my given task.

After I resumed writing the discomfort in my ear continued, and then changed. When I shut my eyes briefly to heighten my awareness of it, a distinct picture arrived somewhere between my ear and my mind's eye. First there was the sensation that my ear was opening wider and wider ... painfully wide ... and that all my attention would soon be taken up by the space just beside it ... an endless space, blue and darkening. Then there was a visual image that I knew well, but couldn't place. Minutes later I remembered that it was the icon from my computer that denotes volume.

The Sensory-motor phase of learning: a rocket launcher or part of the rocket?

Body intelligence has many connections with what is termed sensory-motor learning. Babies and children up to about three are often referred to in the literature of early years education as being in the 'sensory-motor' phase of development. This acknowledges the extent to which they must, and do, learn about and relate to their world through their senses and their movement. A human being's experience of the world begins in movement and sensation. Ask a child of two to say the word jump and they will probably jump as they say it. Ask them to say nose and they'll touch their nose. Babies and children embody their world in the most direct way. At around three, as a child's intellectual capacity begins to grow independently from their body, our society changes its educational concerns from things physical to things intellectual. A child is deemed to be 'passing through' the sensory- motor phase, with the implicit assumption that it is going on to higher things. Human beings, however, do not pass through the sensory-motor phase - we take it with us. It's not a rocket launcher, intended to fall away at the start of the journey, leaving the main rocket intact. This is one of the essential systems that will maintain health, balance and wellbeing throughout our lives. Jettison it at this early stage and we will always run under-capacity. The fact that we are no longer compelled to jump as we say the word is not a signal that we should forget the body's involvement in our learning and our experience. It is a sign that we are ready to move on to a more developed relationship between our physicality and our intellectual capacities. We must continue to refine and develop our ability to make use of sensory-motor intelligence at the same time as we develop other forms of intelligence and functioning.

3

Body Intelligence
and the prevailing culture

'All curriculum models reflect a set of beliefs and values about what is
considered to be educationally and developmentally worthwhile
in terms of children's immediate needs, their future needs
and the wider needs of society.'

Elizabeth Wood and Jane Attfield

Many years ago I worked in a Gateway Club with a young man who had a learning disability. He loved to dance (particularly with floaty scarves) to soaring, romantic music. When he danced he opened up. He had limited speech, but was very articulate in movement. He had a body intelligence that was totally different from his intellectual intelligence. Everyone at the club was delighted and supported this love of dancing wholeheartedly. Then, one night, he took home two of the scarves he loved so much and danced for his father - who was horrified. The more the young man danced the angrier and more desperate his father grew. The more the young man was rebuffed the more he wanted to make his father understand. The evening ended tragically when his father, unable to cope any more, locked him in his room and refused to let him come down for many days, except to go to his Social Education Centre. Every evening when he returned he was sent back to his room. Meanwhile, the father contacted the club and asked what his son had been doing that had made him 'go mad'. He genuinely believed that something had turned his son's mind. The father was both angry and frightened.

This is an extreme case, an isolated incident, but it makes a point. We had encouraged this young man to take pride in a skill for which his family had no context and no comprehension. We had failed to undertake the kind of liaison that might have prevented this thoroughly unhappy incident. In developing a child's ability to make use of their body intelligence we have to consider the ramifications. Seized with the urge to declaim poetry at the Tesco's checkout we probably do it quietly in our heads rather than out loud for everyone to hear; so too, we can work with physical messages in appropriate ways. In this chapter I want to take a closer look at body intelligence against the backdrop of the prevailing culture - both the challenges and the opportunities.

The ultimate goal for the development of body intelligence is clear: that children will become body literate as well as verbally literate and thus truly embodied people, living fully in their bodies as well as in their heads. An embodied person is someone who involves every cell of their being in everything they do; they know how they feel; they are obviously comfortable in their body; they can identify their symptoms and sensations with brevity and precision; they know how to celebrate physically as well as intellectually. These are desirable attributes, but as a culture we do not prize them highly enough to nurture them within our education systems. Born embodied, we lose it along the way.

We no longer know it but there was a time when movement was our language. It was a long time ago and we can't remember, but we were born into an alien world in which the first movement was breathing - that sharp inflation of the lungs that brings the first cry. From then on, we struggled and grew into movement, learning on our own, without being taught, how to stretch out and double up, how to hold up our heads, roll over, sit up, creep, crawl and, one triumphant day, to stand, walk. Our learning was nothing we did on purpose ... We were busier moving than anything else in the world, and long before we had words we communicated how we felt through our bodies. Our smiling was total and explosive. When we said 'Yes', everything in us said 'Yes'. When we said 'No', everything in us said 'No'. We were undivided.

Where did it all go? What happened? How are we now? Well, for one thing, the teaching which was of our own selves gave way to being taught ... We picked up the set of our parents' bodies, absorbing, without knowing it, their attitudes and connections with the body. We succumbed to the requirements of our teachers, their insistence on a certain

kind of behaviour, requiring, without knowing it, restrictions and limitations. Worst of all, we learned very slowly, but almost completely by the time we were in our teens, to move for a reason, to isolate our motions ... the bodily stir, the total action of the whole organism, broke up into separate gestures. The lovely flow of energy, the connectedness, was gone.

Mary Starks Whitehouse

An embodied child or adult oozes that 'lovely flow of energy'; they feel the 'bodily stir' in the midst of everyday life. But full embodiment is relatively rare in our culture. It is much more common to be disembodied, to struggle for a glimmer of 'bodily stir', to find the worlds of sensation and feeling somewhat remote. It is common to see adults, lacking the understanding to make sense of the spontaneous movement play through which young children explore their physicality, put an abrupt stop to it with a crushing 'Stop being silly'. 'Silly: lacking sense; foolish; imprudent; unwise; weak-minded' (Oxford English Dictionary) is how the mainstream culture labels spontaneous movement.

THE CURRENT PHYSICAL DEVELOPMENT CURRICULUM

Physical education is an important strand within the curriculum and, of course, we have created an approach that is in keeping with the mainstream culture, avoiding 'silly' spontaneous movement.

Thinking about the current P.E. curriculum I'm reminded of a picture someone once showed me to make a point. He covered most of it with a piece of paper leaving only a segment available for me to see. 'What is this a picture of?', he asked. I could see the face of a small boy in tears and, bearing down directly above him, a man with a terrible look on his face. I concluded that a father had beaten his son. When the rest of the picture was revealed I could see that in fact the father was being beaten by another man whom I couldn't previously see and the boy was crying in terror for his father. When I saw the whole picture I could see that I had missed the point altogether - of course.

The existing P.E. curriculum seems to miss an important point too. It addresses two areas of our physical development. The first, and dominant area, is functional movement focusing on fine and gross motor skills. The second, much smaller area, is expressive movement: dance. The lived experience of the body is completely missing from the current curriculum and it's important to look at why this is in order to move on.

Piaget's Theories

The current curriculum is based in Piaget's hierarchical theory of learning that suggests each stage is replaced - *superseded* - by the next. Piaget believed that the first stage (sensory-motor and exploratory play based on physical activities) is the stuff of the *first two years of our lives only*. Here we find an academic basis for the 'Grow up and stop being silly!' reaction to spontaneous movement as children pass the age of about three.

Piaget suggests that Symbolic Play (pretend, fantasy and socio-dramatic play involving mental representations) takes over between two and six, and that Games with Rules supplant Symbolic Play from seven or eight onwards. In keeping with this, the P.E. curriculum loses anything approaching spontaneous movement play very early on and replaces it with some imaginative work and a lot of games with rules. Whilst I have no quarrel with the notion that children can play in new ways as they grow older, it is not my experience that they leave the stages behind. As I watch adults of all ages rediscover their ability to play in movement and sensation, and I hear their delight and relief, I am convinced that this way of learning travels with us. Ignore it and we shut down a key resource available to us.

I wonder if Piaget, living in a time and culture that ignored the body, was unable to make use of spontaneous movement play for himself and was, therefore, unable to give it meaning when he saw it in growing children. Perhaps Mr and Mrs Piaget even said to him 'Stop being silly!' from time to time, as he attempted to hop home backwards from school.

Two physiotherapists (40 something and 50 something) came on a training course. After coffee break on the first morning I invited them to dip into 'kinesthetic awareness', to find out what it might be. Sitting back to back, eyes shut, with gentle music on the cassette recorder they were charged with the task of listening in to see what they noticed through their backs, as they sat still or moved together as they wished. Ten minutes later, with not a word spoken and not a look exchanged between them, they swung round, bleary eyed and soft-bodied, to share some thoughts in words. At first they could hardly speak; they had entered the world of their sensibilities so completely that they had left words and the intellect behind. Quietly, gently, they started to share what they had felt. They discovered they were both amazed by how much they could read of the other's desires through the tiniest movements. They said that they had become intensely aware of the smallest shifts and changes, had uncovered a totally new way of communicating that they adored from this first go, and could they have another go immediately please!

Lack of experience of the lived body amongst curriculum makers

Perhaps I'm being overly presumptuous, but I suspect that the men and women who devise and revise this curriculum probably don't have much experience of spontaneous movement play for themselves. They know a great deal about moving for a purpose, dance even, but perhaps not much about spontaneous movement play that opens up the layers of inner awareness for their own sake. Perhaps some of them do Yoga or T'ai Chi and know about body listening, but haven't found a place for that kind of moving amongst the Early Learning goals.

Looking at a teacher's resource book on the theme of 'Myself' recently, it was remarkable to discover that nowhere did the activities focus on the lived experience of the body. All the activities involved externalised representations. The first activity, called 'My Body', involved each child making a model of themselves with a stick for their trunk and a paper plate for their head. No-body looks or feels like a stick or a paper plate! Other activities included painted hand and foot prints, songs about my body, stories about other people's bodies ... but never the body itself. I showed it to a group of dancers, movers ... people utterly familiar with working in their bodies. At first they hooted with laughter. Then they grew sad, and then angry. 'Why <u>don't</u> people work with the body?', they said in various ways. 'It's so simple. How has it got lost?'

Lack of experience of the lived body amongst other adults

There are many Early Years workers who believe that children need more time for spontaneous movement, but when it comes to organising something different within their curriculum they often feel anxious about their lack of skill with movement. Deep down, they know that young children are more readily able to connect with spontaneous movement than they are, and this leaves an uneasy potential for lack of control.

'One of the most thoroughly neglected areas of body education is the awareness of what is happening inside: the dialogue between inner and outer experience in relation to the whole person. We spend much of our time involved in outer perception through the specialised sense organs of sight, sound, taste, smell, and touch. We are generally less involved in developing our capacities for inner sensing which is the ability of the nervous system to monitor inner states of the body. How and why do we progressively close down our capacity for body listening?

... Consider the amount of time we spend feeling good about our bodies. How often do we communicate with ourselves? Do we enjoy our physical capacities and efficiency? Our many years of schooling bring a separation of mind and body (sit still and learn). Cultural stereotypes and advertising emphasise the body as a youthful sexual object. Physical training techniques and medical practices can lead to a view of the body as a machine, needing to be repaired by someone else when necessary. There is often a sense that one is either the master or the victim of one's own body. When communication breaks down, we are left polarised within ourselves. It becomes important to understand that the body has its own way of functioning, its own way of telling us what's going on inside, its own logic. Much of our task is to learn to listen'.

Andrea Olsen. Body stories.

Absence of understanding about developmental movement patterns

The current curriculum doesn't include any support for developmental movement activity. How can this be, since the work is very simple and, seemingly, can have a profound effect on future learning? A consistent body of evidence has been built since the 1940s but much of it remains within closed academic circles. Where information has become more widely known, it has often been mistrusted, because people are reluctant to believe that slithering along on your belly when you are six months old can have any significant effect on your future ability to read.

Moving On

An intelligence is only useful if the surrounding culture values it. There is little point in developing a high degree of body intelligence if people laugh at you when you draw on it, or if there are no opportunities to use it. So is it worth pursuing this idea of body intelligence within our existing cultural framework?

Although spontaneous movement isn't currently at the heart of our culture, there are many changes taking place which suggest that physicality, and body intelligence, will become increasingly relevant; signs that we must balance our sophistication in intellectual and rational matters with a more developed understanding of the body. The foundation stage curriculum is a key place for such changes to begin.

Early Years workers are beginning to ask about the links between early movement and future learning. There is an increasing interest in, for instance, the links between crawling and reading. Many teachers, play workers and child minders would be ready, willing and able to incorporate new ways of working with babies and young children if only they had information readily available. Many are finding that academic skills are simply too heavily weighted and are eager to redress the balance in appropriate ways - especially within the revised emphasis on play in the curriculum guidance for the foundation stage.

Within education, policy makers are increasingly concerned with education for life - with developing broad based thinking skills and with promoting 'Citizenship'. As a society we have an urgent need to address rising levels of challenging behaviour. Being too single-minded, concerned only with learning through intellectual means, we miss important opportunities for personal and social education offered by learning through direct perception.

On holiday this year my children got to know the two other English kids at the pool. One of them, on the brink of his eighteenth birthday, was facing a court case on his return to England for grievous bodily harm. Over the week they spent flopping about in the pool together he told them about the wild things he had done in his life, including drugs, theft and a previous spell in a young offender's prison. Then one afternoon, the bravado phase over, he told them that he wasn't wild until his second year at High School. 'I was crap at everything', he said, 'so I started to do this stuff. Now I've had enough ... I want it to change.'

Watching this young man in the pool I was pretty convinced there were some developmental movement issues that needed clearing up; issues which may well affect his ability to work at the level of his intelligence, his ability to make relationships and his ability to control his temper. (His court case was the result of an angry attack.) It was distressing to hear how excluded he felt by the academic drive of the school and to see how our sophisticated society can let someone down so badly.

Behaviour modification programmes based in rational explanation and reasoning will not have the same impact as learning by direct perception through the senses. We must ensure that children's neurological wiring is in good order (by completing the necessary developmental movement patterns) and that they have opportunities to learn by direct perception, rather than always by reasoning and rational thought.

In the middle of the circle is a chair. Each child can go into the centre and make three shapes - anything they like as long as they a) touch the chair with some part of their body and b) keep themselves safe. Today, several girls go in one after the other. Jenny flies like an angel; Wallace kneels on the seat, holding onto the back and leans his head back delicately. The children decide whose turn it is; they have managed this from the start.

Then Mickey (6), who has asked repeatedly for a turn and been turned down, cannot contain himself any longer. Despite protests he gets up, goes into the centre and leaps onto the chair to perform a risky balance at great speed. The group complain. 'It's not your turn' ... 'We didn't say' ... And to the teacher, 'It's not fair ... it's not his turn'. Mickey, ignoring them, tries another tricky balance that looks as if it will bring him and the chair crashing to the ground. The teacher steps in to steady it and to point out to Mickey that he might hurt himself, or someone else, if he continues.

Undeterred, he goes for a third shape using the teacher's arm to give him more support. He does a stunning reach and balance that looks terrific. The teacher comments and the group gasp in spite of themselves. 'He looks like Peter Pan when he's flying', says one. He does.

Then Mickey begins a fourth shape. The children are furious; he is breaking their closely guarded group rule. The teacher steps away and asks Mickey to listen to what the group are saying to him. He ignores them all, sits down stubbornly and looks defiantly around. 'What shall we do?', the teacher asks. They are unsure. 'Pull him out', says one. 'We can't do that', says another. 'I want my turn. Get out', says someone else. Mickey settles further into his chair. Then Laura suddenly says, 'Put another chair in the middle and we can get on'. They do and Laura has her turn amid many comments about what a good idea it was. Mickey is ignored. Suddenly he feels the pain of being the 'outsider'. He swings his legs a bit, trying to look confident, then slithers his chair just outside the circle. It mirrors how he must be feeling ... outside. He spends a lonely playtime immediately afterwards, even though the teacher has welcomed him back in before the end of the class.

Mickey learned fast. Some weeks later, one of the other children tried to take a very long go. Mickey explained patiently that it wasn't fair because if someone takes a long turn, another child won't get a go at all. Then he said, 'Why don't we have three people in the middle today, no four. Then we won't have to wait and we won't get so cross'.

Movement Play offers another, different, opportunity to address personal and social education within the Early Years curriculum. Different, in that it mixes movement and words and gives strong visual feedback of the processes at work in groups. Mickey feels, as well as hears, what his peer group make of his behaviour. He sees his own 'outsider' role, sitting outside the circle. This is ordinary, everyday learning, heightened within the context of the Movement Play activity.

As the number of young people being excluded from school increases, as young children are being excluded even from nursery in growing numbers, we need to think again about how to work with very young children and young people with 'behaviour problems'. Movement specialists, movement analysts, movement observers, community dancers, dance therapists and ordinary people who know about moving have much to offer in an attempt to widen understanding of the significance of movement play in addressing these issues. These are people who know what it is to think in their bodies as well as in their intellects; people who can help to develop new ways of working with the body.

New approaches to population health

Current government initiatives are concerned with developing the ways in which public health can be improved and with the need for health promotion to play a major role. At present we can only guess at the impact of developing skills in children that will help them to live embodied lives. Evaluation is a long term issue; but experience suggests that children who have a close relationship with their physicality are likely to be able to monitor and maintain their health better than those who have a remote relationship with their bodies.

A curriculum revised to include attention to the lived body is likely to have a more profound effect because of its ability to help children to discover and utilise their self-healing powers through an active and close relationship with their bodies. As the central place of the medical model within our health services becomes increasingly problematic, it is crucial to find ways of involving people in the maintenance of their own health.

A friend of mine went to the doctor recently when he experienced an on-going, uncomfortable sensation in his chest. He didn't know exactly how to describe it. 'Is it a stabbing pain in a particular place, or a generalised, all-over pain?', asked the doctor trying to find out more about my friend's bodily-felt experience. My friend, without thinking, shut his eyes and focused inwards. Like Jack, he was moving into kinesthetic awareness mode, temporarily shutting out the visual sense and the outside world, in favour of the inner world of his body. Unfortunately, the doctor reacted as many adults do with children, as if my friend had somehow nodded off. He prompted rather brusquely. 'Is it a stabbing pain in a particular place, or a generalised, all-over pain?' My friend was stopped in his tracks; he hadn't arrived at an answer yet and neither 'stabbing' nor 'all-over' quite cut the mustard. He became flustered at the speed the doctor was going and said the first thing that came into his head. 'It's sort of throbbing.' (It wasn't, particularly. But he didn't feel able to take the time he needed to really work out what it was.) He came away three minutes later with a prescription for an antibiotic that he threw in the bin.

Let's spare a thought for the poor GP here. He had approximately seven minutes (maximum) to receive this patient, listen, diagnose, prescribe, and bid farewell. He needs my friend, and all his other patients, to be able to identify bodily-felt experience (symptoms), to differentiate between sensations, and to articulate them clearly, accurately and quickly. In short he needs them to draw on their body intelligence. The more body-literate they are, the more successful their consultation is likely to be.

If we equip children to work with feelings, with sensation and with movement they are more likely to be able to monitor and maintain their own health. Malcolm Rigler, a GP from the West Midlands in England, who is well known for his enthusiastic embracing of new and innovative ways to address issues of health says, 'A doctor's best aim is to help patients to learn from their illness'. An important aim for us as teachers, play workers, parents and carers could be to help children learn from their bodies. There is a role for movement specialists in developing new ways of working with movement; but maintaining young children's enjoyment of their physicality, their capacity to embody their lives and their natural ability to learn by direct perception is a task for all those who live and work with them.

Despite the fact that spontaneous movement and learning by direct perception are at the moment relatively alien activities within our culture, there are many reasons to believe that the tide is turning. There is a role for movement specialists in developing new ways of working with movement; but maintaining young children's enjoyment of their physicality, their capacity to embody their lives and their natural ability to learn by direct perception is a task for all parents, nursery workers, teachers and childminders.

4

Movement Play: learning through direct perception

'... play, like dreams, serves the function of self-revelation.'

D W Winnicott

Enabling children to make use of their body intelligence requires a new physical education curriculum. Since children are well used to directing their own movement play (Jack's hopping home being an everyday example) it is ironic that the movement activities we organise in Early Years settings are often so controlled, so adult-led. Ironic, but not surprising. A fundamental anxiety about spontaneous movement leads many adults to think that it must be tightly harnessed or chaos will ensue, and that too much free movement will inevitably lead to injury. Outdoor play (which is well-resourced) is the exception; and there are individual teachers, who themselves delight in movement, who extend the curriculum with wholly positive results.

In this chapter I want to look in detail at Movement Play, which emphasises learning through direct perception - in sensation, feelings, movement and image. It is an approach which begins in the Early Years and continues through adulthood, placing its main emphasis on the lived experience of the body - what it is like to *be* a body, rather than *have* a body.

Children don't stop indulging in discovery through sensory-motor play because it is not in the Foundation Curriculum. They do it anyway - in their mother's arms, in the high chair, in the cot, on the rug on the floor, climbing on Dad's back, hopping home backwards along the pavement, in the Tesco's trolley, in the buggy, at the childminder's, at playgroup, at nursery, in early years classes at school - and just occasionally in specific Movement Play sessions. It isn't a specialist subject;

everyone who has anything to do with young children gets involved with, or sees, movement play. It is a family affair, as well as something to put in an organised curriculum. The more those around notice and value movement, the more open to movement, and to their body intelligence, a child will become. Developing ways of supporting this learning, therefore, begins with the understanding that children play and learn in movement and their bodies whether adults get involved or not.

Play is variously identified as a deeply creative activity with high levels of personally motivated learning, something we do to let off steam or relax, or simply as messing about. Movement Play incorporates all these things and each is equally important. Movement Play is not creative dance. It is not teaching children how to move in response to imaginative ideas; it is not interpreting music; nor is it providing structures to help children make up their own dances: 'Be a tree' is the classic example.

> Many years ago my grandmother (84) rang me enthusiastically. 'I've been doing your sort of thing today', she said. 'Modern dancing! A young lady came to entertain us at WI ... and she said we all had to choose a type of tree ... and move like it. Well, my mind was a blank ... so I chose a dead one then I didn't have to embarrass myself with all that moving.'

Movement Play is not about providing a controlled environment in which children can 'indulge in rough and tumble' in order to refresh themselves for more serious learning. It is a mindful activity every bit as useful as the learning they do sitting at a desk with a pencil in their hand.

Movement Play encourages children to indulge in movement and sensation for their own sake, free from any need to make something either useful or beautiful. Children move spontaneously and idiosyncratically guided by their internal sensations, feelings, images, body-thoughts and rational thoughts. As they follow their own internal body logic they may well move in ways that are not immediately recognisable or understandable to others, but they are encouraged to supply their own personal meaning for the movement. Movement Play activities sometimes set out to focus on the acquisition of new skills or understanding, but the less focused 'messing about' can throw up new understanding just as often.

Closing my eyes and beginning to focus on my body rather than the chatter in my head is like stepping into a dream-pool. I don't know where I will 'go'. I know that mostly something turns up ... extraordinary stories, images, feelings. Today it was dinosaur-bird. As I settled into noticing how my body wanted to move, rather than telling it what to do, there was a long period of nothing very much. Then suddenly I was aware that my body had started to mould, with slow determination, into a particular shape. I was aware of my hips moving backwards and dropping; my mouth opening. I felt feathery and scaly all at once and very tall. My neck elongated and my arms had become wings. (I told you this would sound peculiar.) These feelings and images were so strong ... so real. I was dinosaur-bird, huge and ancient. I loved my neck. Long and strong, pink and rough. I had the sense of knowing something about this ancient creature that I couldn't begin to know by looking at a picture in a book. And a sense that I knew more about myself as well.

In the studio I can play. I don't have to justify myself to anyone. I can be dinosaur-bird any way I like, with no embarrassment and no questions asked. If I had to imagine a dinosaur-bird in my head and then dance it ... there is no way I could do it! I'd rather die! This comes from my body into my head, not the other way round.

Extract from a journal. Woman (41)

An aside

Before going on I want to address the key issue of what makes it Movement Play with a big M and a big P, as opposed to the movement play that children engage in on and off all day. I think the answer is simply one of intention. When an adult deliberately creates a focus on the content or process of a child's physical exploration, it becomes Movement Play. When a child deliberately and persistently follows a body-thought, or explores sensation or movement, this is Movement Play.

Movement Play can happen in a variety of different ways, and with different levels of support from adults and other children. Since the primary piece of equipment is always available (the body) it can happen anywhere, at any time. It can happen in a fleeting moment, or over an extended period. It can involve others, or just ourselves. We can use props or just our body. It can happen with eyes open or eyes shut; it can happen with a lot of movement or in apparent stillness (there is always movement in our bodies, even if it is only the flow of our blood, the pump of our heart, or the peristaltic action of the gut as it moves our dinner along). Sometimes we might want music as a support; other times we will simply move. Sometimes we will be very conscious of what we are doing; sometimes the playing will be at the edges of our consciousness - like the doodle we do on the phone-pad as we talk on the phone.

Discovery through play

There continues to be hot debate about the role of play in our lives, from early years through to adulthood. As someone who has worked in the arts all my life, I have had both a reason and an excuse to go on playing. I have always been paid to play with other people, but I also play for myself. I mostly like to play in movement, but I write, draw and make things as well when it feels appropriate. I don't show these things to anyone, they are simply a part of my on-going life, part of me. In fact I feel quite shy as I start to write about them here. But since there is such a lot of academic writing about the nature and role of play, I want to stay firmly in my own experience as I too write about it. I want to write about the richness of Movement Play from within my own experience, in order to shed light on its nature, complexity and usefulness.

As an adult I always have to make particular times to play and I do it very consciously. This, of course, is different from a child. Sometimes I note the urge to play spontaneously - to skip about the garden, or roll on the floor, or twitch my hands in front of my face as I sit on the train to see what it feels like - but I note it, and set it aside, as decorum, my children ('Mum! You're so embarrassing!') and my own sensibilities require. From the work that I have done with adults and children I see little difference in the nature of the learning in play between the two. Adults often have more insight into their own learning processes; young children often have easier access to a spontaneous flow of movement. But the learning occurs along the same spectrum. So although the examples that follow are about adult play, they are wholly relevant to the development of Movement Play for young children.

There are two starting points. Sometimes I simply want to indulge in goal-free exploration. Roll around for the sheer delight of it. Be in my body because mostly I exist in my head. Sometimes I decide to play like this just because I haven't for a while; or because it is another thing I like to do - like gardening. Here I surrender to the flow of movement that is waiting to unfold given the

opportunity. At other times I have issues or questions that I want to address and I play to find answers.

Let me give you an example. In the first scenario I might go into a large space, or my front room with the furniture pushed back, shut my eyes and wait to see what happens. This is like surrendering to the movement impulses or sensations in my body and waiting to take a ride, free from the pressure of having to decide how to move. I follow whatever emerges, just for the experience of it. I have no plan and no need to make anything of it. What will be will be. Sometimes, afterwards, I realise that as a result of playing something has changed - how I feel, what I understand. Other times, I play and that is the end of it. At least, the sensations, feelings, images and thoughts that I have experienced simply enter the rich texture of my on-going life and I may or may not refer to them again.

With the second route I play in the hope that I will find something out, learn something. In this instance, a question, an issue or a bodily-felt sensation rises into my awareness and I make time to focus on it, to see if my movement, or writing or drawing, illuminate it in any way.

I have a particular pain in my upper arms, both of them, from time to time. It happens when I reach slightly awkwardly, like turning into the back of the car to collect an abandoned lunch-box, or reaching up to get the clean sheets off the top shelf of the airing cupboard. It has been going on for several weeks and I realise that I am fed up with it and I wonder why it's there.

When I can make the space, and there is no-one in the house, I go into the sitting room and push the chairs aside. How shall I begin? I shut my eyes and wait. My head is full of chatter about domestic arrangements and work things; I wish I could focus on the task in hand. Braced, I think. So wide. And as I notice this my trunk starts to twist slowly around so that I am facing left, and one of my arms hangs lower than the other. With my eyes still shut I notice the sun stream into the room. I notice my legs. I wait, barely moving. I wish my body would get on and address the issue of my arms. I wait. I notice I am rocking. I wait. And then my fingers begin to twiddle and twitch. Ah ha, I think - action. But after a while the twiddling stops and I am just rocking again. Rocking and waiting for something to happen. It's nice. I like the rocking. I rock for several minutes.

And then, suddenly, I realise that I am seeing the hall in the house where I lived when I was three. And I am standing in it, rocking. And my Mum isn't there; I know where she is. She's busy in the kitchen just out of sight. I want to be picked up but she isn't there. I have an urge to drop down to the floor onto my knees. It takes me a moment to follow it, rather than think about it. When I do, I find myself kneeling with my weight divided between my knees and forearms. I am still rocking, pressing my head into my upturned hands on the floor, bum in the air. I like the feeling of the weight of my head pressing down into my hands and into the floor. And then I find myself pulling my arms in so that I am curled into a round ball, with my arms tucked right underneath me. I find the word 'resting' in my thoughts. And still I am rocking. I notice the thought, 'I could stay here for ever' playing around the edges. A picture of an amoeba forms in the dark and I feel as if my body is rolling in space. Without front or back, just rolling. After an age I say to myself, 'I wonder what will happen if I'm only allowed to move my back, and not my legs?'. And then fantasy arms appear from the middle of my back, gossamer thin and impossibly long, stretching effortlessly upwards into space, and as they do so, I become more aware of my real arms cuddled into me, closed, surrounded, held.

This particular playtime had other bits to it and then I finished by drawing (or doodling, really) with some crayons and writing a few notes to myself, to capture things I might want to come back to. I noted my pleasure in being curled up and protected; and the fantasy arms doing the stretching whilst 'I' did the protecting. I noted the memory of being three years old with no-one available to pick me up, and how much I wanted to be picked up. And I remembered that when I was three, if I wanted to be picked up, I would always lift up my arms. I can interpret these thoughts if I wish, or just let them wash around. I'm not trying deliberately to work out what the pain in my arms is about - to end up with an answer - but allowing my body thoughts to become conscious rather than unconscious. Now, when my arms ache, I remember the fantasy-arms doing the stretching and I have tried pulling my real, aching-arms inwards and resting them as I did on the floor. This is not a reasoned strategy. It is something else to try; another way to be as I try to soothe the ache.

This Movement Play involved a process of exploration (indulging in a flow of spontaneous movement) followed by a period of focusing (the drawing and doodling) and then one of reflection (remembering things that happened as I had moved and recalling things from other parts of my life that the movement play brought to mind). Once the direct perception has become conscious I can let the information gained in sensation, feeling, movement and image mix and mingle with my rational thoughts, adding to my experience of myself or to any strategies I may choose to create for responding to the pain. The two tributaries (intellect and body) become continuous with one another and feed the river (mind).

Back to the Body...
Some starting points
In Chapters 1 and 2 the Back to the Body sections offer prompts to rediscover the flow of spontaneous movement that exists at the edge of our consciousness, moment to moment. Here are a number of simple structures that can help to get bodies 'thinking', just as we might use external props to waken up our intellects (word games; puzzles; books; conversations with ourselves). They are play structures; use them lightly, bend and reshape them according to your fancy. Reject what you don't like. Above all, don't stick doggedly to them if something else comes up. They are only intended to get you started.

Back to the Body...
Will or surrender
Ask yourself how you want to get going? Do you want to turn your focus towards your body and see what sensations/feelings/movements are there ... and then follow what comes up surrendering to the flow of spontaneous movement? Or do you want to start with your will - with specific questions or issues that you'd like to find out more about. See if you are clear about either of these. Sometimes neither will leap out and your moving may be an interweaving of the two. At other times, it may be clear which interests you.

Surrender: Begin by checking in with the sensations, feelings, movement and images in your body. Make the transition from 'head' to 'body' and see what you notice ... what you want. If there is nothing calling for your attention, stay with the movement as it unfolds. Allow your intellect simply to notice what happens. If the voice in your head persists in trying to take control ... make suggestions about how to move ... insist on something different / more / better, notice, but don't feel you have to take its advice. There is absolutely nothing that you have to do, or should be doing. Your movement doesn't have to look a particular way, or achieve anything. This is for your body to do as it pleases. Many adults, when they come back to this kind of moving, worry that they can't stop doing things for the sake of it, or that they don't

know whether they are really surrendering to the flow of movement or not. Don't worry ... just do what you do. And look for something you enjoy ... something that feels comfortable. You don't have to please anyone but yourself.

Will: If, as you start, there is something occupying your mind (What is that twinge? ... Why do I keep getting this headache? ... I wish I hadn't shouted at the children last night?... How come I feel so great today?) let that be the focus for your moving. Resist the temptation to make something happen. Instead, allow things to happen - if they will. You may start by asking: 'What will happen if I move my head like this?' and follow the sensations and movements that begin in this way. Or you may simply let the question or issue roll gently around in your focus as you move ... and notice what happens as a result of this light connection between thought and movement. It may well be that, after a beginning that clearly revolves around either will or surrender, you soon have no idea which is in the ascendancy and the two will interweave of their own accord.

Back to the Body...
Getting stuck ... getting unstuck
You may find, as you move and explore, that you suddenly have no idea what to do next. You run out of steam. No matter: rest, breath, refocus and start looking for the sensations and movement that might start you off again. Or the question that you would like to explore. Focusing on your breathing - the movement that is always present - can help you find your way again. If nothing occurs, don't make yourself go on. Above all, be comfortable.

Back to the Body...
Freeze Frame
If continuous movement doesn't feel easy; if you find yourself feeling daunted by the prospect of having to keep up this spontaneity, try a freeze frame structure. Aim to move only for as long as it takes to discover a shape, or feeling, or sensation that feels 'right', and hold it there. You're not trying to create something that looks right, but that feels right to you. If you work with your eyes shut it might help you to focus on this kinesthetic aspect. Once you have the still shape, notice as much as you can about it ... the images that accompany it, the sounds, thoughts, sensations, feelings, memories. When you're ready, move on to another.

Back to the Body...
Repeated phrase

Try finding a sequence of movement that you can repeat over and over again. Just a short movement. Resist any attempts by your intellect to insist that nothing short of a small, searingly beautiful ballet will do. Any wriggles or rockings, bounces or wobbles that feel right are just fine. As you go round and round the movement simply notice as many layers of accompanying experience as you can, including the intrusion of shopping lists and pressing engagements.

Back to the Body...
Making Bigger

When you arrive at something that feels right, or interesting, try making the shape or phrase bigger. Or take one part of it (the fingers of one hand, a leg, the jut of a hip) and exaggerate it. How can you make it bigger, or intensify the sensation, or trigger more picture or sound images? Try different ways until you hit upon something that feels right. Notice as much as you can about all the different layers of experience prompted by this process.

> *Tom (4) is at the water tray. He is filling a pan with water, lifting it above his head and letting the water trickle out. Each time he lifts it higher and higher. He is staring into the middle distance and appears to be absorbed in the sensations of the movement as he lifts and lifts again ... the weight of his arm ... the rhythmic action ... the twist of his wrist ... the inner experience prompted by the action.*
>
> *As I watch, I feel this is more a dance than an experiment with water. He seems to be learning more about himself than about the water.*

Back to the Body...
Opposites

If at any time you feel stuck, and you don't want to be, find a shape or a movement and ask yourself 'What's the opposite of this?' In some ways this is a daft question, of course. There is no definitive answer. Everyone would come up with something different. But challenge yourself to see what your opposite might be. Tackle the challenge in any way that occurs to you: either with relentless, intellectual logic. (This is high, the opposite is low. This is shaky, the opposite is smooth) or with the unpredictable ways your body might answer the question - moving and noticing what happens. When you have arrived at what you feel is the opposite, move from your starting point to your finishing point, finding the journey that takes you from one extreme to the other. Notice as much as you can about all the stages along the way. When you have become familiar with the journey, decide where you think the mid-point is and play there for a bit in any of the ways suggested above that feel comfortable.

Movement Play and relationship

The examples of my own playing and the Back to the Body sections in this chapter have all been about solo play. Our relationship with our self is clearly central, but we don't learn about who we are and who we want to be in isolation from those around us. We test our understanding and our behaviour on others and adapt what we do in the light of the responses we receive. We must also develop a flexible relationship with our environment if we are to keep ourselves safe and maximise our learning opportunities. We must get to know it, learn how it helps and hinders us, discover what opportunities it affords and how to take advantage of them - and what it needs from us.

Playing with others offers an opportunity for us to learn about ourselves in relationship with others, as well as about the nature of relationship itself. Through Movement Play we can develop and practice our ability to notice things about other people and make discriminations - to detect mood, to read intentions and desires, to measure others' desires against our own and to respond appropriately. Our first relationships are made through sensation, feeling and movement. Movement Play provides us with focused opportunities to develop this learning from the direct perception of ourselves in relationship with others, as adults or as children.

Lizzie (6) and Sarah (6) are best friends. They play together at school and, as their families are friends, they play together at home as well. But Lizzie has been upset recently. She is finding the relationship hard going, but can't say why. Both her Mum and the teacher are concerned.

Today ... everyday ... Sarah is desperate to dance. The activity is a News Time Circle (see page 143) and the children are invited to choose someone to dance with in the centre. This gives a very focused, yet indirect, structure for two children to negotiate their relationship.

Sarah chooses Lizzie and dives into the circle to begin. She whispers to her about the kind of dance they will do, leaving no doubt that she is calling the tune. As they get going, Sarah keeps Lizzie in line with little gestures that indicate when and how she wants Lizzie to change what she is doing. Lizzie watches intently and works really hard at following.

Sarah is full of life. She swoops and rises, changes the movement and the patterns frequently. As I watch her I imagine that she is dancing with the energy of the whole world. I feel uplifted and delighted. When I watch Lizzie I discover I am feeling a little anxious, and full of hope that she can keep up. I find myself filling with tenderness as I watch her conscientious efforts.

In the comments afterwards someone says, 'Lizzie was really good at following Sarah', and Lizzie looks at the carpet and smiles.

Several days later it is Lizzie's turn to dance. She chooses Sarah. I remind them gently that this is Lizzie's dance and that Sarah has been invited to join in. Lizzie chooses to dance with Ribbon Sticks. She chooses red for herself and blue for Sarah. They move into the centre to begin.

They stand side by side. Lizzie dances with a downward focus of her eyes watching her ribbon move slowly on the floor whilst Sarah waves her ribbon in the air in front of her. Lizzie is watching out of the corner of her eye. She sticks to her movement; then she changes it to small circles above her. Sarah has discovered a whipping movement that is giving her great delight and doesn't see the change. When she eventually notices, she joins Lizzie briefly, then discovers that she can do her own whipping in the same position above her. Lizzie sticks to her own movement.

The dance progresses. Lizzie finds movements that she likes. Sarah sometimes joins her, and always makes her own embellishments. I feel quietly strong as I watch Lizzie throwing sideways glances at Sarah, but staying with her own movement. I feel glad that she isn't thrown off by Sarah's dramatic actions. I laugh with pleasure inside as I watch Sarah - always something new to try, such vibrant energy.

After the dance is over, I invite the circle of children to speak about what they have seen and specifically suggest that they may wish, amongst other things, to comment on the relationship between the two. 'How did they dance together? Did you see one of the girls leading and one following? Or did you see some other way of dancing together?' Amongst many comments Peter says, 'It was Lizzie's dance and she did her moves, but Sarah didn't do them much'. Ryan says 'Sarah did big moves and Lizzie did little ones'. Andrea says, 'They were side by side not looking at each other'. Imran says, 'Lizzie did look. She looked sideways'.

I don't comment, just remind us all that each person sees what they see ... they can't see everything. Then I say, 'Lizzie. It was your dance. Do the comments feel right?' She nods and smiles. Sarah is winding her ribbon around its stick. 'And Sarah?' 'I liked my whirly movement', she says.

Movement Play, carefully structured by an adult, gives these two a chance to negotiate their relationship in a different way. Sarah is dominant, Lizzie is struggling. Movement Play allows them to be with each other, to talk with each other without the complication of words or a subject matter. Leadership, subject matter, the degree to which they can share ideas, yield to the other, and see each other is negotiated directly through movement, sensation and feeling. The feedback from the watching children gives them information about their relationship that they won't get otherwise.

It might be tempting, in this case, to ask Sarah to try copying Lizzie to see if she could learn from that experience. My guess is that she would probably have been able to carry out the task pretty well. However, this would place the activity within a teaching context, rather than a play context. Sarah would be addressing a task provided by me, rather than discovering, at her own pace, in her own way, through her relationship with Lizzie. My task here is to provide opportunities for focusing and reflecting, but not to control the outcome.

Movement Play and Lifelong Learning

There are a great many similarities between my adult play and the play that children indulge in. As an adult, I get tricksy with my reflection and analysis and I make a conscious effort to use the learning potential of my play. But I am always surprised at the degree to which young children can articulate their experience when they know that I am interested and value what they have to say. When I ask children about the sensations, feelings, images, body-thoughts and rational thoughts that arise from their spontaneous movement play they often have a great deal to say.

Palvinder (6) runs around a bit, lies down a bit and rolls around a bit. After his allotted three minutes in the middle I ask him if he would like to tell us about anything he noticed while he was moving.

'I was running and I could feel my knees going wobbly so I lay down and then I was a crab under the sea and I was looking up at all the fishes going by. I was sad to be at the bottom of the sea 'cos my snappy-fingers didn't work. Then I thought I'd be a fish instead and I swam and swam to the edge of the sea.'

Palvinder was able to involve himself fully in the movement and then to focus on the experience in recall, describing and differentiating several different layers of experience. He identifies sensation (wobbly knees), feeling (sadness at the bottom of the sea), a movement action (running), fantasy (being a crab and then a fish) and visual images (looking up at the fishes).

We provide children with a wide range of play activities (sand play, water play, block play) and a selection of 'corners' in which to indulge in self-directed discovery (home corner, dressing up corner, painting corner) but only outdoor play comes close to providing self-directed Movement Play and by its very nature it tends to have less adult attention than the indoor equivalents. Movement Play and a Movement Corner create opportunities for children to focus on their inner experience in sensation, feeling and movement and thus to inch their way towards being able to make use of direct perception as one of the ways they develop understanding.

Indulging in free flow, spontaneous physical play allows us to experience our body as our first and fundamental home and to discover our rich inner worlds. It allows us to get to know the unique interplay between the different parts of us, and to experience the intertwining of reality and fantasy, both as potent as each other, as we try and make sense of our lives and find meaning in our experience. These are useful things to do no matter what age we are.

I was working with a group of very frail, elderly people in a residential home recently. We were wafting huge 'flags' through the air - swathes of light, floating material on long sticks. Dolly (87) took a very long turn and whilst she wafted others in the group started to say, 'Doesn't she look lovely. Like a great floating bird'. 'Well I was a bird', she said simply when she finally finished. 'A big white one flying over the trees. Swooping and diving ... I could do anything'. Then she started to laugh, a tiny, frail laugh that brought tears to her eyes that she dabbed at with a lavender scented handkerchief. 'Listen to me!' she said. 'What am I saying?'

I think the reason that the others had started to comment as they watched, was that Dolly had become embodied. She had really started to play, to indulge in the sensations, feelings and fantasies inside her. For a while she <u>was</u> a big white bird. And she said she felt better for it.

5

Movement Play and the Foundation Stage Curriculum

'During this time we cannot afford to get things wrong.'

Foreword to Curriculum guidance in the foundation stage

Margaret Hodge MP

'Early Years experience should build on what children already know and can do.' So says the curriculum guidance for the Foundation Stage published in 2000. There is nothing more familiar and natural to young children than learning through their bodies. Supporting what comes naturally, rather than supplanting it with other less familiar ways of learning, is an excellent way to 'encourage a positive attitude and disposition to learn and aim[s] to give protection from early failure'. (*Curriculum guidance for the foundation stage*)

Movement Play is a planned and purposeful child-centred approach that offers structures within which children 'explore, experiment, plan and make decisions for themselves'. Activities vary between those planned and led by adults and those planned and directed by children. In Movement Play there is no distinction made between play and work. The adults' role is 'crucial in planning and resourcing a challenging environment' and in 'extending and supporting children's spontaneous play'. The Early Learning Goals suggest eight ways in which play can support effective learning. Movement Play can help children to:

- explore, develop and represent learning experiences that help them make sense of the world
- practise and build up ideas, concepts and skills
- learn to control impulses and understand the need for rules

- be alone, alongside others or cooperate as they talk or rehearse their feelings
- take risks and make mistakes
- think creatively and imaginatively
- communicate with others as they investigate or solve problems
- express fears or relive anxious experiences in controlled and safe situations

Movement Play will make it easier to meet these aims by encouraging children to learn through direct participation with their senses, alongside the other means they are developing.

Personal, social and emotional development

Movement Play gives children the tools to listen to their bodies and to become confident in the use of their body intelligence alongside their intellectual intelligence. As they explore their bodily-felt experience through spontaneous movement play they gain greater access to their feelings, and learn a new way of addressing social and emotional issues that arise in their lives. They become self-possessed and able to act upon *felt* experience.

Carmella (4) trailed into the kitchen with a dejected look. 'I want something awfully bad and I don't know what it is', she whined.
'What makes you say that?', said her Mum.
'I've got this feeling in my middle.'
'What sort of feeling?'
'A pulling feeling ...'
'What does your pulling feeling need', asked her Mum. 'Does it need a cuddle?'
'No! Not a cuddle! I don't want a cuddle!' Carmella was scornful.
She shut her eyes and examined the pulling feeling in her middle. First she rotated her tummy slowly, then lay down on the kitchen floor and jiggled on her back for a bit. She turned on her side and drew her knees up to her chest in a tight ball. Then, all of a sudden she arched backwards into a fully stretched banana shape. Just as suddenly she drew back into the curled ball and shot out into the banana shape again. She did this over and over which had the effect of turning her slowly through 180° on the floor. At last, tired, she rolled onto her back and stared at the ceiling.
'That's better', she said. 'That's what my pulling feeling wanted.'

Carmella has addressed her problem in sensation and movement, rather than reason. Working in direct participation with sensation and feeling she has identified a problem and resolved it quickly and efficiently. In Movement Play, children learn to value movement as another way of addressing problems, and they develop the skills to make use of their body intelligence at will.

> *Imran (3) sweeps all the Duplo off the table in a rage. Julie the nursery worker sees it. She catches his eye and with complete seriousness, and no blame, she mirrors his gesture sweeping her own arm through the air in front of her. She does it again being careful to mirror not only the shape but also the quality, which speaks of the inner attitude. Imran stops and watches her. 'I know that feeling', she says. Imran gives a half laugh.*
>
> *Julie invites him, through her movement, to join her in repeating the gesture in mid air. They do it together and it changes slightly each time until it has less force. The last time she does it Imran doesn't copy her. 'Now, let's pick up the Duplo. If you sweep it off the table no one can use it. If you want to, we can do some more moving later.'*

Using movement this nursery worker acknowledges what Imran is feeling and reflects her recognition back to him. She also lets him know that the consequence of his actions is unhelpful, without blaming him. She is working with direct perception (to let him know that he is seen and understood) and reason (to reiterate important nursery guidelines). Movement Play provides the structure within which to acknowledge and then address the feelings he has, rather than simply asking him not to display them. Imran has more chance of learning about his feelings if there is a way to explore them.

Movement Play provides a highly focused opportunity for children to notice those around them. In self-directed play and with support from adults they can enhance their ability to detect mood, to read other people's intentions and to have an influence on other people - all skills which depend to a large degree on reading body movement.

> *Preeti (3) came running into nursery, screeching round the corner by her tray and*

straight up to the circle area. Plop! She sat next to Michael (4) with a bump, her legs sticking out in front of her and her arms by her side. 'Pheeeeeew!', she announced to no-one in particular, jiggling her toes together and patting the ground beside her. Michael looked, then stuck his legs out too, jiggling his toes like Preeti. She didn't seem to notice. He jiggled his toes more obviously and said 'Pheeeeew!' too. Preeti turned.

He bounced his feet on the floor and slapped the ground beside him once. Preeti slapped. Michael slapped again. They laughed.

Michael had really noticed Preeti and found a way of acknowledging her, and of joining her. This had been a first conversation of the day.

Movement Play allows children to engage with, and take responsibility for, complex social negotiation within their peer group. Using direct perception of what they see and feel, carefully supported by adults, they can learn about aspects of group relations that would be very challenging if dealt with only in thought and words.

There are twenty five children (5 and 6) and two adults (40s) beginning a Movement Group. We are all sitting on the floor in the corner of the classroom, having piled the tables and chairs out of the way. The class has 22 girls and 3 boys. The boys have chosen to sit together. As we begin, the teacher explains the rules. Everyone can do a movement with the elastic and all the rest of the group will follow them. When the leader wants to, they will say 'Pass' and then it will be the turn of the next person round the circle. The first fifteen in the circle are girls. I am surprised at their confidence in taking control of passing it on when they are ready. When adults do this activity they often contrive to leave that bit to the teacher, feeling uncomfortable about taking responsibility for how long a turn to have. These girls are quite happy. Then comes the first boy in the circle. He grins madly as he offers a very testing idea involving leaning backwards and waving our legs in the air.

We puff and pant and grunt and just about keep up with him. He takes a very long turn.

After a while one of the girls cheerfully complains. 'O, Alex, you're taking ages.' Alex grins some more but doesn't pass. Another girl complains. 'Hurry up.' After a while, the girls stop doing the movement with Alex. Their bodies show directly that they have had enough. They continue to complain. 'Pass', he says. The next boy offers something even more complicated and difficult. The girls groan, but they join in enthusiastically in their bodies.

When this boy also takes ages, and then the third as well, the girls start to reflect upon the fact that all the boys have had longer turns than they 'should'. In fact the third boy goes on moving throughout the subsequent conversation.

The teacher says to the boys, 'Did you notice? You have all taken long turns, boys.' They grin some more. 'Well, we wanted to', says one of them.
'Why shouldn't we?', says another.
'Because Sophie has to wait ages for her turn and that's not fair', says a girl across the circle.
'So?'
'So you should take the same length turn as everyone else.'
'No one said we had to. Mrs H said we could take as long as we wanted.'

The teacher, still moving with the third boy, says to all of them: 'Perhaps some days any one of us might want a longer turn and some days it's all right to have a shorter turn. I know some days I feel like moving more and on other days I'm happy to pass almost straight away'. They all think. Then another girl says, 'What if the boys always take longer turns'.

'Well, there's more of you than us', says one of the boys. 'We always get less time than you girls!'

A theme that was present in this group, but hidden, has become clear. The boys say that because there are twenty two girls and only three boys in the class, the 'girls side' always 'wins'. Because of this basic imbalance, the boys feel they should be able to move for as long as all the girls put together. Later, in the staff room, the teacher confirms that she has felt a them-and-us undercurrent for some time, but hadn't realised that the boys were feeling this way. She is glad to have it out in the open.

These children were beginning to get to grips with aspects of the new citizenship curriculum - 'developing concern for common good and learning to resolve conflicts; developing a disposition to work with and for others, and a proclivity to act responsibly'. The girls were showing 'tolerance', starting to address issues through which they can begin to 'develop a moral code for the group'. Several of them were showing the 'courage to define a point of view'. Only time will tell if the boys will develop an 'openness to change their opinion in the light of discussion and evidence'. Movement Play offers appropriate opportunities for very young children to become involved in robust social negotiation.

Communication, Language and Literacy

Eighty per cent of human communication happens without words. Approximately fifty five per cent happens in movement alone. And yet when we teach 'speaking and listening' skills to young children we do so almost entirely in words.

In Movement Play children learn to speak and listen in movement as well as words. Through movement they 'talk' about how they feel, they tell stories, they ask questions and give answers. Through direct participation with sensation, feeling and movement they 'imagine and recreate roles and experiences' and 'organise, sequence and clarify thinking, ideas, feelings and events'. Children develop confidence in their ability to express themselves through movement and in being watched by others. As they watch others move, they develop keen 'listening' skills. They learn to differentiate functional and expressive movement from exploration of inner experience. They develop the language to make both felt and rational responses.

Throughout this book there are many examples of young children 'speaking' their experience, communicating their wants and needs, and 'listening' to others doing the same - in movement. When children can do these things with insight and awareness, they have extra tools for making and maintaining mature relationships, expressing themselves and communicating with others. Movement Play gives children the opportunity to become body literate - able to work with movement just as they learn to work with words.

Maisie (4) crawled around under the tables showing the other children what she had been doing as she played.

'I saw my baby sister', said Naomi afterwards when their teacher asked them to respond to what they had seen. 'She crawls.'
'I saw a tiger', growled Lee.
'I've got a big yellow bruise on my knee', said Reece. 'My knee hurts when I crawl'.

'Try crawling just like Maisie', said their teacher, 'and listen to what it feels like when you do that crawling.'

Afterwards they talked again, and then drew two pictures - one about watching Maisie crawl and one about their own crawling.

Knowledge and understanding of the world

Movement Play emphasises discovery of the world by sensing and feeling our relationship with our environment and the things in it. It encourages children to ask questions about how things are and to seek answers from their body intelligence. This might be a simple issue, like learning through touch, or something altogether more complicated and inexplicable like the woman's exploration of the 'dinosaur-bird' through movement (page 61). In the story below, a small child explores something that is beyond his intellectual understanding, but which he can embody - in order to learn in a different way.

Arthur (6) stands in the middle of the circle with his eyes shut. He waits. I wonder if he will move at all. Then I notice that he is blinking in a very exaggerated way. He is screwing his eyes up tightly and then opening them, over and over again. This is the beginning of his dance. He is totally absorbed and focused. After a while he stamps one foot, then both feet. Big stamps, rhythmic stamps ... and still he opens and shuts his eyes.

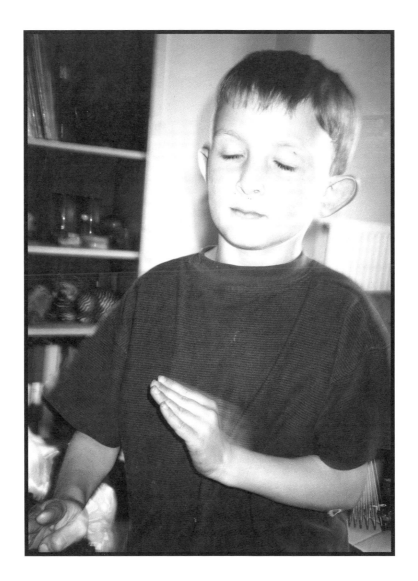

Then he starts to run round in a tight circle in the middle. He leans inwards and runs as fast as he can without falling over. He lifts his arms in a diagonal stretch. Then he slows, and stops, and stands very still in the centre. His dance is over.

'It was the Great War', he says. I am surprised! Can he really mean what he has just said?

'I saw it on television with my Granny last night', he says gravely, and there is much sombre nodding from the others.

Sometimes intellectual thinking is too remote; children must go back to sensation and movement as the source of their learning. Movement Play encourages children to embody problems and challenges in order to find new, effective ways to solve them.

Susie attends a special school where she has a weekly session with a dancer. Susie likes writing and has a lot to say. But until recently, her teachers could only read a portion of what she wrote, because Susie didn't notice the edge of the paper. As she wrote she worked her way across the page, then onto the desk until she came to the end of her reach. Then she returned to the page and started all over again. No amount of talking about it helped; bigger paper didn't help. Then her teacher asked the dancer if she would work on the page problem.

Together they worked with an aspect of movement called 'flow'. It concerns the way a person allows energy to pass through and out of their body (or the way they hold it in). Susie moved with lots of 'free flow'. Her movement seemed to go on and on. If you clapped your hands and said stop, it took her a long time to come to some sort of stop ... and even then there'd be some tiny movements remaining. They played 'flow' games - letting the energy go, then trying to stop it and hold it in. Gradually the games moved closer to the skill of stopping at the end of the page. They played 'Move your arm along the floor, now Stop!'. They got out paper and played 'Move your arm across the paper and then, Stop!'.

Susie returned to the classroom and never wrote off the paper again. She needed to learn this through her body, not through a process of reasoning.

Creative Development

Movement Play introduces children to the ways in which visual images, stories and fantasies can be uncovered in direct participation with sensation, feelings and movement. It introduces children to practical ways in which they can locate, explore and share their inner world of image through movement. Adults help children both to notice their inner world of image, and to develop ways of 'entering' and working with these images at will.

There are no external imaginative ideas in Movement Play; unlike a creative dance approach, the subject matter is always created by the child. 'Working imaginatively' in Movement Play doesn't mean taking an idea from the intellect ('Be a Tree'), and exploring it in movement. Children explore images of their own that arise as they play, and learn to work with felt responses.

We read a story called The Winter Bear - about a bear who is discovered hanging in a frosty tree on a cold winter walk. We talked about it; about how the bear might have been feeling when it was alone, and how it might have felt when the children carried it back to their house. Rian listened carefully. Then we made a circle and anyone who wanted could go into the centre and move - with the idea of the winter bear in their minds. They didn't have to act it out, or be the bear, just move with the thought of the story somewhere about them. Rian dived in. She lay on the floor on her side and lifted a leg in the air. Then an arm. She stayed there in this position, stock still, while we watched. After a minute or so she opened her eyes and said 'Finished', and came to sit in the circle. 'I wanted to be hanging in the tree', she said. 'It was lonely. I was blue'.

In Movement Play children explore ways to form their experience - so that it is both their own, and separate from them. They can do this in movement, drawing, words or other art work. The representations they create are made through direct perception, rather than through a process of reasoning. Children don't have to decide which movement to show, or what to draw, they improvise - following the flow of a movement and allowing the 'representation' to evolve spontaneously. They learn about felt responses, rather than reasoned responses.

Lucy (6) was eager to dance for everyone. When invited, she chose fast music and she wanted me to partner her. She began ... I followed as best I could. At first, she tried lots of different things, groping her way towards a subject matter. She hopped around in the middle, then crossed the circle in straight lines - first one way and then the next. Finally she came to the centre to meet me. A pattern emerged and we repeated it, settling it in our minds. We finished in the middle.

The next child in the centre picked up on Lucy's theme; she crossed the circle then added her own bit - a little jump as she reached the edge - before turning to cross the circle again. Once again there were many journeys back and forth before she finished in the middle.

The third and final child for the day built on both the previous dances. He crossed the circle, put in that jump, and then added a turn of his own. He also added a running bit in the middle of the circle at the end.

I was amazed. These children displayed a perfect understanding of choreographic progression - found a movement idea and developed it. I set no guidelines as to how this would happen; we spoke of no techniques or movement ideas. They simply used an innate understanding that I didn't know they had.

In fact, as the term progressed (we met two or three times a week to dance for 20 minutes) the whole class (with the exception of two children who offered other ideas) used Lucy's first dance as a springboard. It became the theme for our work together for fourteen weeks.

Physical development

'Physical development in the foundation stage is about improving skills of coordination, control, manipulation and movement. Physical development has two other very important aspects. It helps children gain confidence in what they can do and enables them to feel the positive benefits of being healthy and active. Effective physical development helps children to develop a positive sense of well-being.' (*Curriculum guidance for the foundation stage*)

The foundations for the development of physical skill, and for gaining confidence in ourselves, are twofold. One is the developmental movement patterns that give children the neurological and physical basis for each subsequent stage, and the other is a sound relationship with bodily-felt experience. Movement Play places these two at the centre of a physical development curriculum, in the knowledge that the other skills will follow.

Baby Zack is up on his feet at ten months, delighted to pull himself to standing and stagger around the edge of the room. His Mum is concerned though - to date he has spent virtually no time on his tummy and very little on his hands and knees, preferring to bottom-paddle his way about. As he stands, she can see that his feet are rolling inwards and his knees are close together. Knowing that I 'do something with crawling' she seeks me out in the playground to ask what I think of all this.

Over the next few weeks we spend happy mornings crawling around the floor with Zack, persuading him that it is just as fun to be on the floor as it is to be upright. He is not so sure, but reluctantly agrees to join us and eventually develops a splendid crawling pattern (though he still resists lying on his tummy). I also discover that he has a 'lazy eye', which his mother, understandably, hadn't connected with the crawling issue.

Zack needs all the belly-crawling and all-fours-crawling he can get to ensure that his hips rotate correctly into place allowing his legs to align correctly underneath him when he walks. Similarly, he needs to spend time on his tummy and knees to help his shoulders to align properly. Adults who have skimped through these early stages may well walk with slightly turned out feet in future. They may have niggling knee problems throughout their lives, or shoulder aches and pains. Zack's eyes

too need the particular movement experiences that go along with belly crawling and crawling on all fours, to help them come into alignment. If he crawls enough, it may help to correct his lazy eye.

If he goes back and revisits the belly-crawling, his Mum may never know what problems she has avoided.

Being Seen: affirming self

Movement Play contributes to each of these areas of learning, but it also addresses another area of fundamental importance to the developing confidence of a child. Our capacity to learn is inseperable from our emotional wellbeing. We can be highly intelligent and skilled people, but if we are not acknowledged for who we are, (rather than who people would like us to be) we are unlikely to be able to build a deep comfort in ourselves.

> '... inherent in being a person in the cultures of the West is a deep longing to be seen as we are by another. We want to be witnessed, without judgment, projection, or interpretation.' (Body and Soul. Janet Adler)

Getting praise, or rewards, for specific accomplishments is an important part of building self-esteem. But beyond this lies a driving need to be acknowledged simply as the unique person we are. This acknowledgement seems to provide a basis from which we can dare to be ourselves. The more acknowledgement we get, the more fully ourselves we are able to become.

The frequency with which some children say 'Look at me Mummy' or 'Come and watch me' tells us that they need to be seen. They make clear verbal requests. Children also make non-verbal requests to be seen. Postures and gestures can deliberately draw attention to specific feelings or attitudes - the child who loiters close to you with a particular hang-dog expression may need you to notice how she feels today. She may need you to ask how she feels, or acknowledge that you have seen her by mirroring her movement in an appropriate way. (Adults are not excluded from this kind of behaviour; when spouse wants you to acknowledge the nasty cold he has, there may be copious rubbing of the chest and an exaggerated droop of the shoulders that invites a tender inquiry and some sympathy.)

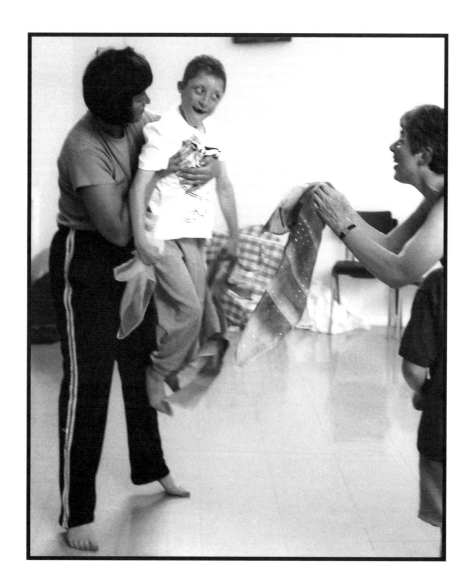

Experience that *takes place* in our body sometimes needs to be acknowledged *in* our body. Words will do, but a physical acknowledgement may be better. Spouse may feel better if he gets a tender rub on his chest - the painful bit - and a cuddle, rather than verbal sympathy and a cold remedy. For children, acknowledgement through Movement Play addresses their physical communication more directly than words.

Beth (5) had a splinter painfully removed from her finger before she arrived this morning. She holds up her finger for me to see the wound. Her body is stiff and her movements rather held and tentative. She has a generally wounded air and doesn't speak.

We are just about to dance and I suggest that she might like to go into the middle of the circle and dance the Dance of the Wounded Finger. She smiles cautiously and nods her willingness. I don't give her any ideas as to how this dance might go. (See page 363 for a fuller description of this structure.) She knows that she has our full attention and she may do whatever she feels like doing ... as long as she doesn't hurt anyone.

She walks slowly into the centre, still holding her finger with her other hand. She circles slowly, just walking round the edge past all the other children who are sitting in a circle on the floor. As she comes round for the third time she holds out her finger for everyone to look at as she passes; then she gathers pace and starts to run round, gradually raising her finger as she does so until both hands are held high above her head. Then she makes her circles smaller, spiralling into the centre, finger held aloft. When she reaches the very centre she suddenly lets go with the supporting hand, and begins to whoosh her sore finger through the air, her hand diving and darting rapidly around her head. With a sudden dive, she crouches down and drops her hand, palm up, on the floor in front of her. She is still, and breathing heavily.

She looks up.
'It's all tingly', she says seriously. 'But it doesn't hurt anymore.'
She is no longer stiff and held in her body as she goes to sit down.

Within learning settings we usually require children to divert their need to be seen into being heard. '*Tell me* what's wrong', we say, refusing to acknowledge that we can read the body signals perfectly well. We trust words when we don't trust movement. '*Tell me* about the splinter.' But this is something that has happened to Beth's body and perhaps it is best shown, rather than spoken.

Her teacher and I did wonder, after the splinter dance, whether I had opened the floodgates for every minor injury in the class to be displayed in the circle. Certainly a few showed me bruises and grazes and inquired as to whether they might do the Wounded Knee or the Bumped Elbow dance next time. We decided that, if necessary, we would support each and every one, feeling that if this was how the children needed to be seen, then there wasn't a problem. As it happened, none of the children took up the option of doing an injury dance until one child broke an arm at home and did the most daring Plaster Dance to rapturous applause from the other children - and a missed heartbeat or two from me and her teacher.

Some children have a more urgent need to be seen, a need that presents itself in challenging ways. The 'challenge' (and it is the adult's challenge not the child's) is this: can we find an appropriate structure that will allow the child to express what is most urgent, even when it is uncomfortable? Movement is one of the ways in which a child communicates their deepest needs and Movement Play can be the medium through which this communication can be directly acknowledged and worked with.

Barry (3) has trouble joining in. He is aggressive to other children and demanding of adults' time and attention. In a group situation he often shouts out and hits children who get in his way. He is part of a small Movement Group with five other children. Here, he wants to be the centre of attention all the time.

Based on experience, the nursery worker has taken to inviting Barry to come to the room first and they spend ten minutes playing together before the others arrive. In this time, she gives him all her attention. He leads, she follows, mirroring his movement as closely as she can. Today his movements change frequently; first he jumps, then he hops, then he crashes to the floor and spins round. He bangs his legs on the floor and crawls under the table, then he curls up small. In mirroring what he does, she lets him know, directly, that she sees him and that she can join him as an equal. It is a direct

form of approval. Sometimes she underlines what they are doing in words as well. 'You're jumping ... now you're hopping and now we are both crawling under the table.'

After a time of simply following him, she looks for points of contact ... of relationship. They meet under the table and push their heads together briefly, then pass on; as they bang their hands on the floor in a rising crescendo of sound, she makes sure that they share a rhythm as closely as possible ... she tries to make sure that her hands bang the floor at the same moment as Barry's. 'Listen', she says. They are banging as one ... it is the equivalent of a feeling of agreement in a conversation. And then their feet meet as they sit in the middle of the room. Barry pushes; she pushes back. Barry pushes harder; she pushes back harder still. He laughs. He pushes as hard as he can. She has to use all her strength to meet him. They groan and grunt and laugh with the effort. Then they finally burst apart and Barry lies on his back panting and laughing. She lies next to him.

The others arrive. During the group Barry makes frequent movement references to the time they have spent together - he bangs his legs on the floor, crawls under the table - reminding them of their special time together, their 'secret' conversation but he lets the others have attention as well.

Movement Play extends the foundation stage curriculum in many areas. It gives us a way of harnessing the incredible energy in young children that we often feel compelled to squash. It provides structured opportunities for making the most of those wriggly, jiggly moments and provides reasons to encourage children to move, rather than fighting the inevitable and trying to get them to keep still. It is intended to extend the ways we support learning, but to do so within the guidelines that all Early Years settings are struggling to keep abreast of. This isn't another new thing to do; it is a different, effective way of working towards existing goals.

Hopping Home Backwards

SECTION 2

Organising Movement Play

Hopping Home Backwards

6
A framework for learning through Movement Play

Experiencing ... Focusing ... Reflecting

All children have the potential for body intelligence. It has nothing to do with physical agility or 'natural grace'. It is about participating directly with sensation, feelings, movement and image and making use of the information found there.

Body intelligence is a natural potential, but children have to learn to make use of it; in the Early Years we help them to learn to learn from their bodies, just as they learn to learn from their intellects. Section One was about the ideas behind body intelligence and Movement Play; this section is entirely practical. It looks at how children learn in direct participation with the senses, and the role of adults in supporting and extending this learning.

Style of learning

Movement Play, the place in the curriculum where we can focus on body intelligence, isn't a taught subject. It is a process whereby adults help children to become more fully themselves through exploration, reflection and growing self-awareness. A traditional relationship which casts the adult as the controlling party, and always the more knowledgeable, is not appropriate. Movement Play requires an open, compassionate interest from adults who look for ways of helping children to learn in the fabric of their everyday lives and to explore more of themselves, others, and the world around.

The subject matter for Movement Play within the curriculum is each child's personal experience. In creative dance activities, adults first offer external themes (stories, images, particular ways of moving) and children explore them through their bodies. In Movement Play, children's spontaneous movement comes first, and themes are drawn out. The framework for structuring this learning begins with the experience itself. Adults offer open activities within which children explore what it is like to *be* a body. When children are able to dive into this exploration wholeheartedly and at will, adults help them to 'focus' on the experience (notice more about it) and then to 'reflect' (to draw out things that will be useful, or enjoyable, to them in their lives). This three part process forms the framework for learning through Movement Play.

EXPERIENCING

In order to turn body intelligence from a potential into a useful resource we must start with a child's ability to engage with their bodily-felt experience. Children need to be comfortable with their physicality, willing to take their focus to their inner experience, and confident that their desire to explore their experience through movement will be supported. The first phase of the learning framework is simply providing opportunities for children to get to know the lived experience of their body

'Experiencing' is about being, rather than doing. Many children do this naturally as part of their everyday lives; some do not and require extra support. Bringing spontaneous Movement Play into a *learning* context requires some special considerations from adults.

Bridging

Although most children move a great deal they are not used to focusing on their movement and they don't expect adults to join them in a purposeful way. In fact they probably know that movement play is not 'normal' for adults and that much of their own is generally ignored. If Movement Play suddenly enters a more formal agenda, the adults must let the children know how they can behave in this new situation.

When I first met this group (4 year olds), they came into the room warily. I was sitting on the floor in the middle of the room with my legs stretched out in front of me. I patted the floor and invited them to sit in a circle with me. Gradually we put all our toes together in the middle. The children were subdued and cautious. They didn't know me and didn't know what we would be doing together. After we had looked at the pattern all our legs made, and everyone had been (unusually) still, Kirsty wriggled. I mirrored the wriggle and said, 'You've got wriggling legs Kirsty', as I wriggled. I invited the other children to try Kirsty's wriggle. They looked surprised. Did I really mean I wanted them to wriggle? They took some persuading. 'Can anybody else do Kirsty's wriggle?' One by one they wriggled too. When I looked pleased, they wriggled some more until the wriggles and giggles grew quite wild and we had to stop in case we hurt each other ...

Physical Safety

Moving bodies can hurt and be hurt. It is important that the adults help children to understand, from the start, that it is their responsibility to take particular care of both themselves and others as they indulge in Movement Play.

As Ramone (4) ran round with the ribbon stick, the children sitting in the circle were obviously anxious about being hit, yet none of them either said anything, or made any move to protect themselves. The teacher reminded them - 'If you are anxious, it is fine to protect yourselves'. And she held a hand in front of her face in a protective way. Several of the sitting children followed her example. Others didn't feel the need. At the end of this dance the teacher spoke further about it. 'Although the mover will always try not to hurt or frighten anybody, it may happen accidentally. So the rest of us must take responsibility for protecting ourselves. And sometimes we might want to say to the mover, please move further away, or lift the stick up. If we don't tell them, they may not know that's how we feel.'

Emotional safety

The creation of a non-judgmental atmosphere is as much to do with safety (emotional safety) as it is to do with maximising the potential learning from the Movement Play. Children need to feel safe before they can show who they are. If children feel accepted without judgment, they are more likely to embody their experience and to share their own meaning for that experience. Creating such an environment is not easy, but it is the vital foundation for Movement Play. Adults need to develop their own capacity for responding without judgment and help children to do the same. They also need to encourage children to supply meaning, and vocabulary, for their own experience. We have become used to asking open questions about children's art work, in order that we support, rather than crush it. ('Tell me about your picture', rather than 'That's a lovely rabbit' - when the child has actually painted a castle.)

Many adults are familiar with helping children to separate what they think from what they feel; within literacy work children practice identifying fact and opinion as they find it in written work. 'I Saw, I Felt, I Imagined' is a simple framework developed by Tina Stromsted and Neala Haze within Authentic Movement work, which helps to structure the complex range of things we think, feel and imagine so that we are clear that they are our thoughts and feelings (subjective) and not the Truth (objective). (See pages 193 - 196 for further details)

I have watched all kinds of people grappling with the 'I Saw, I Felt, I Imagined structure', from sophisticated groups of therapists with many years experience, to a group of four, five and six year olds who came to it for the first time as part of their Circle Time. Adults often come to it with much baggage and angst. The children accepted it with a simplicity and willingness that seemed to feed their ability to make it work. The adults have to be repeatedly reminded to locate what they see in the movement rather than going off on their own flight of fancy. The children almost never missed this simple, and generous link. 'When I saw your tummy moving I imagined a dog in my garden rolling about.'

Physical comfort

Over the years that I have worked as a dancer or movement specialist in school and community settings I have developed a passionate commitment to working wherever I am put, because I want movement work to happen as an ordinary part of life. But the bottom line is that it must be clean.

How can anyone develop a delight in physical exploration if it means crawling through the squashed peas and mashed potato left over from lunch? If you have to clean up first - so be it. I have discovered that hoovering and sweeping are often an integral part of the Beginning section of Movement Play activities. (See page 157)

Establishing Appropriateness

Adults must help children to understand when Movement Play is appropriate and when it is not. Clearly there are times when stillness is vital; just as there are times when voices must be quiet. This requires a consistent policy for each setting. Rehearsal of these guidelines may need to be routine or even ritualised as part of Movement Play itself. Children need to be encouraged to notice and consider the things that might affect their choices - the space, the comfort of people around and existing rules for that environment.

> The wriggly, jiggly group who start with me, move straight on to pre-writing and drawing skills with their teacher. So, having been invited to display and develop their wriggles, they are then required to 'sit on your bottom while you are writing'. I was anxious that the Movement Play would make things difficult for their teacher. Was it fair to encourage them to wriggle for half an hour, when they were expected to sit still immediately after? (Particularly as they are a very wriggly and excitable group anyway.) Since I was anxious I decided to go back to their classroom to see how it would be. I was delighted to discover that they seemed unperturbed by the possible inconsistency. Penny always asked them about their wriggles. Their teacher always asked them to sit still while they wrote and drew. It seemed simple as long as we were both clear.

Structures: Boundaries and space

The purpose of providing structure for Movement Play is not to impose, but to enable. The best structures provide a combination of 'boundaries' (to reassure the mover that they are safe and held) and 'space' (within which to explore). If the space is too open children can feel lost and unable to act; if the boundaries are too tight, they can feel restricted.

Providing structure doesn't mean determining subject matter, or telling children what to do. There are a number of things that shape spontaneous movement.

NOTES FOR LEADERS:

THINGS THAT STRUCTURE SPONTANEOUS MOVEMENT

YOUR INVOLVEMENT	
Verbal feedback	Talking about an individual's or group's movement while they move, or afterwards
Movement feedback	Mirroring, Reflecting and Patterning. See pages 168 - 170
Watching	Impromptu or prearranged
Moving with someone else	Impromptu, prearranged child and adult, children together
THE SPACE	
Establishing a specific place where children can go when they want to move, or which they go to at specific times	For impromptu play For Activity Groups For Circle Time To watch others
MUSIC	
Tapes and CDs	Simple choice of fast and slow music

NOTES FOR LEADERS:

MORE THINGS THAT STRUCTURE SPONTANEOUS MOVEMENT

PROPS	
Anything that stimulates movement. These can be specifically for Movement Play (Ribbon Sticks, Elastic Ropes) things around (chairs, hoops) and things children bring from home.	A variety of items that support attention to different kinds of bodily-felt experience
ACTIVITIES WITH RULES	
Open structures that allow children to provide both the subject matter and their own ways of moving.	Lots of suggestions in Section 3

Adult Participation

Adult participation is a hugely important part of a successful learning environment. In Movement Play adults need to be active participants. Moving with children is ideal. However, many adults feel thoroughly daunted by the idea of crawling around under tables, leaping enthusiastically to reach the ceiling or banging their legs up and down on the floor, and need to find other ways of being actively involved. It is perfectly possible to be fully and actively involved through watching, talking and drawing.

Taking children seriously

Movement Play is uniquely suitable as a learning medium for children; for many, spontaneous movement is their home base. As we encourage children to discover and explore this aspect of themselves and their learning, we have to be able to support them, stick up for them, advocate on their behalf and translate where necessary. As adults we must overcome any discomfort we feel about spontaneous movement. If children are to learn all they can from Movement Play, we must take them and their movement seriously.

Knowing when to get out of the way

Lastly, and just as importantly, adults need to know when their support isn't needed; when to withdraw and let children get on with it for themselves.

NOTES FOR LEADERS:

SUMMARY OF WHAT WE ARE TRYING TO ACHIEVE IN THE EXPERIENCING PHASE

BABIES & CHILDREN	ADULT ROLE

Attitudes
• enjoy spontaneous movement play for its own sake
• take pleasure in their physicality as an important part of their lives
• are interested in the many different layers of experience prompted by the body as well as functional and expressive movement
 	
Skills
• able to move spontaneously at will - on their own, with other children and appropriate adults
• able to notice how much people move in everyday life
• able to be in their bodies - in sensation, feelings, movement and image
	• Make, or support, lots of opportunities for spontaneous movement play with babies and young children:
	  ○ in fleeting moments as part of everyday life
	  ○ playing mirroring & follow my leader games letting children be in charge
	  ○ by making a special movement corner just for Movement Play
	  ○ by providing resources that encourage Movement Play (music, equipment, yourself)
	  ○ by organising structured movement games for groups of adults and children - that support spontaneous, free-flow movement where as much movement as possible is initiated by the children
	  ○ introducing turn-taking into the play
	
	• lots of positive feedback on movement of all kinds
	• if you can, let them see you enjoy different sorts of Movement Play. This will give the most positive message of all

FOCUSING

In the second part of the learning framework adults bring children's attention to the many layers of physical experience contained within their play and help them to develop ways of focusing on this experience.

'Focusing' concerns the child's ability to make conscious, and differentiate between, different kinds of bodily-felt experience. Most of us notice the body when something goes wrong - an injury, a pain, an unsatisfied thirst - but have only a patchy awareness of it at other times. In this phase of learning through Movement Play, a child is encouraged to *notice* bodily-felt experience (sensation, feeling, movement); visual experience prompted by the body (still images and visual imaginings); aural experience prompted by the body (sounds, rhythms and melodies that emerge in the imagination) and thought-processes (stories, fantasies and memories).

Adults have a specific role in helping children to become more focused as they play.

Watching

If adults give their full attention to children as they move it helps them to focus. Children also learn, by example, how to watch in a mindful way, and how to share their thoughts and feelings about what they see.

It is hard to watch purposefully with no structure. Adults, therefore, provide the structures that enable children to separate and articulate their different responses. The 'I Saw, I Felt, I Imagined' structure applies particularly to watching movement. (See pages 193 - 196) Inviting children to draw as they watch also helps to create a focus for both watcher and mover (See page 385).

Developing an inner witness: noticing WHAT happens in the body

In order to learn through direct participation with the senses, children must learn to notice their bodily-felt experience. Adults help them to develop an inner witness - an internal voice that notices rather than directs. The inner witness is a link between our intellect and our body; between our rational thoughts and our body thoughts. It notices, but does not judge. Adults encourage children to pay attention to two things: the direct experience of sensation, feeling and movement, and the indirect experience of these same things when they reflect on them (inviting them to speak about,

or draw, their experience afterwards). Children will quickly become used to the fact that adults are interested in their experience and develop their own strategies for focusing on and remembering.

Adults need to develop their own inner witness in order to develop their ability to work with children in this way.

Back to the Body...
Noticing the voice in your head as you move
Dip back into your inner awareness of bodily-felt experience. Give yourself time to leave words and thinking processes and discover what sensations, feelings, movements and images float to the surface. Give yourself time to settle in. Can you locate the voice in your head - your intellect - that comments on what you do? Can you move and listen to the voice at the same time? It may take a few 'go's. When you feel you can move and listen, start to separate the different kinds of things that the voice says. Can you separate directions (I must move like this ... sit down now ...) from judgments (I look silly ... I'm too old to roll around the floor ...) from things you simply notice (I'm jumping ... my left leg is shaking ... I'm tired). It takes a lot of practice to become clear about all the different things the voice says, and the ways that it says them.

Back to the Body...
Noticing the voice in your head as you watch
Watch someone moving. It doesn't have to be a long piece of observation. In fact, this isn't an observation exercise at all. Think of it instead as 'witnessing' and know that you will have many responses in your intellect and your body, most of which generally go unnoticed. Allow yourself to be stirred and affected by what you see. Can you locate the voice in your head - your intellect - that comments as you watch? Can you watch carefully and listen to the voice at the same time.

When you feel you can watch and listen to the internal voice in your head, try watching and listening to the sensations, feelings, tiny movements and images that occur in your body as you watch. What do you feel as you watch?

Developing an inner witness: noticing HOW things happen
As children play within a given structure it quickly becomes apparent that each child behaves

differently - of course. In addition to the movements they perform in order to complete their task are the less conscious movements that happen around the edges - the tiny gestures and postural shifts that speak of the person separate from the activity. In these bits - the process rather than the task - there is a wealth of potential learning, for it is here that we can gain insight into how we organise ourselves, and how we respond to our environment. In busy lives it is important to be able to focus on the task in hand, but it is equally important to be able to switch our attention to the *way* we do things, for this is the stuff of future self-knowledge and self possession.

In Movement Play adults encourage children to notice the way they do things, as well as the things that they do.

> ### Extracts from a diary
> *... Keith is a fabulous dancer, a joy to watch. He seems to know how to structure a dance and how to find shapes in his body that will delight both himself and others. When I dance with him he encourages me to really dance - not just to move, but to stretch into that other part of myself that wants to communicate everything I am in every gesture ...*
>
> *... Keith loves to dance so much he doesn't want to stop. Each time he dances he seems to fill with longing and yearning and being-alive ... and he doesn't want to stop. Every cell of him seems to quiver with emotion, his body an Aeolian harp vibrating with the whisper of the wind as it brushes over him ...*
>
> *... He will do anything to avoid finishing a dance. His teacher says he avoids lots of endings and often cries when he realises someone is leaving, or he must finish something he is enjoying. He cries many times during a day and especially piteously at the end of a day. Tears accompany most transitions ...*
>
> *... Keith has had a troubled life. I wonder if endings hold pain and anxiety for him? Or whether he is simply a troubled chap, compelled to search for something that will relieve an inner turmoil ... compelled to go in search of himself. He seems to relax so when he dances with all his body and soul ...*

... I focus on endings a lot in the Movement Play we do together. Here is a good place to practice them, free from words or the necessity to reason or explain. I have taken to giving him very clear signals about which bit of the dance we are in - beginning, middle and end. I hope this will a) help him to relax when it is not the ending phase and b) have positive experiences of ending that help him to build an easier relationship to them ...

... As I say 'And now we are near the ending of our dance', Keith always restimulates the most exuberant and involved part of our moving and urges me, in movement, to dance on. As I take my movements to the floor, and reduce them in size (gradually trying to bring the dance towards a close) he grows bigger and rises. He senses my every attempt to close and mirrors it with a request (in movement) to continue. This is like a battle of wills. I diminish, he increases. I fall, he rises. Any verbal prompt only serves to stimulate more urgent moving and he clutches my hands tighter lest I get away. And he cries ...

... I love endings. I can feel frustration mounting in me as Keith tries to sabotage my attempts. Today, as I went about the professional business of carefully winding down, I could feel my own desires fighting for attention. With my eyes shut, I could see images of shadowy figures running away from something ... pushing and shoving things out of their way in their urgency to be away ...

... Keith cries less when we dance together now. Tears still sometimes roll down his cheeks when I say 'We must find an ending soon Keith. In the next few minutes we will finish this dance. We will dance together again soon'. But he is managing it all a lot better in Movement Play sessions ...

...Today Keith finished a dance before me! I was just starting the whole ending routine and he sank to his knees - pulling me down too - rocked a bit holding my hands then dropped his head to his chest and stopped moving. It was definitely the end! ...

...Today Keith and I did a little dance in the corridor as he was on his way to something else ... and he didn't cling. Well, only a tiny bit. I wouldn't have done that six months ago because it would have been so difficult ...

NOTES FOR LEADERS:

DEVELOPING ATTITUDES AND SKILLS IN THE FOCUSING PHASE

BABIES & CHILDREN	ADULT ROLE
Attitudes • children *believe that human beings learn in their bodies* **Skills** • able to play with attention, and with awareness of what they are doing and feeling • able to play in different ways, in response to different stimuli • able to separate different bodily-felt experiences (sensations, feelings, different kinds of movement and accompanying visual images and inner sound) • able to show what they have been doing or talk about it with others	• find opportunities during any activity for children to focus on different aspects of bodily-felt experience: touch, sensation, feelings, visualisation, images, stories ... (what it feels like in their body) • watch children move (in fleeting moments, in fully fledged games, as they use play equipment) and ask them about different kinds of bodily-felt experience • offer different stimuli (music, props, structures) • make opportunities for children to share their experiences in whatever ways they choose • reflect children's movement back to them, in movement or words • *be a role model for interest in bodily-felt experience by talking about your own experience*

REFLECTING

In the third phase of learning, adults help children to work with, and make use of, information from the body. 'Reflecting' concerns the child's ability to recall and remember, to sort and sift through the information gained in movement experience, to make comparisons and to comment on their own movement and movement they have seen in others. Children can reflect both in direct perception and through intellectual processes.

Within this phase the child is developing the ability to externalise their growing awareness and to engage with their own learning process.

Body Memory

Adults help children to revisit things that have taken their attention as they played in movement. Body memory does not necessarily entail a child in doing the same *movements* that they did before but in finding their way back to the same *inner experience*. Body memory is used in order to learn from experience and to find out more about any of the layers of experience contained within Movement Play - a particular movement, a sensation, a visual image, an inner sound, a story, or a particular relationship with someone else.

Sorting and sifting

Adults help children to scan through all the different experiences they have in their play and to draw out ones they would like to revisit. This sorting can be done in their bodies; they don't have to stop, make rational choices, and only then go back to movement. It is possible to slip-slide through bodily-felt experiences and arrive at short movement phrases without thinking them out in an intellectual way.

Making decisions

Sometimes it is important to encourage children to decide on a particular aspect of their Movement Play to share, draw, write or talk about. These decisions can be arrived at through direct perception as well as by reasoning. Adults help children to arrive at decisions through movement by asking them to revisit, prioritise and decide as they move.

Drawing

Drawing, doodling, making marks on paper with a variety of different kinds of crayon or paint are all important ways of reflecting on a bodily-felt experience without having to resort to reason or words. Adults encourage children to find their own ways of doing this, without necessarily resorting to representations of what happened. Through drawing they can make felt responses to sensation, movement and relationships, and they can explore particular feelings.

(Young children sometimes find this easier than adults. Adults, hidebound by their preconceptions, are often anxious about how well they can draw.)

We did drawings altogether at the end of term to celebrate our Movement Play. (Actually, I like to call them 'drawdlings' - a cross between doodling and drawing - to emphasise that we're not trying to make good pictures, but to respond to our experience.) Thirty one pictures were displayed on the wall at the end ... glorious bold shapes and patterns, squiggles and daubs, all singing with life. I invited the Head Teacher to look at them. 'Which ones are the adults'?', I asked (knowing that there were four amongst them).

'No idea', she said.
It was impossible to tell.

Drawdlings like these, where no technical skill is required, are a fabulous way of emphasising the similarities between us, young and old, when we make feeling responses to the things in our lives.

Word-poems

Adults can show children how to use words to capture something of their experience without having to describe it. Word poems are collections of words and phrases, written down in the order they occur without trying to create 'a poem'. Like drawing word poems can represent some part of the experience, or be a felt response. Only the writer will know why those words are there. To anyone else they may appear random and unrelated. To the mover, they will be full of meaning.

Talking about movement

Adults create safe, non-judgmental environments in which children can talk about their experience of Movement Play. Open questions may be needed to start children off. Questions like 'Tell me about your moving' rather than 'You looked like a lion' are necessary to ensure that children are free to name and describe their own experience.

Watching and talking

Adults encourage children to watch each other move and to engage in a shared process of reflection. Always encourage movers to speak about their experience first; then invite watchers to respond within a structure.

Back to the Body ...

Get some big sheets of paper and a variety of crayons ready before you move. Have some really interesting crayons, not just the stubby bits left over; not just felt tips and markers. Include some oil-pastels in a good range of colours. After you move, spend some time drawing something of what you have just experienced. Throughout the Back to the Body sections there have been suggestions to draw, or doodle. You may be very comfortable with this; if not, here is your chance to explore the possibilities. If you are anxious about 'not being able to draw', put the crayon in your non-preferred hand and shut your eyes ... draw from your felt-sense not from your rational thoughts. You may only want to put a few marks in the paper. You may want to do a full response with a great deal of marks and colour. Give yourself plenty of 'go's. Each time: move then draw.

Back to the Body ...

Try moving, then drawing ... and then moving again, this time using your last picture as the starting point for your movement. Try to avoid interpreting the picture in movement. Make a felt response. Just go for it ... don't get stuck on what on earth that might mean. Go for it. And quickly let the movement settle into something that feels right. When you reflect on this process, consider whether it led you to something new, or whether it just got in the way.

Using the Framework

Whatever opportunities you plan to make available for children to learn to learn from their body, this three part framework - experiencing, focusing, reflecting - always applies. Sometimes you will work with words and sometimes with movement as you encourage children to notice and reflect upon their 'bodily stir'. Sometimes you will create a wall display of drawings and doodles, and sometimes children will stand up and speak about their Movement Play. The more you bring movement into your setting as an everyday, valued part of what you do, the more children will expect to notice, sort, sift, remember and recall the things they experience in their bodies and the more readily they will interweave body learning and intellectual learning.

NOTES FOR LEADERS:

DEVELOPING ATTITUDES AND SKILLS IN THE REFLECTING PHASE

BABIES & CHILDREN	ADULT SUPPORT

Attitudes
• Know that *sensation, feeling and movement hold information*
• Know we can make choices about what we share and what we keep private
• Know other people's experience is to be treated with respect and difference is to be celebrated
 	
Skills
• able to remember and differentiate the various layers of experience in movement play
• able to remember and reproduce shapes and movements that they have made
• able to use a range of methods to recall and share Movement Play - talking, drawing, making things, word-poems and so on
• able to watch others' movement with focus
• able to give feedback within a set structure
• able to use sensory information to make deliberate attempts to solve problems and answer self-generated questions
	• refer to movement in all areas of the curriculum
	
	• help children to become aware of the processes involved in their learning in Movement Play
	  ○ following body-thoughts in sensation, feeling and movement
	  ○ setting a task, problem or a question and seeking information in sensation, feeling or movement
	  ○ making choices about what to share and what to keep private
	  ○ finding out more from movement ideas using drawing, dialogue, word poems, feedback and 'tell me about...' structures
	  ○ using opportunities to practice recalling and replaying movement
	
	• encourage children to be actively involved in identifying their movement preferences

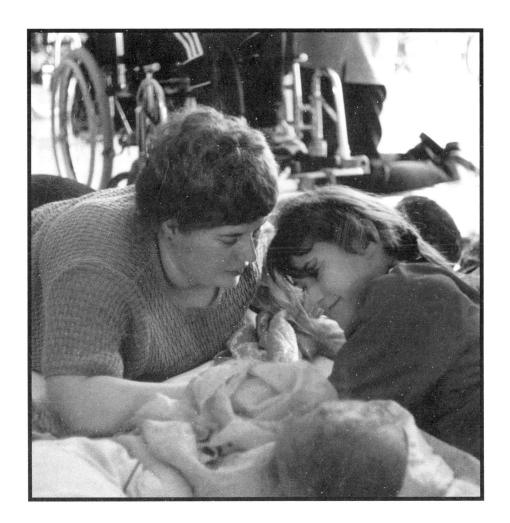

Hopping Home Backwards

7
Organising Movement Play

'We cannot increase learning by destroying the defences which block it. What we can do is create the situations where people will not need to stay behind their defences all the time. We can make it safe for them to sally forth from behind the moat, secure in the knowledge that while they are exploring the countryside no-one will sneak in and burn the castle.'

Richard Harrison

Movement Play places a clear emphasis on spontaneity and on child-centred learning, but it requires a high degree of background organisation from adults. This chapter suggests three contexts within which adults can help children to learn from their bodies. The first is everyday life: adults draw attention to movement and bodily-felt experience in all aspects of children's lives. The second is child-led activities: adults create opportunities for children to organise and direct their own Movement Play. The third is adult-led activities: adults structure specific Movement Play activities to *extend* children's learning and to ensure they develop a wholehearted relationship with their bodily-felt experience.

NOTICING AND VALUING MOVEMENT IN EVERYDAY LIFE

Since movement and bodily-felt experience are so often ignored we need to start by making a determined effort to notice and value the body and movement as an ordinary part of life. This doesn't require any special activities, just a particular frame of mind. Movement is happening in every nursery, playgroup and school, throughout every childminder's day and in every aspect of family life. If adults make reference to the body, bodily-felt experience and movement, children quickly come to believe that these things are important and a valuable part of their own experience. They soon bring aspects of bodily-felt experience into their conversations and their creative projects - as a matter of course.

It is dinner time. Painting, gluing, doing jigsaws and playing in the home corner have all stopped and the children are either sitting in chairs at the dinner tables, or making their way towards them. The room is full of noise; amongst the chatter there are whoops and cries, hisses and screeches, gurglings and garglings. Everywhere you look there are children rocking, hopping, bouncing on their bottoms and slapping their knees. It is an ordinary hullabaloo. Gareth is hanging down sideways from his chair. 'If you can't sit properly in that chair you will have to sit in a high chair', says a hot and flustered nursery worker. A voice rises above the hubbub. 'Er, excuse me ... will you all be quiet and sit still.' It is hard to organise the practicalities of lunch in this level of noise and activity.

But look again: here is a room full of children singing and dancing. If you set aside the very real practical considerations (just for a moment), it is possible to see a room full of children exploring the world and themselves through sound and movement. Here is singing and dancing of the most spontaneous and creative kind; these children are using this time to pose questions and explore possible answers. What happens if I lean out of my chair? How far can I go before I feel unsafe? How can I make that screeching noise again? Where does my tongue need to go in order to change the sound from an eeeeeeee to an uuuurrrrrr? Often, to the frustration of the adults around, leaning and screeching are just more relevant than sitting nicely.

NOTES FOR LEADERS:

WHY BRING MOVEMENT INTO THE EVERYDAY CONTEXT?

- So that children notice, acknowledge and value movement and bodily-felt experience as part of everything they do.
- To help children to develop a curiosity about movement and bodily-felt experience.
- To help children to become more articulate about bodily-felt experience, developing the language to discuss sensation, feelings, movement and image in everyday life.
- To help children learn to differentiate between functional movement, expressive movement and spontaneous movement.
- So that children develop an understanding of what kinds of movement are appropriate in different contexts.

NOTES FOR LEADERS:

ADULT ROLE IN THE EVERYDAY CONTEXT

- Adults take a fresh look at movement and develop an interest in bodily-felt experience as a part of all learning.
- Adults look for opportunities throughout the day to point out and talk about sensation, feeling, movement and accompanying images.
- Adults use simple language to describe bodily-felt experience and give children opportunities to describe their own experience.
- Adults point out, and differentiate between, functional, expressive and spontaneous movement.

Page 130

Nursery 1

As the children arrive for the start of the day Mrs Stone asks them to come and sit on the carpet. 'Hurry up!', she calls. 'Quickly, quickly. Sit on the carpet, legs crossed, nice straight backs.' The children come to the carpet in all the different ways that reflect how they are feeling this morning. Rashid flies in all jumps and bounds; Morag slithers slowly, scuffling the toes of her shoes along the floor. Ned turns circles as he goes and arrives dizzy and unfocused. Martin sits down with his legs out in front of him. 'Come along. Walk properly everyone. Cross your legs Martin', says Mrs Stone. 'Come along. We need to get started.' 'I don't like sitting with my legs crossed', Martin complains. 'It hurts!' 'There isn't much space here', says Mrs Stone. 'We all need to cross our legs so that we make room for the person next to us.'

Nursery 2

As the children arrive for the start of the day Mrs Cole asks them to come and sit on the carpet. 'Let's see how you are all arriving today', she says. 'Jo and Fiona are walking together, Dan is hopping with his arms out and Jamila is going as slow as slow ... it'll take a long time to get right across to the carpet! Dean is going round and round. He'll have to walk further than everyone else to get to the same place!' When most of the children have sat down (and Jamila is now delighting in taking as long as possible) Mrs Cole says, 'Look around at all the different ways we are sitting ... all the different shapes we are making with our bodies. What can you see?' After they have spent a little time practising their movement observation skills Mrs Cole says, 'Right. Get comfortable everyone, make sure you're not taking up the space that belongs to the person next to you, and change from looking to listening'.

Mrs Cole uses the opportunity of the children's arrival to notice and value the movement they are doing. She uses her own words to structure the learning possibilities. She is working with spontaneous, child-led movement but she is still firm and directive in order to maintain order.

CHILD-LED ACTIVITIES

Children, left to themselves, organise and indulge in a wide variety of movement play activities, anything from bouncing on the bed to hopping home backwards. Adults get involved in only a small percentage of this activity. In organised settings, however, children tend to have fewer opportunities for spontaneous movement games, which have to be reserved for the playground - where the adults have least involvement.

Taking body intelligence seriously means providing a range of different kinds of support - both formal and informal. Think about the amount of informal support we provide for literacy and numeracy skills from the earliest age. You have to work very hard to avoid nursery friezes, changing-mats and dungarees with the alphabet and numbers on. The importance of supporting reading and counting is clear, but we don't give equal attention to ensuring that babies belly-crawl and crawl on all fours, and that toddlers roll down hills and spin round and round.

Movement Play in the midst of ordinary life

Once we have understood the many levels of experience a child may be exploring within their seemingly random wriggles and jiggles, there is no limit to the amount of time we could spend supporting them. (Except our own very real exhaustion level.) Whenever we have the energy, and an appropriate setting, getting down to Movement Play is a wholly positive thing to do. Paired-crawling is as important as paired-reading; a few minutes of Movement Play is as valuable as a story; a second or two of mirrored movement as affirming as a reassuring word.

As we develop the 'serious' ways we support child-led movement activities as well as good, fun, rough and tumble ways, we must ensure that children learn what is appropriate and what is not. Today it is all right to hop home backwards, tomorrow it may not be. It's alright to roll around the floor at home, but not alright in the middle of the frozen-food aisle at Asda. It's fun to play; it's also important to be able to say no when you don't want to play. It may be all right to watch telly upside down and jiggling when no one else is sitting on the sofa, but not all right when someone else is sharing the sofa with you.

These boundaries need to be created with consistency and without recourse to the 'Stop being silly' attitude to movement. Acknowledgement of the child's desire accompanied by 'I'm too tired to help you today', or 'There are too many other people on the pavement' is much more helpful than 'Stop being silly!'. Once we understand the potential learning involved we may be more tolerant of much of the spontaneous movement children indulge in; but even though we understand, we must still ensure that children are aware of the need to take care of other people and to keep themselves safe.

> As I was writing today, sitting at the kitchen table, my daughter (12) was lying in bed in the room above my head, with a slight fever, feeling 'absolutely terrible'. The whole day long, she had been lying across the bed with her feet wedged against the wall, idly bang ... bang ... banging with one foot, over and over again. If I hadn't been writing about the importance of idiosyncratic movement, and 'allowing', I would have been up those stairs straight away shrieking, 'Will you please stop banging!!'. But as it was, I felt duty bound to be understanding and trust there was some reason she needed to repeat this movement over and over again. After all, it's an odd thing to do when you feel 'absolutely terrible!'.
>
> When I finally asked her about it at 7.00 at night (with an exaggerated carelessness about my manner) she said, 'Have I been banging my foot? O yes! So I have. It feels really good ...' And she banged some more.
>
> 'I'm glad it helps', I said nonchalantly, 'BUT CAN YOU PLEASE STOP. IT'S DRIVING ME INSANE !!!'

Outdoor Play

If you work in an organised setting you will probably already have clear structures for children's outdoor play. The value of this can be extended by taking another look at the relationship between adults and children during outdoor play, and the relationship between what children do in the playground and the rest of their learning. Is this a kind of time-off for adults to have a (much needed) cup of tea and a chat while they watch over the children? Is there an opportunity for adults to engage with children's movement play? Is there any way that a child's experience of movement play can be fed back in a serious way into classroom, playgroup or nursery activities? Do children have an opportunity to celebrate their playground experiences, discoveries and achievements?

Movement Corner

The fact that very few Early Years settings have a Movement Corner - a dedicated place for children to go when they choose to move - says a lot about how we generally think about movement and learning. A Movement Corner is a simple way to let children know that moving is an important part of their learning and a way of supporting their spontaneous need to move at various times during the day. There is a tendency to think that movement equals chaos, but many young children, given clear guidelines and support from adults, can organise their own use of a Movement Corner safely and appropriately. Of course, babies and very young children will always need an adult with them; and some older children will need extra support, even if it is only through being watched. Other children can quickly learn to use a Movement Corner effectively and safely.

NOTES FOR LEADERS:

WHY SET UP A MOVEMENT CORNER?

- To give movement an equal place within the learning opportunities you provide

- To make a place where children can move spontaneously at times they choose, as well as at specified times

- To make a place where children can focus on their body-felt experience, where inner focus is as acceptable as outer focus

- To make a place where children create and organise their own Movement Play structures

NOTES FOR LEADERS:

SETTING UP A MOVEMENT CORNER

- Make a movement corner (a particular place that children can go if they want to move or take their focus inward to their bodily-felt experience) in the same way as you make a special place for painting or home-play, sand and water play.

- It can be permanent or temporary, available all the time, or only at specified times.

- It needs to be clearly marked - with a floor mat, a chunky rope laid out around its edges or with chairs placed strategically ... anything you can manage.

- Any clear space will do. Ideally, however, it will have some of these elements as well:
    - some clean floor space with a slippery surface children can slide on
    - a soft surface that children can curl up on comfortably
    - some props that support different kinds of movement (ribbon sticks, hoops, beanbags, lengths of fabric, scarves and so on)
    - some props that support different kinds of tactile experience (fabrics with different textures, make up brushes and massage tools, natural objects like fir cones and sweet chestnut shells)

- If you want to support developmental movement patterns (belly crawling and crawling on all fours) have a length of vinyl flooring available to provide a clean, smooth slightly slippery surface that is ideal for these activities.

- Have an easy to use cassette or CD player available and a small selection of music (some slow and some fast).

- Have drawing things readily available so children can change from moving to drawing.

NOTES FOR LEADERS:

CREATING GUIDELINES FOR A MOVEMENT CORNER

- Create guidelines with all the children *before* anyone uses it.
    - When can they use the Corner? At any time, or only at specified times?
    - Are there times when they may not use the Corner?
    - Do they need to ask an adult *before* they go there?
    - How will they share the available time for the Corner?

- Is it possible for children to use music at all times, or will it be disruptive? Help them to understand an acceptable volume.

- Are there times when adults will be available to play in the Movement Corner?

- How will you ensure that children use the Corner, and the props, safely?

- Remind children to leave the Corner as they found it ... ready for the next person.

Although this is a space in which children themselves organise the play, they may need help in the early stages as they discover how to make use of it. Start with whole group sessions in which you discover together some of the possibilities for playing in the Movement Corner, including stillness, quiet moving, more boisterous moving, playing with the different props, playing with one or two other people, making up movement games, and moving and drawing. Create guidelines together about what level of the boisterous and energetic Movement Play the Corner can contain. Once the Movement Corner is established as a regular part of your activities, children may be keen to tell you about things, or show you things, they have been doing there. Make time for showing movement, talking about sensation, feelings, movement and image and celebrating the experiences that the Movement Corner prompts - by making wall displays using words and drawings gathered from group feedback times.

Developmental Movement Play

Given perfect conditions, babies and young children will naturally complete each pattern as it arises. They know what to do. However, since conditions are seldom perfect and many things *do* get in the way, it is important for adults to ensure that children have plenty of opportunities to practice the patterns, and keep a weather-eye out for any gaps.

We don't have to be experts to do this. We need to know the kinds of movement to support, and things to look out for that might indicate a child has gaps. If we suspect significant gaps, then we can involve a specialist. Bette Lamont, from the Seattle Developmental Movement Centre, uses this analogy. If we suspect that a child has a cavity in their teeth, we don't expect to fill it ourselves. We go to the dentist for the filling while we make sure the child brushes their teeth to reduce the risk of another cavity in the future. In Movement Play we are doing the equivalent of teeth-brushing.

NOTES FOR LEADERS:

ABOUT DEVELOPMENTAL MOVEMENT PATTERNS

- The patterns *begin* in the womb and continue until a child is about eight or nine.
- Each pattern leads on to the next. Thus, crawling on our bellies prepares us for crawling on all fours ... which prepares us for walking and so on.
- Each pattern addresses many aspects of future functioning.
- We do not necessarily complete one pattern *before* progressing to the next. It is a spiralling process. Thus, just because a baby likes to crawl on all fours, it doesn't mean they have finished with crawling on their bellies; if they are walking, that they have finished with crawling.
- Adults do not have to teach children how to do these patterns. They need to provide support and children's bodies will do the rest.
- Both sensory stimulation and movement are important in promoting the patterns.

NOTES FOR LEADERS:

SUPPORTING DEVELOPMENTAL MOVEMENT PLAY

SENSORY STIMULATION
Make sure that children get as much sensory stimulation as you can give them. Look at the sensory activities outlined in the Activity Section. (Pages 279 - 297)

TIME ON THEIR TUMMIES
Ensure that they spend time on their tummies (looking at books, drawing and painting, doing puzzles and so on). This is especially important now that babies are put to sleep on their backs to prevent cot-death.

BELLY CRAWLING
Plan activities that encourage them to crawl on their tummies - belly down. on the floor. Whenever possible, let them have bare feet so they can feel them on the floor more easily. If they are reluctant, get down with them.

CRAWLING ON ALL FOURS
Change your environment, if necessary, to encourage children to crawl - either in pure Movement Play (see Crawling games page 354) or as they do other things. Gayle Loyd of the Seattle Developmental Movement Centre suggests that you organise activities so that children have to fetch things from one end of the room (toys, bricks, jigsaw pieces, word cards and so on) and play with them at the other. In this way, children get crawling practice without noticing.

SPINNING
Encourage children to indulge in the spinning and dizzy-making play that they are often very keen on. The fancy name for this is 'vestibular activity' and children need to do it. (See Spinning page 356)

NOTES FOR LEADERS:

WATCHING FOR GAPS

Given the fact that so many exciting things happen in the adult world, away from the floor, it isn't surprising that babies are eager to come up to join us. This, coupled with the amount of time they spend in chairs, can make it difficult for them to complete the patterns.

BELLY CRAWLING

Watch out for babies who want to rush on to crawling before they have spent time getting about on their tummies. Encourage their interest in crawling by all means, but also return them to their tummies and play with them there. If they are very reluctant, and cry or show distress, build up their tolerance very gradually. Don't give up ... it may be difficult now, but it would be very much harder in future - you'll never know. Persevere! Put babies on their tummies for just a few seconds and give them lots of rewards. Then repeat the process. It is probably important to get down on the floor with them.

By the time a baby has completed all the work to be done in the belly crawling pattern, you will see a smooth travelling movement with full involvement of legs and arms, and a cross-pattern as they travel along, ie. left arm working with right leg.

CRAWLING ON ALL FOURS

Watch out for babies who rush on from crawling to pulling themselves up onto their legs, hanging onto the furniture. Encourage their interest in standing, but make sure they return to crawling as well. Once again, you may have to get down with them to make it interesting enough to stay on the floor.

By the time a young child has finished the crawling on all fours pattern you will see a smooth travelling movement with arms and legs directly under the body and legs and arms both involved in a 'stepping' motion in a cross-pattern ie. left arm working with right leg.

NOTES FOR LEADERS:

WATCHING FOR GAPS

The early patterns provide the foundation upon which walking, hopping and skipping are built.

WALKING AND RUNNING

If you notice that a child continues to walk or run with a wide stance (like a toddler) when they get older, support lots of belly-crawling and crawling on all fours activities, which may help them to align their body in the best way for walking.

HOPPING AND SKIPPING

If a child has difficulty with either of these activities, support lots of belly-crawling and crawling on all fours activities. It may be that they haven't organised the balance, or the cross-lateral patterns that will enable them to do one thing with one side of the body and something different with the other - a vital skill in either hopping or skipping.

A 'CLUMSY' CHILD

If you notice that a child bumps into things more often than you might expect, if they appear to have a faulty perception of where their body is in space, support lots of sensory activities that might help them to develop their sensory feedback systems. Once again, go back over the belly-crawling and crawling on all fours as well, to support their balance.

A CHILD WHO FINDS EARLY READING ACTIVITIES VERY CHALLENGING

Encourage as many spinning and dizzy-making activities as they enjoy. Don't <u>make</u> them spin. They may find it makes them feel sick rather quickly. Take it steady and increase their tolerance slowly. This may help to organise the convergence of their two eyes in a way that makes looking at words on a page more acceptable for them. Belly-crawling and crawling on all fours are very important as well.

ADULT-LED ACTIVITIES

Adult-led activities provide opportunities to extend children's learning in Movement Play. Adults get involved in order to help children make more of something they already do. Adult-led activities have a strong focus and are organised in similar ways to other activities; they continue to emphasise children's own ways of moving and describing their experience, and make a bridge between children's natural learning through spontaneous play and more formal learning experiences. In adult-led activities, issues that come up in child-led play can be dealt with - the necessity to think about safety again, for instance, or helping children to work together more constructively. Adults encourage older children to get involved in their own learning processes and to understand the relevance of learning in their bodies so they can make active use of their body intelligence in future.

CIRCLE TIME

Children need to show us who they are as much as they need to speak about who they are. Early Years settings use a variety of focused structures through which young children practice presenting themselves, their ideas and their experience to others. Generally speaking, these activities (News Time, Show and Tell Time, Circle Time) rely heavily on words and the showing of objects. A movement version of the same activity encourages children to share themselves and their experience through movement, and to share felt-responses as well as rational responses.

> On Monday morning, Reggie (5) begged to be allowed to go into the circle. 'I want to show about what I did on Saturday', he yelped. Once in, he jumped and leapt and dived for the floor in a succession of high energy bursts. Then he stood right in the centre of the circle and - feet together, knees slightly bent, eyes shut, and his clenched fists drawn up to just above his head - he shook his arms for all he was worth in a gesture of sheer delight and triumph. Then off he went again with the high energy leaps and dives, finishing once more in the centre.
>
> 'I went to Alton Towers', he beamed. 'And I _loved_ it!'

NOTES FOR LEADERS:

ORGANISING CIRCLE TIME IN MOVEMENT

- Circle Time activities put the emphasis firmly on one child moving and the rest watching. (This may develop into pair work and even group work over time).

- Movers have about three minutes in the centre. They can choose to move alone, with an adult, or with a prop. (As they get used to the structure, they might choose to move with a partner).

- Movers can choose to have music or no music.

- Watchers are encouraged to watch actively; to notice as much as they can.

- As watchers become used to the process, they are given structures within which to organise their responses (I Saw, I Felt, I Imagined ... Think of some questions to ask ... Think about how you would move in response to what you see ... Draw something in response to what you see).

- When the time is over, the mover is invited to speak. They may or may not want to speak.

- When the mover has finished speaking, the watchers are invited to respond - talking, showing a drawing, or moving in reply.

This structure can be used with children from four upwards. Younger children can prepare for it by having 'dancing in the centre' time, without the sophisticated feedback structure. Adults need to make sure that the watchers are happily and actively engaged and not just sitting around.

NOTES FOR LEADERS:

WHY USE A CIRCLE TIME STRUCTURE ?

- To build children's confidence in themselves as movers.
- To make it ordinary to be watched.
- To value and develop children's ability to express felt responses as well as rational responses.
- To value and develop communication through direct perception as a complement to verbal communication.
- To develop children's ability to watch with focus and intent.
- To develop children's ability to notice and share their felt response to what they see.

NOTES FOR LEADERS:

ADULT ROLE IN CIRCLE TIME ACTIVITIES

- To create a clear, strong structure to contain the movement.
- To create, and help children maintain, a non-judgmental, wholly positive atmosphere.
- To place an equal emphasis on moving and watching.
- To provide structures that enable children to be fully themselves - in safety.
- To be a role model for offering and sharing felt responses, by noticing and sharing your own.
- To include opportunities for focusing and reflecting, as well as for experiencing.

This style of movement activity works best on the carpet area - the contained, safe place where children usually gather for register, or news, or stories. You need a space that is just big enough for all the children to sit in one circle. Don't feel anxious if it is a little cramped - this isn't like a dance activity where you might want a lot of space. In fact, it is best if the children are well contained by the surrounding walls, tables and other furniture as it will help to focus their attention on the centre of the circle. Many of the problems you encounter with traditional dance and movement activities might be considerably eased by working in a small space. As long as there is enough room for the children to move in the middle, the activity can work well.

When this activity is not appropriate
This activity might be extremely difficult for a group who find turn-taking too difficult. If a session requires repeated verbal controlling from the adults, or individual children cannot contain their desire to move, don't battle on. In this instance, it is important to use a different structure that enables all the children to move. There is no virtue in pinning them to the spot when activity is what they need.

NOTES FOR LEADERS:

HOW LONG IS A SESSION?

- This works well if it is run just like Circle Time - a twenty minute or half hour slot between other things. (Inevitably, you will probably need a little time to move tables and chairs aside at the beginning).
- Twenty minutes is long enough for about three children to move in the centre of the circle and for the others to give feedback on their responses to the moving.
- A half hour session is long enough for four or perhaps five children (or pairs) to have a go.
- If you have a particularly boisterous group, position the session with a playtime after it, enabling children who haven't moved (but who are longing to) to run about before a quieter activity.
- In a school setting, it makes a very good follow-up to Literacy Hour. It allows the children to balance the intellectual work with some focused physical work.

Supporting children's learning

Accept whatever a child chooses to offer. You are not looking for 'beautiful' shapes and movements that look like ballet or creative dance. Remember that the movement each child offers is a reflection of who they are, to be treated with respect. At the start of this Circle Time structure it is often enough for a child simply to be in the centre and hop about a bit. If they feel that this is acceptable, they will be safe to go in again and their confidence (and the amount they move) will grow. Don't force anyone to have a go. If a child doesn't want to, so be it; acknowledge their right not to take a turn. If you offer a variety of activities most children will find a way to take a turn eventually.

> *Sam (6) says, 'Can I dance in the centre with Messy?'.*
>
> *Messy is a small, yellowish-brown toy rabbit, a treasured friend. Sam has not yet asked for a turn in the centre of the circle, but today, emboldened by the thought of dancing with his friend he is eager to have a go.*
>
> *Over the last few weeks we have built up a number of things that the children can choose to dance with - the chair in the centre, the Ribbon Sticks, they can dance with each other and they can dance with me. But Sam has not been enticed by any of these. I wasn't sure if he would ever want a turn. I have been watching and waiting for a clue. But now Sam has found his own way ... better than I could ever have thought of.*
>
> *He chooses fast music (an Irish Jig today) and, holding the rabbit in both hands, swoops it about in front of him. Then the rabbit rolls round his shoulders and appears to do a little jump in the air. Sam stands perfectly still, only his arms (and the rabbit) are moving. They repeat the movements. After a little while he shrugs, turns to me to indicate that he has finished, and hops back to his place.*
>
> *'I saw Sam and the rabbit and I imagined someone dancing with their friend', says one of the children simply. There are lots of quiet nods of agreement around the circle.*

Remind children to feel what a movement or a shape is like as well as to see what it looks like. Make opportunities for them to move with their eyes shut as well as with them open. Encourage children to accept, and value, all kinds of movement and to take delight in the different things people do when it is their turn. Give lots of verbal feedback so that movers, and watchers, know that they are seen by you. Remember to give feedback to the children who only move a little, or perhaps just watch ... they will always be making shapes just as they sit, so there is plenty to reflect back to them. Notice and remark on the everyday dancing that happens all the time in the circle, not just what happens in the centre.

Oscar is very quiet and never asks to have a turn in the middle. I am anxious about him; anxious that what I am offering is irrelevant to him. During one whole term he has one go and looks somewhat uncomfortable. Is he compromised by the fact that his twin sister is forever in the centre, always asking for another turn - as happy as can be when she is moving and being watched?

In the last session of the term we get out huge rolls of paper and draw things we remember - all of us together in one big swirling mass of colours and shapes. Then we draw individual pictures of the things that have taken our fancy. I watch Oscar with trepidation. This is where I will find out what it has meant to him. He is head down, turned away from the group and I can't see what he is doing ...

When we all bring our doodlings back to the centre to share them with each other Oscar is looking intense. It emerges that he has paid great attention to drawing the observers. All term, it appears, he has been observing the observers! He has many and detailed things to say about the process of watching ... he has been fully involved, not in the moving, but in the watching.

Safety

Help children to learn how to keep themselves and each other safe by discussing the issues, creating shared guidelines and sticking to them.

NOTES FOR LEADERS:

SAFETY & THE MOVERS

- Remind children of safety issues, especially if they want to come close to the edge of the circle near to the watchers, or if they are using a prop that might catch someone.

- If a child is highly charged and moving in a way that might cause them injury, stop the activity. Help them to notice the risks they want to take and to think about the possible consequences for their own body. Find a way of supporting them so that they can express, or experience, what they need to, without damaging themself.

- Encourage children to ask for support when they think they are going to need it.

- Ask watchers how they feel as they watch high risk movement. Let them know how you feel about their high risk movement. Ask them how they feel.

- If a child repeatedly uses high risk movement, find every opportunity you can to massage them and work on noticing sensation (to build up their sensory feedback). Get them belly-crawling as often as possible. It may help them to develop better self-care strategies.

NOTES FOR LEADERS:

SAFETY & THE WATCHER

- Start by noticing the people on either side and take care not to invade their space.

- Talk to the whole group about the right they have, and the need they have, to look after themselves when others are moving.

- Give explicit permission to the watchers to protect themselves. Encourage children to put up a hand to cover their face, or fend off a flying ribbon when they feel anxious.

NOTES FOR LEADERS:

SAFETY AND YOU

- There may be times when you feel anxious about what children are doing. We all have different tolerance levels according to our past experiences. Be open about your anxieties ... let children know when you are uncomfortable. Try to find ways of letting them get on with their movement whilst taking care of yourself at the same time. Hold onto the back of the chair ... take time out to talk about the dangers of waving a stick ... say you can't manage that movement today ... Make sure that both you and the children are comfortable.

ACTIVITY GROUPS

Movement Play activity groups offer a variety of different structures; some enable all the children to move at once and some involve moving and watching, or turn-taking. (You can include any of the Circle Time activities in an Activity Group.) Activity Groups are suitable for all ages, from tiny babies upwards. In the Movement Play Activities section at the back of this book, suggestions are given for children from birth up to eight. If you are running groups for babies and younger children (up to four) you will need a higher adult-child ratio as many of the activities will need to be supported on a one to one basis. One adult can organise a whole group of older children. However, in all cases apart from whole group celebrations, small group work is more beneficial. An ideal number is between six and eight children.

A Movement Play session can be a short interlude or a fully fledged activity lasting up to an hour. It can be just one activity or a number of activities linked together.

NOTES FOR LEADERS:

WHY RUN MOVEMENT PLAY ACTIVITY GROUPS ?

- To support babies' and young children's pleasure in being in their bodies.

- To extend children's learning by offering carefully chosen structures.

- To introduce new structures to stimulate their interest and curiosity.

- To involve older children in recognising the learning processes involved so that they can use them at will.

NOTES FOR LEADERS:

ADULT ROLE IN SETTING UP ACTIVITY GROUPS

- Ensure that Movement Play is given sufficient time within the curriculum.

- Watch children move in order to discover which layers of bodily-felt experience they are engaging in.

- Plan a range of activities that involve sensation, feelings, movement and image as well as developmental activities (belly-crawling, crawling on all fours, and spinning).

- Make opportunities within these sessions to encourage persistence, curiosity and delight.

- Make links between these Activity Groups and other aspects of the curriculum.

- Make opportunities to re-establish guidelines and address issues that arise in other Movement Play activities (safety, appropriate behaviour and so on ...).

- Talk with all the other adults involved with the children about what you are doing together.

- Include information gained in observation of Movement Play in children's records.

- Make opportunities to celebrate and share the work you do in these sessions with a wider community.

Where to run activity groups

There are some common misconceptions that surround movement activity groups - the most common is that you need a large space. This may not be the case, even if you are working with a large number of children. Choose your space to fit your aims and the energy level of your children. If you run Activity Groups in order that children can all move at the same time (unlike Circle Time), then you may need to move to a large room. Small groups are almost always better in a small room.

If you are forced to work in a large room, and children can't resist charging about, partition off part of the space with chairs (or aything handy) to create a more focused atmosphere.

Peter (8) has Downes Syndrome and in response to particular circumstances in his life he has become very withdrawn and shy. The staff are concerned about his isolation, his sudden refusal to speak and his apparent abject sorrow. They ask if movement work might help. When a group come to the hall for a Movement Session Peter dives for cover under the grand piano and refuses to come out. But he lets me slide under with him. Fortunately there are enough staff to cope with a split focus. So we decide that, for a while, it is here that Peter and I will do our own movement session, both of us huddled under the piano for safety. We start slowly, tentatively, inching our little fingers towards each other, intertwining them and tugging a little whilst we stare ahead at the others. By the end of the session, still under the piano, we are crawling around, pushing the tops of our heads together, sitting back to back and rocking, giggling, sliding down onto the floor side by side. All in the few square feet that the piano allows us ...

Structuring sessions

Traditional advice about physical education and dance teaching suggests that any session should begin with a physical warm-up, go on to explore particular kinds of movement in order to extend range, follow this with some creative work using the movement ideas and finish by sharing what the children have done. This is a standard format that shapes different content each time. Movement Play doesn't need to adhere to this standard format since it follows the content that the children bring to it. Whatever your particular style of leadership (planning all the activities in advance, or responding to what you see at the time) Movement Play activities need to be organised in a three part structure - beginning, middle and end. This provides an ordered, careful learning atmosphere in which each child can both prepare for, and separate from, the activities you are engaging in together. This is important for the emotional wellbeing of children as they indulge in activites that may stir them deeply.

NOTES FOR LEADERS:

STRUCTURING ACTIVITY GROUPS

BEGINNINGS	MIDDLES	ENDS
- Gathering - Preparing the space - Preparing yourself - Sizing each other up - Letting go of other concerns - Seeing how people feel today - Remembering last time - Giving information about this time - Remembering guidelines and rules - Setting new guidelines	- Getting stuck in - Experiencing - Focusing - Reflecting - Taking risks - Challenging - Opening up - Sharing	- Winding down - Reviewing & Remembering - Preparing for what comes next - Re-energising if relaxed - Calming down if excited - Separating from one another - Looking forward to next time - Giving information - Celebrating successes

Although an ideal session will contain a good balance between beginning, middle and ending activities, some groups will need to spend much more time on one rather than another. Plan activities that ensure they have at least a taste of each.

The Warm up

But shouldn't children do a physical warm-up before engaging in physical activity - for safety's sake? No-one does a physical warm-up before children go out to the playground, where they are likely to do some of the most demanding physical activity of all. A physical warm up is necessary when we are telling children to perform specific movements directed by their heads rather than their bodies. Where children are choosing their movements guided by their body intelligence it is much less likely that they will damage themselves.

A 'warm up' for a Movement Play session, therefore, is concerned with a wider 'warming up' of children's attention to their bodily-felt experience, to each other, and the environment rather than with physical jerks to stretch and loosen the body. A warm-up helps children to focus internally (on the inner voice that says 'I want to move like this today'), externally on the space they are moving in and its potential dangers, and on the other people in the room.

If the children in your group find it difficult to take care of themselves you may need to structure this first aspect of a session very carefully and continue to help them to move safely. Try some of the 'Body Wake Up' structures (pages 334 - 338) at the start of an Activity Group.

Choosing activities

In Section 3 there are lots of ideas for activities. Some of these may be helpful in getting you going; in time, as you get to know your children, you will find that you discover your own structures. This is the nature of working with spontaneous movement. It isn't a question of doing an activity, but of finding a structure that supports the ways that children want to be.

At the start, let the aims for your session guide which activities, or props, you choose. Depending on your style as a leader, you may choose activities that glide one from the other, or you may hop from one game to another. Try to avoid choosing activities that are completely random. It is best if you know why you have decided to use Ribbon Sticks, or to work in pairs (although everyone will grasp a prop sometimes without knowing why and use it to good effect).

I went into the session quite undecided as to what I would do. Should we use Ribbon Sticks again, or should I suggest that we use a Gymnastic Ball? I just couldn't make up my mind. As I was pushing back the tables, still uncertain, Gilly hopped up and said, 'Can I move with Tara today?' And then I knew what to do. Here was a clear request to move onto pair work, something I had been considering for a while. It worked perfectly and others moved in pairs as well. In fact, we used this theme for another six weeks.

So often in this work the group lets me know what to do.

Most of us, when we start working in new ways, are eager to make firm plans in advance, even if we do not use them. You may want to plan the first activity for a session, see how it goes and plan on the hoof from there. Or you may want to plan a progression of games and activities taken from the back of this book and stick to them - until you find your feet with movement.

Size of groups

As with any activity, young children benefit from being in a smaller group. Six to eight children is ideal for Movement Play activities. If this is not possible, the smaller the group the better as this allows the adult to pay careful attention to each child, and for children to have a lot of time for moving, rather than waiting. However, large groups are fine too, but do temper your aims and expectations accordingly. Large numbers always necessitate more verbal instructions from the adult in the beginning, which detracts from the time available for moving.

BALANCE OF DIFFERENT APPROACHES

It is important that, as we adults learn more about supporting spontaneous movement, we do not take over. There needs to be a balance between child-led and adult-led activities within the Early Years curriculum, supported by an appreciation of, and respect for, bodily-felt experience as part of everyday life. Most children love to play in movement with adults, from simply larking about to playing games with focused intent. But they also love just to mess about with their peers, and to spin themselves silly all on their own.

Each of these has real value, and, if we watch carefully, each provides us with information upon which to plan child-centred activities within the curriculum.

Hopping Home Backwards

8
Moving with children

we sing before we talk

we dance before we walk

All the suggestions in this book can be organised without the need for you to move yourself. However, the best way you can let children know that their movement is valuable is by moving with them. If they see that you value it and enjoy it they will know that it has value for all human beings.

The purpose of this chapter is to make movement, and working with the body - *ordinary*. Dance and movement work have an air of exclusivity and specialism, but you don't have to be a specialist, or be able to make movements look a particular way, to make Movement Play an important part of the way children learn. It has nothing to do with teaching dance; you don't have to be a developmental movement expert. Movement Play is about the languages of the body - the things that weave in and out of everything we do. Just as everyone has a voice in their head that chatters away non-stop, so everyone has a body that chatters away in sensation, feeling and movement. These are constant sources of information and feedback about our experience no matter how young or old we are, how boisterous or frail. Each of us, whatever we feel about the *idea* of expressive movement, is already engaged in it on a daily basis. Although we are barely conscious of it, we 'choose' postures and gestures, and perform them with particular qualities - all the time. We also observe and read movement on a moment to moment basis. You know when you see that particular teenage slump over the breakfast table to leave well alone. You know as you glance through the window at spouse getting out of the car whether it is going to be a cheerful evening or whether you need to find an urgent prior engagement. You know because you read movement.

This chapter is about how to adapt your existing speaking, listening and communication skills to work with the languages of the body.

Movement as a language

You are already skilled at using verbal language to communicate with young children. You know how to listen so the child feels attended to; you know when the child is saying something really important and when it is happy chatter; you know how to prompt, how to encourage, how to help them stick to the subject; you know how to help them to round up and finish what they are saying and when to encourage them to be quiet.

You also know how to hold a good conversation. You know how to pick up and join in with a subject that the child offers; you can judge when to stick exclusively to the child's experience and when it is appropriate to feed in your own experience of the same subject, letting the two versions mix and mingle so you both learn something about each other.

These are the skills you need to work in movement. Conversations happen in movement just as they happen in words. In everyday life, movement parallels the words as we speak to each other, even if we don't notice it.

> *Ricky wants to go outside. He asks and is told 'Not now'. 'But I want to!' he repeats, stamping his foot hard on the floor, curling his fingers tightly into his palms and jutting his chin out. Deidre, the nursery assistant, turns so that she is facing him fully. 'You can go out later', she says with a little beat of her hands in the air in front of her as she says the word 'later'. She brings both hands together and curls the fingers of one hand round the back of her other hand. Ricky punches the floor with his foot again and twists his body backwards and forwards around his tummy and up to his shoulders. 'Now.' This is a strong twisting, as if he is pushing through thick, setting concrete. Before Deidre says anything she opens her hands, palm upwards and spreads her arms to her sides, elbows tucked in. Her hands are like the pans of a set of scales. 'if you go out*

> *now', she says as one hand lowers and the other rises, tilting her body slightly to one side, 'You will miss your snack. If you go out later' - her body tilts the other way - 'you can have your snack as well as going out.' Her body looks as if it is weighing up the options.*

The two bodies talk to each other through movement at the same time as they speak the words. In this case they are using very different kinds of movement because they have taken up very different positions. When two people are in agreement verbally, their movements may also agree.

> *'Shall we play in the home corner?', says Ben with a little jump. 'Yes!', says David mirroring the jump exactly as he speaks. 'Shall you be on the phone?', says Ben, giving two little jumps and jiggling his arms. 'Yes!', says David mirroring exactly once more. The two boys, as one, hurtle over to the Home Corner and sit almost on top of one another, squeezed together, both with their hands pressed into their knees.*

The movement both emphasises the agreement the boys come to and seems to heighten the pleasure they feel in their togetherness. Ben has provided the subject for the movement bit of the conversation - a little jump. David has joined him by mirroring it. Ben then develops the subject by offering two jumps, and once again David mirrors, displaying agreement. When they run, they do the equivalent of saying exactly the same words at the same time. As they sit down together, their physical proximity mirrors their emotional closeness. Take out the words and here is a dance with a beginning, a middle (movement theme developing into a *pas-de-deux*) and an ending.

Movement conversation

There are many circumstances in which you might want to move with a child. It may be a fleeting part of everyday interaction whilst you stand at the painting table together, it may be during a movement activity group, or it may be part of a specific strategy of one to one work with a particular child. Whichever it is, the same guidelines apply. You will choose to move with them for all the same reasons that you choose to talk to them - to show them that you care, to show interest in them and

their concerns, to show them you agree with them or that you disagree with them, to help them to develop their voice, their ability to share their experience, their sociability. You will do this through conversations - movement conversations.

Movement conversations work just like verbal conversations. First, either you or the child will come up with something to say. One of you will start, the other will reply. Your conversation will probably develop as you go along. You might get sidetracked into something completely different from your starting point, or you might stick doggedly to the point. You might agree with each other, or you might disagree. One of you may throw challenges or questions to the other, to see if they can reply. It may be mostly a monologue, or it may go backwards and forwards between you.

Movement conversations are the first conversations we have. Watch a baby in its mother's arms. She will communicate her approval and agreement, or her adoration of the baby by mirroring the tiny movements the baby makes. She will communicate her disapproval through movements that oppose the baby's, that show difference. She tunes into, and communicates with the baby through movement. Mother and baby do this unconsciously; it is part of the human package and we continue to use the same methods of tuning in, communicating agreement and disagreement all our lives. We have movement conversations with each other even though we choose to ignore them.

Don't think of spontaneous movement as totally alien. Think of it as another means of having a conversation or conducting a monologue. If you apply the rules that you already know, you will realise that you are not a novice at all.

Settle in ... notice more

Always give yourself time to watch and to settle into the language of movement. The more you use it, the more you will be able to focus on movement as well as everything else that's going on at the same time. When you start watching, you may need to block everything else out. (Try watching the television with the sound down as a practice exercise. Or watch people in the street as you sit in the car. Tune in to the movement and notice how much you see.)

When you start watching children, tune into all the *little* movements that they do as well as any more obvious ones. Just as you expect to listen carefully to what they say and *how* they say it, watch what children do and *how* they do it. The little bits are just as important as the more obvious bits. Notice the shapes, the phrasing, the quality of the movement. Without the details you might have the movement equivalent of a misheard statement: 'It's very mild for the time of year' changed to 'He's very wild when he's full of fear'.

WORKING IN MOVEMENT

The following descriptions outline ways of responding in movement. You will recognise them as things you do with words as well. Choose a way of responding based on the type of conversation, or relationship, you want to have.

Attunement

This is the process whereby you focus your attention - ready to notice and act upon movement signals. It's the equivalent of listening carefully, which involves making sure that you can hear well and that you communicate that you are listening. In movement, make sure that you can see well and that you communicate that you are really watching.

You can also 'listen' to movement through your body using your own direct perception, or kinesthetic awareness, to give you information about movement. Some people will prefer to use visual watching and others, although they are looking, process most of their information kinesthetically. If you find yourself moving along with the child you are watching, doing tiny movements that give you a flavour of what they are doing, then you probably like to use your kinesthetic sense. If watching is enough, then your visual sense may be your strongest asset. Most of us probably mix the two.

As you tune in to movement, words tend to get in the way. Generally speaking, talking to anyone other than the person you are working with is not helpful. Words keep us in the verbal realm and whether you favour the visual, the kinesthetic, or both together, you will be more focused if you don't talk.

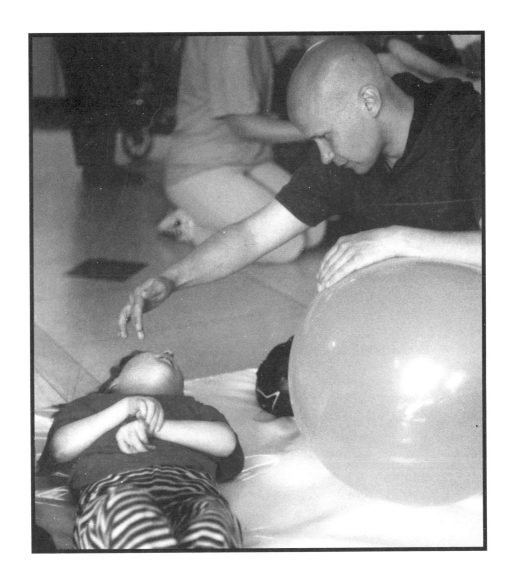

Holding

'Holding' is everything you do to facilitate a focused, mindful, safe atmosphere for learning through movement. Different situations will require different kinds of holding. You will be: giving the child the right quality of attention, creating the appropriate forum (public or private), helping them to stay on track with what they are saying, helping other children to respond appropriately, helping them to shape what they have to say into a beginning, middle and end structure, helping them to complete what they have to say appropriately. If they have expressed something that has touched their feelings deeply, you will also keep an eye on them afterwards.

Only if we do all these things will it be safe enough for children to reveal themselves and focused enough for them to learn. You can do this holding in movement or in words, or both.

Mirroring

This is a way of showing a child that you notice them, that you understand what they are saying, or how they are feeling. The verbal equivalent might be saying 'Yes ... yes', as you listen. The feeling of it is 'I'm right with you' or ' I agree'.

We 'mirror' all the time as part of everyday communication, but we do it unconsciously. If you watch a group of adults sitting around having an argument or a debate, you can often see that two people who agree with one another will adopt the same posture. You can sometimes see one person's body move into another's physical posture as they start to agree verbally - the body gets there before the words. If you are talking with someone and you suddenly notice that you both have your arms behind your head in the same posture, you will probably find that you are in agreement with each other at that moment. Try taking your hands down and the other person may well follow - if you are still in agreement.

Using mirroring consciously as a way of affirming a child's experience involves picking up the movements that they make, and doing them yourself. It isn't copying or mimicking; there is nothing more infuriating than having someone copy everything you say or do. This is about wholeheartedly joining in with their subject matter. It is a direct form of agreement - not agreeing with what they *think*, but *being* like them.

Use it as a specific structure, or, as you would in verbal conversation, as a way of letting a child

know that you are ready to talk ... in movement. You can mirror for a few seconds (a quick exchange) or for several minutes (a whole conversation).

Reflecting

This is another way of letting a child know that you have seen them. Here, you are not trying to be just like the other person, but staying separate - whilst still offering as much support as they need. It might be paralleled by saying: 'You are you and I am me; let's talk'.

'Reflecting' is picking up the essence of what a child is doing, but doing it in your own way - maybe with a different part of your body. If the child is stamping, you might slap the floor with your hands, using the same rhythm and quality. If they are trying to bite, you may snap with your fingers, using the same quality but in a very different way. Thus you reflect back to them that you have seen, but do it in your own way.

Patterning

This is a way of communicating with a child who is not focusing on you. They may be resistant to social communication, or it may be that you want to support the child, without imposing too much. The verbal parallel might be 'If you want me, I'm here'.

'Patterning' involves taking your inspiration from the child and trying out, and enjoying, the movements for yourself. You do not try to get their attention, but, if they care to notice what you are doing, they will see that you are available. The movements you do will not be exactly the same as the child's, as in mirroring. Nor are you reflecting the child's movement back to them. You are amusing yourself in the vicinity of the child and are ready to move towards a conversation if it is appropriate. There may be fleeting moments where you notice one another, moments that dissolve into self-absorbtion again.

This is like *being* with, rather than *doing* with, the child.

We worked with Molly in a Child Development Unit. She was labelled autistic and resisted attempts to communicate directly with her. She consented to stay in the same room as us (some times with persuasion) but never joined in with the rest of the group. She would not tolerate any physical contact whatsoever, although I knew she would accept hugs from a few people she knew very well.

For several months we arranged to have two facilitators, one to lead the session with the group and one just for Molly. Whilst the others were happy to do things together, Molly padded round the edge, pat-patting the walls, the curtains, the windows, the doors ... shooting quick glances at everyone else and muttering to herself. It was my job to be there for Molly. I began by watching. What was Molly doing while she wasn't joining in? I tried out some of the same movements to see what they felt like to me. I quickly discovered the pleasure of being on the edge, of feeling my way round the edges of the room rather than being engaged in all that activity in the middle. And as I was pat-patting for myself, across the other side of the room, some of my attention was available for Molly - I looked across at her frequently, beamed, said her name quietly and directly mirrored the occasional gesture as she did it. Then I returned to my own exploration. The aim was to give her the space she demanded, but to let her know that I shared something of her way of being in the world.

The leader of the sessions, meanwhile, always left two spaces in the circle, one for Molly and one for me, so that we could join at any time we felt ready. Molly was always recognised as part of the group - welcome when she felt like joining.

Over weeks and months I got to know the edges pretty well. There was always plenty to amuse myself with and Molly looked at me more often and came closer during the sessions. She was intrigued by me. She recognised that there was something running between us. Then one day, perhaps six months in, a ball flew out of the group activity in the centre and she hurled it back in. It was the first time she had acknowledged them. The leader rolled the ball out again, to Molly and to me and we both rolled it back in. A few sessions later, Molly came right up to me and stared intently into my face before retreating to pat some more walls. Later I went close to Molly and held out a hand. She looked for a few seconds, then moved away.

At each session the leader made an opportunity to roll a ball out and each session Molly

came closer to the group as she rolled it back. This became a group ritual. At each session Molly stood closer to the circle and I did the same. One day, she sat briefly in her place - the place that had remained empty so long. I sat in mine. A few weeks later Molly was sitting regularly and for longer periods and I would sit at her feet with a hand out, inviting her to touch me.

Almost exactly a year after we had started, what felt like a breakthrough occurred. As I was sitting at her feet an air of tremendous expectation settled on everyone in the room. Molly was totally still and totally focused.

She was tolerating my presence and showing no signs of running off. I held out my hand. She watched. I extended my hand ... slowly, so slowly. It was a piece of pure dance, a simply gesture full of meaning and potential. I was consumed with it. Further and further went my arm, palm upwards, until my outstretched hand halted just in front of her - offering myself, inviting a response. For a few seconds we were totally still. Nothing moved in the room. And all of a sudden Molly shot out an arm, touched my hand with the briefest of gestures, got up and ran off to the walls. And life started again.

A few weeks later Molly accepted full body contact and grew to enjoy really dancing with one of the two co-leaders. She had taken a long time to join the group, but she became a wholehearted member ...

Opposing

Not all conversations are about agreement. Some children show an intense need to push against you, to do the opposite, to test, challenge and oppose you. In movement, they can do this directly and appropriately. There is no real verbal equivalent to this since it is seldom acceptable to allow a child to have a thorough-going argument with you or to push you around verbally. If we could speak about it adequately it might go something like this. 'I see that you are angry. I can stand up to that anger. It's fine to be angry as long as it doesn't hurt anyone else and you know how to contain it.' Anger can be a positive emotion that prompts our ability to stand up for ourselves and protect ourselves . Children (and adults) need to learn how to use it positively and not destructively.

Opposing involves noticing a child's need to oppose rather than agree; showing them that this is acceptable and, depending on the strength of their need and intention, providing the boundaries that will allow this to be a constructive, safe exchange.

Opposing is done through movement. You might let the child push against you, provide a steady body for them to pull or push on, or do an opposite movement (when the child is tall you are small, when they run you stay still); you might create a movement pattern in which you and the child face up to each other, even coming nose to nose in a play challenge. Your choice will be made according to what the child offers. Your intention to make this a steady, safe activity will be transmitted partly through the rules you establish, and partly through the mood you relay to the child through facial expression and verbal feedback. Give a clear time boundary: 'We have a count of ten for this push'. Give clear guidance about safety: 'We both have to sit down'. 'Neither of us will try to hurt the other'. 'You can only push with flat hands', and so on.

Flow-bond

A flow-bond occurs, as it sounds, when the flow of your movement - the way you use your energy within the movements themselves - is shared. When you are both using the same quality of energy (perhaps with some similar shaping and rhythm as well) there will be a feeling of accord between you.

Flow bonds occur during everyday communication; we probably feel the accord but don't notice the movement. If you want a child to feel supported and affirmed, creating a flow bond by sharing their flow of movement will let them know that you care about them and that you have things in common. When you mirror and reflect you will be trying to 'catch' your partners' flow.

Synchrony

Synchrony occurs in moments when the flow, shaping, rhythm and quality of the movements of two people match exactly. Synchrony carries with it the deepest feelings of accord, agreement and recognition. It happens in moments rather than minutes. It is very difficult to manufacture synchrony, but it is important to recognise it when you see it. People often comment on those moments after moving or watching movement - they are very powerful, almost thrilling. Sometimes, the watchers or movers laugh or smile immediately after such a moment without realising why.

Safety

Keep them safe - by offering extra physical support where necessary or by channelling the responses, moving or verbal, of other children. If their movement is emotionally charged, help them to contain it appropriately. If you are moving with them take your movements down to the floor; make your movement smaller; use the same quality and put it all into one body part, rather than whole body movement, encouraging the child to do the same. Provide a time boundary for moving: 'We can move for just 10, 20 ... seconds ...', as appropriate. And sometimes, if it really feels right, use your body to contain the child's movement. Be careful: this can serve to prompt more, not less, of the emotional content. Use your knowledge of the child and your sense of what they need to guide your decisions.

Prompting

Children may need verbal or physical prompts to help them to stick to their subject. Your prompts are designed to bring parts of the body, or ways of moving, to their attention. You may speak of an area of the body that you think might need to move, or you might place your hand on that part to bring it to their attention. You may do a specific kind of movement that you think is trying to be expressed, to see if this helps them to move on. Only prompt after careful watching.

Bringing movement dialogue to a close

Help children to round off what they have to say. If they seem to be going on and on, remind them about the need to find an ending. Some children, once they have attention of this kind from you, need a lot of persuasion before they relinquish it. Keep reminding them to look for a way to end. Make movements smaller, take them down to the floor, bring them in towards your body, take whole body movement into limbs and then ends of limbs (fingers and toes) - these are all ways of indicating that a movement conversation is coming to a close. Stillness and or parting from physical contact are the final signs of the end.

WORKING THROUGH RELATIONSHIP

All the above suggestions about moving with children assume some kind of relationship. Movement Play places a strong emphasis on learning in relationship. Adults facilitating Movement

Play, therefore, need to focus on, and support, different kinds of relationship so that children will become aware of the possibilities and potential contained within their interactions with others.

What is relationship?

We come into contact with other people constantly, but not every encounter can usefully be described as relationship. When two people engage in mindful interaction with each other, when both people are engaging with the interaction, this can be described as relationship in terms of Movement Play. In relationship, each is aware that they have an affect on the other; they may not be feeling the same things, but they are focused on what is passing between them. The safer the participants, the more they will be able to notice and learn.

Mother and baby display this complex learning mechanism perfectly. Within the safety of the holding relationship (in this case the security of the mother's arms) the baby tries out all sorts of behaviour and the mother responds through facial and physical expressions - mirroring, reflecting, opposing, offering new possibilities. Whatever the baby tries out, she is safe, even if her mother disapproves. Given positive feedback she learns she is lovable and worth knowing. Given negative feedback she learns that there is something amiss, that she is not good to know. Movement Play is similarly direct and physical. When it takes place with a conscious focus on relationship, children can learn both from the experience itself and from the feedback given by others. The basis for these relationships must be total respect - respect for who a child is now, not what we might want them to become.

Different kinds of relationship

Veronica Sherbourne, in her movement work with children who have learning difficulties, suggested three basic relationships - Caring, Sharing and Against. Even though 'Against' might not be as comfortable as the others, experience of each of these is equally important to our learning, growth and development. Movement Play offers a safe structure for exploring each of these in robust and wholly positive ways, not by offering external prompts to do so ('Let's dance anger today') but by providing opportunities that allow children to try all three when they are ready. If adults notice and value all three as part of ordinary life children will be able to explore them when they are ready.

'Caring relationships' involve the child taking care of the adult, as well as the adult taking care of the child. Within 'Caring' play, children can practice the transitions between being cared for, being independent and taking care of others.

In 'Sharing relationships' the participants take equal responsibility for the content of their interactions, for negotiating the way in which decisions are reached between them, and for their safety. Successful relationships pivot around the participants' ability to negotiate with others, as well as their ability to stand up for themselves.

In 'Against relationships' the participants are not in agreement, but explore what it is like to be in opposition. This doesn't have to be an all-out battle; there are many gentle and playful ways of being in opposition as well as rumbustuous pushing-pulling games. Children need places where they can explore, feel and get to know these kinds of relationship, as well as the more readily 'acceptable' caring and sharing.

In addition to these three kinds of relationship, there is a fourth that is particularly relevant to very young children. Babies and young children, by necessity, have to be skilled at manipulative relationships. They wouldn't survive if they couldn't manipulate adults into doing things for them. They have to be self centred and seek support for the things that they want, or need, to do. Adults can help young children to be persistent and confident in their relationships; they can also help them to notice other people's needs so that when they are developmentally ready, they will be well equipped to empathise and adapt.

THE STAGES OF BUILDING A RELATIONSHIP

Learning through relationship thrives in certain conditions. Most of us provide these automatically, but they bear looking at afresh. There are distinct stages to every interaction we make or renew. The mix will be different according to past experience and present context. If children are to feel safe to explore themselves, they will need each stage to be respected so they can feel certain that while they are 'exploring the countryside no-one will sneak in and burn the castle'.

Seeking consent

Adults have a lot of ways of forcing the issue - verbal pushing, grabbing hands and swinging a child into action, pushing them by the shoulders, or simply using adult power to insist that 'It will be fun!' Adults need to remember to seek children's consent.

Making overtures

'Making overtures' involves starting slowly, trying out what you might want to 'talk' about and what you might 'say', offering movements that the child might join in with and 'mirroring' things the child does. In this phase of making a relationship, you may try out lots of different kinds of movement before you find something you are both happy to settle with.

Deepening

Once trust is established and boundaries are in place, it is possible to engage with more serious matters, in more intimate ways, and to share more of yourself. In this phase, you are likely to find a movement theme, or subject, that feels good to both of you. You become clear what the 'game' is to be, or what kinds of movement you will share, and then you extend it. This is where you get to the heart of the matter ...

Review

In this phase you exchange something of how you feel as a result of what you have done together. This is done within the movement - not by talking and rationalising afterwards.

These stages are all important and we adults will 'favour' some over others. Some of us like to dive straight into the nitty gritty, whilst others like a good, long lead-in before we get to the heart of the matter. Notice your own preferences if you can. Young children's preferences are only just beginning to form, but watch out for the ways they choose to build relationships in movement.

Movement relationships and conversations follow the same pattern as verbal relationships and conversations. If you are nervous about spontaneous movement, start by following your children. They are usually experts and not short of ideas for things to do. Adults are definitely active learners in Movement Play. We are always responsible for creating and maintaining a focused atmosphere, and for everyone's comfort and safety, but beyond that we can pitch in and learn alongside the children we live with or work with.

Hopping Home Backwards

9
Watching Movement Play

'dance like some happy little fly, I
and sing like the wings of a bird.'

poem written after dancing

A new way of working with movement requires new ways of looking at movement, and new expectations about what we might see. Existing physical development activities in the curriculum are based around functional or expressive movement, in which balance, coordination and ease of movement are the primary goals. You may be used, therefore, to looking at 'what moves, where and how', checking that the major gross motor skills (walking, hopping, skipping, jumping) and fine motor skills (using scissors, holding a pencil, using a cup and so on) are all in place.

In Movement Play, however, we are encouraging children to engage fully with their physicality, to engage with sensation, feeling and image as well as with the functional and visual aspects of movement. As we watch children indulge in the free flow, spontaneous Movement Play through which they explore these felt experiences, we need to see more so that we can support and extend their learning. To see more we need to be able to observe in detached and analytical ways, and to 'witness' in involved and personal ways - to gather information and notice how we are moved as we watch. We need to use both our intellect and our direct perception as we watch; to engage our thoughts and our sensations, feelings, movement and images.

In this chapter I want to offer new structures within which you can address these two aspects of watching movement - observation and witnessing. Below, you will find several simple structures (two that I have borrowed and adapted from specific areas of work and others that I have formed for my own use over the years). Use them to extend your existing systems. I find that I duck and dive between them depending on what, and why, I am watching. All of them aim to help us to see more of children, not by dissecting what we see but by looking further into the whole.

It is in the way we watch children, as much as in the way we move with them, that we create the non-judgmental, open atmosphere in which they can be more fully themselves. We don't just watch in order to fill in the records. We also watch in order to be actively involved in the learning process - to help children to learn, and to learn ourselves.

Some basic guidelines

You can watch with your eyes, looking at the particular kinds of movement that a child is doing. You can 'watch' with your body, using your kinesthetic awareness to feel the movement that you see. You can 'watch' with your heart, letting what you see speak to your own experience - move you, inform you, delight you, and challenge you. Information gained from these processes will both inform your plans for future activities, and help you to build wholehearted relationships within which children will learn.

When you first come to watching Movement Play you may feel that there is so much to see and feel you don't know where to begin. Having a structure in mind, within which to watch and reflect, can help you to see more. Don't expect to switch on your ability to watch like a tap. It requires focus and attention, just like really careful listening.

NOTES FOR LEADERS:

STARTING TO WATCH MOVEMENT

Settle in. Give yourself time to make the transition from listening and talking to watching. Don't expect to start seeing significant things right away. Just watch and let the movement seep in.

After a while, decide which structure you are going to use to guide your watching. Then start applying it gradually.

You may need to be clear about your reasons for watching: observing in order to gather information, or witnessing in order to develop the relationship between you and the mover.

You may want to slip-slide between structures in order to gain information as part of a relationship-building process.

If you need to note down anything you've seen, try to make time to do it as soon as possible. There are charts provided later in this chapter that help to round up information quickly and easily. They are a sort of formalised 'post-it' system since there is always so much we could write, and so little time to do it.

Make time to share things you have witnessed with the mover.

If you are using structures that encourage attention to you own inner experience as you watch, don't be surprised if you feel very moved sometimes. Do give yourself the space to acknowledge your feelings if you can.

Choose the kind of structure that is right for you today. If you are weary, stick to the more detached approaches and leave your inner world to rest.

NOTES FOR LEADERS:

STRUCTURE 1: SAY WHAT YOU SEE

This is a way of easing into watching the language of movement, with help from the language that is most familiar to you - words. You may also find it useful if your attention is wandering - a kind of wake-up call.

There's a quiz programme on television in which the host tries to help the contestants to get the answer to picture clues by saying, 'Just say what you see'. This structure invites you to do just the same. It invites you to put into words (in your head) what you *see* in movement. It is a creative game, not an analytical structure. Use it lightly and play with any images that may arise.

As you watch a child move, or a group of children move, run a commentary in your head describing as many different elements of what you *see* as you can. You are not trying to be a movement expert, just 'say what you see'. Try as many different ways of describing it as you can think of - it will be a little like a stream of words out of which pop one or two that give you a fresh insight. As you find the words, listen to what you *say* and *see* if anything rings out or reframes what you think about a child or group of children.

'All the children are moving. The room is full of different ways of moving. Some have got out props and some are moving without anything. <u>Dion is right in the middle of everybody</u> in a squash of girls. A group of boys are doing sporty-type movements over by the window. <u>Paul is on the edge</u> of the room. There seems to be <u>a lot of movement going upwards</u>; arms and elbows breaking the surface of the water. Two children are on the floor - different from everyone else.'

Speaking what we see can bring to the fore what we might otherwise only dimly notice. The example above is an extract from a description of a chaotic room full of moving children, quickly scanned, saying instantly what I saw - *without trying to make interpretations*. The bits that are underlined are things that leapt out at me as I spoke them in my head. They provide information about emerging movement themes (upwards movement / boys doing sporty stuff) and about the position in the group of particular children (Dion in the middle and Paul on the edge). There is also the indication of a contrast, a balance in the chaos (two children are on the floor).

I can use this information in many ways, either to note particular movement preferences or to give me a pointer towards my next step - allowing an organic development of the movement. I could bring everyone's attention to the two on the floor and suggest we all take their example, thus grounding the movement and changing to something that might be less anxiety-provoking. When we look - and see more - the next step is often waiting in the group, if only we can recognise it.

NOTES FOR LEADERS:

STRUCTURE 2: SAY WHAT YOU FEEL

The same as the 'Say what you *see*' structure, but this time you are trying to identify your own *feelings* in response to the movement. Some of these will be professionally based (I am afraid someone will hurt themselves) and some will be personal (I really long to sway with Glen on the cushion).

This is practice for you in locating your feeling response.

It invites you to notice the feeling responses you have in relation to individual children or to the group as a whole.

It generates lots of information - some of which you might want to share with a child, or the group. ('I felt really happy as we moved' ... 'I felt anxious when we were all moving a lot in this small space ...').

NOTES FOR LEADERS:

STRUCTURE 3: WORKING KINESTHETICALLY

This structure invites you to use your body intelligence as you watch. Take your attention to your bodily-felt experience - sensation, feeling, movement and image - and feel your response to what you see.

As you watch, <u>imagine</u> the movement that you see in your own body. Imagine what it would be like to do that leap, or that shuffle.

As you watch, <u>try out</u> things you see in your own body. You may need to adapt the movement in some way, staying true to the quality, but doing it in just one part of your body for instance.

<u>After you watch,</u> try out movements that you have seen and listen hard to see what you find out about them when they take place in your body. You may discover that when you watched you thought the hips were the focus for the movement, but now you try it, you feel it is the neck. There can be dramatic differences in the observed experience and the felt experience.

NOTES FOR LEADERS:

STRUCTURE 4 THREE OPEN QUESTIONS

This structure invites you to choose three different things to focus on as you watch: what is happening, what is not happening and what is trying to happen.

As you watch for what is happening, stick to what you actually see. 'I see her left arm flapping.' 'I see a great many jumps.' 'I see lots of rolling.'

You may also become aware of something that is not happening - no stillness, no movements that lift away from the floor, no small movements, no big movements.

And through the centre of these observations you may begin to get a feeling of some movement that is trying to happen. The role of the adult is to provide opportunities that may help the child to move on. These opportunities may be accepted or rejected.

What is happening?

Notice as much as possible about the ways a child chooses to move on any particular day. (The more you practice asking yourself this question and trying it out, the more you will see.) Notice things like particular actions (hopping, walking, rolling and so on, or spontaneous, idiosyncratic movement that is unique to that child). Notice whether it is slow or fast; high or low; where a child likes to be in the room; whether they like to use a lot of space or a little; whether they seem to like moving or not. Gather as much information as you can without getting anxious about whether you are doing it right.

Gather information of this kind over a number of Movement Play sessions. Notice any themes, patterns or marked differences.

What isn't happening?

What kinds of moving do you not see in a child's Movement Play? Perhaps nothing jumps out, but perhaps, after you have watched for a while you realise there is no stillness, or no changes of pace or level. Perhaps a particular part of the body never moves. Think widely and carefully and treat your answer lightly. This question isn't designed to give you something to 'fix'; just to help you to see more.

What is trying to happen?

This is the most intriguing question. As you watch, over a single session or over a number, can you get a feeling for what might be trying to happen in a child's Movement Play. What would they do if only they could? What is in the 'zone of proximal learning' for this child? Again, this is not designed to give you something to 'fix', but it might help you to plan opportunities, or ways of moving with this child, that will extend their learning - opportunities that may be accepted or rejected depending on the readiness of the child to move on.

Ripton (4) has a movement theme that becomes apparent over many observations. I become interested when I notice that he 'shuffles' when he walks. He doesn't lift his feet fully off the ground, but drags them along. In the playground one day I see him dragging one foot round and round in circles as he stands watching the others playing. Another day, I find him 'roller skating' round the edge of the room, dragging one foot along after the other. In Movement Group when we move together I slip in a little foot shuffling and we enjoy 'roller skating' together for a minute or two. Then I see him bouncing as he stands beside the book box, bouncing as he paints at the easel, watching the way that his brush makes marks as his body moves up and down on bouncing legs.

I try the bouncing for myself and notice that once again the feet are not moving off the ground. I ask myself the questions. What is happening? Answer: Ripton's feet are in contact with the ground a lot. What is not happening? Answer: Ripton's feet do not leave the ground when he is playing in this way.

When next I move with Ripton we bounce together. We start bouncing on our bottoms

(same theme, different part of the body). Then we crawl and drag our knees along a lot. (Like the feet in the roller skating.) Then we stand up and bounce, our toes never leaving the floor ... in circles and then in a sort of Ripton version of the Twist. After we have moved like this I think about the third question. What is trying to happen? I try out some of Ripton's movement in my own body, and replay some of the things I have seen him do in my mind's eye. When I try the movements I feel strongly that I want to leave the floor - to jump, to lift my feet away from the ground. I answer the 'What is trying to happen?' question. 'A jump.'

The next time we meet in Movement Group we bounce and shuffle again. The others notice and welcome the familiar theme. There are several balloon-fish hanging from the ceiling above us, the product of a craft session. As we bounce I start to look up and raise my arms above my head, as if I will try and reach the fish above me. Ripton sees my intention and, grinning, looks up too. I bounce harder and look up more. Ripton mirrors me. I feel that he is happy to go along with this as long as I am not forcing him. Then, quite suddenly, Ripton leaps up and makes an attempt to touch the fish. And again and again. I mirror him, leaping and leaping to touch the fish. We laugh and squeal with the effort. I bring my jumps into rhythm with Ripton so that we leap, land, breathe and leap again together. We can't do it for long. We collapse onto the floor and huddle together on our knees, panting and laughing. It feels as if <u>something has happened</u>. It feels bigger than just a bit of a jump.

NOTES FOR LEADERS:

STRUCTURE 5: I SAW ... I FELT ... I IMAGINED ... I THOUGHT

This structure invites you to allow thoughts and feelings and images to mingle and mix, but to be clear about each as they arise.

It separates thoughts from bodily-felt responses (sensation, feeling, movement and image).

It divides your responses into these four headings.

It encourages you to watch carefully and to be moved by what you *see*.

It provides a clear, non-judgmental structure for things you might want to tell someone after you have watched them move.

I saw

This simply encourages you to notice movement ... what a body is doing. 'I saw an arm out to the side.' 'I saw you jumping.' 'I saw you stamping.' 'I saw your fingers wriggling.' Although this sounds very simple, it can be profoundly important for a child just to know that you saw them. Naming what you saw very cleanly helps them to feel valued for exactly who they are, not who you might wish they were.

This structure emphasises the fact that we don't see everything; we see what jumps out at us, what resonates with our experience as a fellow human being. So we make sure that children understand (when we feedback) that we did not see everything they did, but this is what jumped out at us. 'This is what I saw.' In a group situation it is useful to let several children feedback, emphasising that each of us sees different things.

I felt

This is the hardest one of all. As you watch, can you identify the feeling inside you, prompted by the movement you see. Once again, don't try to second guess how the mover is feeling. How do you feel? 'When I saw your fingers wriggle I felt curious. I wanted to know what was going to happen next.' 'When I saw you still I felt sleepy.' 'When I saw you stamp I felt anxious.' The temptation to interpret, to make a reasoned response, is strong. 'When I saw you stamp I felt you were angry.' This is a sneaky way of saying 'When I saw you stamp I *thought* you were angry'. When we use this structure with children we need to take care about what we feed back in order to keep it wholly positive, and encourage others to do the same. In this structure we are trying hard to identify how we are moved and to let people know their affect on us. We adults generally find it hard to keep away from the interpretations under this heading.

I imagined

As you watch, notice the images, or stories, or memories that float in to your awareness prompted by the Movement Play. Don't be trapped into interpreting what you think the mover might be imagining. This is about you. 'When I saw you jump I imagined a big road digger moving along the road.' (Rather than 'I imagined you were a road digger'.) We cannot know what images and memories are at work for the mover. In Movement Play adults give children the opportunity to make sense of the play for themselves and to find their own vocabulary for their experience.

This structure is about identifying your own inner experience and letting the mover hear how they affect you. (We are so used to interpreting, this isn't as easy as it sounds.)

This is a structure that helps you to identify your own inner world as you watch. I learned it from Tina Stromsted, working in a movement approach called Authentic Movement - a kind of Movement Play for adults. She created this particular structure, along with a colleague, as a simple way to help people to be really aware of their own subjective responses as they watch other people move. I have adapted the original for use with young children, including another section - 'I thought' - to catch the judgments we make. The original was created within a form that encourages 'no interpretation, no projection and no judgment' in order to develop our ability to see others for who they are, rather than who we *imagine* them to be. As such, adults set aside interpretations, projections and judgments. However, for the purposes of Movement Play, in a learning context, I think it is important to have somewhere to 'put' our thoughts.

I thought

This heading is for your own records, not to be shared with children. It is where you record anything that occurred to your rational thinking processes. This box doesn't have any more worth than the others. It doesn't record the truth about the child.

'When I saw Ralph move today I thought that he looked weary.'
'When I watched Merle move today I thought she was anxious.'
'I don't think Oscar likes Movement Play sessions.'

We make these judgments all the time; this structure encourages us to name them as judgments and separate them from other responses.

The structures above provide different ways of looking at what is happening in movement. Back in Chapter 1, watching Jack hop home backwards, I wondered about what he might have been 'doing' in his body. Since Movement Play is about engaging with bodily-felt experience, it is useful to have a structure that encourages us to ask: 'What is this child engaged with?' and to search for clues that might help us to answer it.

Of course, there are many detailed forms of movement observation and analysis that specialists could apply to bring them closer to an answer. But most people working in Early Years settings are not movement specialists, and need something that will help them to watch in broad, not in analytical, ways. We need to watch movement as we listen to words - searching for the subject matter and helping children to explore it.

THE LANDSCAPES

This last structure views the layers of bodily-felt experience in terms of 'Landscapes' that children might visit along a learning journey. I use the word 'Landscapes' in order to suggest places that have an overall identity, but a wealth of individual detail within them - each particular Landscape not only different from every other, but also different each time we go back.

The example of Jack hopping home identified many different Landscapes. I don't want to suggest that it's possible to identify all the Landscapes that a child might visit and round them up into one neat framework. So, perhaps what follows should be described as a frame of mind, rather than a structure. It suggests thirteen different kinds of engagement, or Landscapes, that we might identify as we watch. Some of these are driven by innate programming - things that all children are compelled to seek out (touch as food, opportunities to repeat the developmental movement patterns, gaining physical mastery, establishing a sense of me/not me) and some are concerned with establishing ourselves in the world (making sure we are seen, exploring relationships - what we can get other people to do for us and, gradually, what we can do for them). Others are to do with developing learning strategies (active imagination, developing our ability to listen to our bodies, developing our body memory, taking pleasure in our physicality, our ability to make sense of the world we live in and, ultimately, embodying our learning and our lives).

These Landscapes are only a starter kit, a nudge towards a particular frame of mind. As you watch children you will discover many more. Similarly, the suggestions for things you might see in any Landscape that accompany each description, are only a beginning. It's impossible to give a definitive list of things a child will explore through their body-felt experience. We have to look with care and an open mind. One kind of movement might occur in many of the Landscapes; the way the child engages with it will determine the layer of experience they are exploring.

As adults, we need to have a willingness to keep looking, to try see more of each child and to find ways of supporting their journey. We watch, not in order to tell them which Landscapes they should visit, or ensure that they get round all the Landscapes, but in order to help them to make the most of those they choose to visit. We watch to ensure that we notice and value children's spontaneous Movement Play as part of their learning. We watch as we have learned to listen - with care and attention so that we can join them on their journey.

NOTES FOR LEADERS:

STRUCTURE 6: THE LANDSCAPES

As you watch a child move, do you feel that they are exploring one particular area of their bodily-felt experience? Sensation, feeling, movement or image or their ability to listen in ...

Do you feel that they are keen to explore a particular aspect of that experience? Does it appear in the Landscapes chart (page 233) or is it something different?

Can you use what you see to help them to explore it in more depth?

Can you use what you see to influence how you will choose to move with them, or the opportunities you will offer in future?

SENSATION
Touch as food

In this Landscape a child is seeking vital stimulation through touch that supports current and future health and wellbeing. 'The tactile stimulation associated with tender loving care (is) absolutely crucial to a baby's development. Without it, no amount of food and no kind of medicine (can) produce a healthy individual.' (Job's Body *Deane Juhan*.)

It seems from many studies that the effects of sensory deprivation are very similar to malnutrition - retarded bone growth, failure to gain weight, poor muscular coordination, immunological weakness and general apathy. Sensory stimulation is also vital for the promotion of good neurological organisation at the pons level of the brain, which in turn helps children to experience accurately the life preserving sensations of heat, cold, pain and hunger and supports their ability to sense themselves fully in the world. Babies, young children (and adults), need to be touched and touched a lot. It isn't just pleasant, it is vital to the healthy functioning of our organs, to our future emotional stability and our ability to be effective parents in our turn.

This Landscape is about affirming a first step on the journey that will form the foundation for learning throughout our lives. If we are alive to our senses, our intention and the movement that takes us into action, we are alive to many possibilities for learning.

As a child I used to watch my mother pause in her work ... cooking perhaps, or taking me through my music theory test papers ... and gently run the fingers of one hand up and down the other arm. It was a gesture I grew very familiar with. Her eyes would go slightly glazed for an instant as her attention went inside, and sometimes a tiny shudder would pass through her body as if she were engaged in the unconscious pursuit of waking up her body to herself ... so that she could return to the constant stream of external demands. I have come to think of this as an ordinary, everyday way of satisfying the need our bodies have to 'stay in touch'.

NOTES FOR LEADERS:

TOUCH AS FOOD: watch out for

Snuggling, cuddly behaviour. Climbing on to your knee, sitting in close contact, coming into the bed at night ...

Children who *seek* touch games - stroking, tickling, poking, rubbing, licking and so on.

Children who *seek* activities that ensure their whole body is in contact with things in the environment - who roll around on the floor, roll toys around their bodies, use adults as a human gym.

Children who love to be massaged ... who can be still and quiet when they are massaged.

Young children talking, and asking questions, about the sensations they experience.

A child who is incapable of keeping still. If they haven't had enough touch-food they may need to top up their reservoir to get their sensory systems working properly. Wriggling and writhing about can do this for them. A massage, or sensory games, from you will do this much better.

SENSATION
Sensual Delight

In viewing sensation simply as a stepping stone to learning, we are in danger of missing the equally important source of learning that is sensual delight. Over the years I have been questioned many times about the dangers of arousing inappropriate sexual feelings whilst encouraging people of all ages to move, to touch and to focus on their bodies. There is a clear and important difference between sexual activity and sensual delight. One is entirely inappropriate in learning settings and the other entirely appropriate. But unless we are very clear about the differences there is tendency to close down on both. We need more sensual delight in our lives, not less!

Sensual delight is about delighting in physical sensation and in the sense of one's physicality as a whole. It does no harm to anybody and is an important part of our pleasure in being alive, and in our confidence as a physical creature. In this Landscape, therefore, a child is eager to take delight in being a body and explores things that feel good. There is no sense in which Movement Play attempts to *teach* children about sensual delight. Adults simple support and value children's pleasure, rather than suppress it, as an important aspect of their physicality.

> *Martha (18 months) is sitting beside her mother on the grass, holding onto her trousers. She is still, staring into the middle distance, swaying minutely from side to side.*
>
> *Suddenly, she flings both her arms into the air, tips onto her back and throws her legs over her head, kicking them into the air as she goes. Whooping with delight she struggles to her feet and gallops off to a nearby tree. Whooping all the time she gallops round the tree, her short arms waving above her head. After five careful circumnavigations she hurtles back to her mother and crash lands onto her legs. Burying her head she wrestles her mum backwards until she falls gently onto the grass, laughing and protesting mildly. Martha climbs on, extends herself fully with the whole surface of her front in contact with her mum's legs and belly. She wriggles and writhes so that she can fit as snugly as possible. 'Make yourself comfortable!', laughs her mum. Then Martha bends down and pulls up her mum's shirt, and, pulling up her own T-Shirt she carefully presses her bare skin against her mum's.*
>
> *She lies down, shuts her eyes positively crowing with delight.*

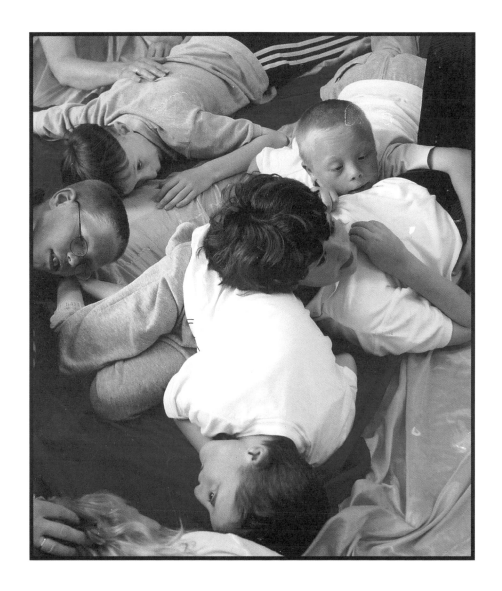

Johnny (4) leans back in his chair and raises his arms above his head. He stretches an exaggerated stretch, and turns his head into his left shoulder. Maintaining the position of his arms he shuts his eyes and blows gently into the fabric of his tee-shirt. Gradually, his arms fold down over his head and he arches backwards in his chair. Then he turns his head and blows into the other shoulder. Moving his arm away he blows on his bare skin below his sleeve, moving his head backwards and forwards to move the air current across his skin. Clasping his hands together in front of him he blows across the other arm and then bends forward to blow on his legs.

A little while later, 'back in the land of the living', he looks up and beams. He has been lost in his own sensual delight.

NOTES FOR LEADERS:

SENSUAL DELIGHT: watch out for ...

A child wallowing in their bodily-felt experience.

A child who is obviously alive to their physicality, to their bodily-felt experience.

Drifting and dreaming: a child who seems to have put mental activity on hold.

Great concentration on particular sensory experiences.

Often, but not always, slow movements. A sense of indulging in time ...

A feeling that the child is really present in their body.

Expressions of delight and pleasure - both physical and vocal.

SENSATION
This is Me

In this Landscape a child is building information about self and other - what is me and what is not me? Since the body, the skin, is our physical container, much of this fundamental understanding about what we are and what we are not is gleaned through the body - through touching, but also through moving. Our skin is the interface between ourselves and the world. As we touch we experience two things - the thing we touch and ourselves touching. Our sense of our own surface is very vague until we touch something. As Bertrand Russell observed, 'Touch, more than any other mode of sensation, defines for us our sense of reality. Not only our geometry and our physics, but our whole conception of what exists outside us, is based upon the sense of touch'.

In this Landscape, babies and children engage in a variety of Movement Play activities that explore and confirm their reality, their separateness and their relationship to the people and objects in the world. A child needs sensory feedback in order to feel themself to be in the world.

Jonathan (6) can't sit still. When he comes to rest, to watch telly, he is always shuffling and changing position, sitting up, lying down, draping himself over the arm. The only thing that helps is if his Mum massages him; rubs his legs up and down, holds his arm and squeezes, strokes the bottom of his feet. Only then can he lose the desire to be in constant motion.

It may be that Jonathan simply doesn't feel his body until he is touched. The movement gives him some of the feedback he needs to feel that he exists.

Silas (six months) lies on his back on the floor with his legs and arms waving in that random fashion that will eventually come together into organised patterns. As he jerks and moves, his fingers suddenly find his toes and he pulls and flicks at them until he loses them again. After a little while he finds them again and a smile flashes across his face and he makes contented gurgles.

Ricky (3) sits on a beanbag entwined with Matt (3), his best friend. It is hard to tell where one begins and the other ends. As they sit, silent except for little squeaks, squawks and gurgles, they struggle and tussle, seemingly trying to make some space between themselves, but hold on tight all the while. Then Matt pulls an arm free and waves it in the air - announcing its freedom, its separateness. Ricky makes a grab for Matt's wrist and pulls the arm back in, sitting on it for extra security. 'Oww', complains Matt loudly. But now Ricky waves a hand free in the air and it's Matt's turn to pull it back in. 'We're twins', he says. 'You can't get away'. Then Matt, with a huge effort, pulls his whole body free and squares up to Ricky, who responds in kind. Both boys face each other foursquare, like a pair of bear cubs. Suddenly, as if they had exactly the same idea at the same time, both boys have shot out their hands in front of them and are pushing each other away, growling and hissing with the effort.

NOTES FOR LEADERS:

THIS IS ME: watch out for ...

A child who likes to play movement games that emphasise togetherness and separation, or a child who finds these games very challenging.

A child who cannot stop wriggling.

A child who seeks firm contact on their tummy - their centre. Lying on the floor, lying over a beanbag, your knee, a big ball, and, so on.

A child who calms, or stills, when you massage them.

A child who calms when you hold their tummy firmly, or when they lie with their tummies in contact with something.

A child seeking firm holding from an adult, or who likes to find places to crawl into that fit tight around their body. In Movement Play they might love to be wrapped tightly in a lycra square, for instance.

FEELINGS
Exploring Feelings

In this Landscape a child is interested in exploring their emotional feelings - what is it like to feel certain ways; how feelings link with events and actions; what is difficult to bear and what is pleasurable; how to manage feelings - big and small; the effect of their emotions on others; the effect of others' emotions on them. In Movement Play, as opposed to creative dance, the child chooses when and what to explore; adults don't suggest that they think about a particular emotion and then explore the idea of it in movement. In Movement Play the child happens upon this Landscape when it is important to do so in their learning journey, and creates their own meaning from their play.

Nick asks to dance with me.

He is six, withdrawn and anxious. He cannot trust his weight at all - will not lean or balance with any one else. He doesn't like being touched; doesn't like anyone too close to him. He refuses to work with other children. He has good cause to be wary ... this is a child who has been sexually abused.

Today we are working with hoops. The room is full of children swaying and balancing, stepping through and round and under, leaning out and balancing one another's weight. Nick and I move the hoop gently backwards and forwards between us.

Then I lean backwards. 'Can you hold me', I say. He laughs and shakes his head, but braces his legs and digs his feet into the floor. I continue to lean and he takes my weight. 'You can', I say and smile. 'You can! You are holding my whole weight!' A huge gurgling laugh erupts from deep within him. He is so surprised he lets go and I have to take a quick step back to stop myself from falling. Nick jumps up and down on the spot and laughs. Then he thrusts the hoops at me, urging me to do it again. I lean back and he holds me. 'You're holding me again', I say. Again that gurgling laugh and as he lets go this time I fall with a little bump onto the floor. He looks crestfallen. 'Here, take the hoops again and lift me up', I say smiling, to let him know this is all part of the game. He takes the hoops and pulls. Instead of rising, I slide along the floor. Nick is stunned.

He, a six year old, is pulling me, an adult, along the floor. I can't tell whether he is more stunned at his strength or that fact that I am happy to let him do it. He repeatedly asks if this is all right. 'It's great', I say. 'I love it,' And he slides me around the room, taking great care of me, but loving the fact that he is 'pulling me about'.

NOTES FOR LEADERS:

EXPLORING FEELINGS: watch out for ...

Children speaking about the emotional content of the play, whilst they are moving or afterwards. (They may talk to themself as they explore in their bodies, explaining things as they go along).

Movements that seem to be full of feeling - rather than about the shapes or patterns.

A child who uses a prop to support exploration of a particular feeling: for example an elastic rope to pull on aggressively, or a parachute to get underneath and hide from people to explore separateness or loneliness and so on.

A child who negotiates situations in which they can heighten a certain emotion through their Movement Play.

A child who is emotionally charged as they move.

FEELINGS
Exploring Relationship

In this Landscape a child is exploring themself in relationship to other people and to the environment. They seek Movement Play activities through which to feel this relationship, test it and see what it offers them. Young children are self-centred; they want to know what's in it for them. This propensity for manipulation is basic to their ability to survive; babies and young children must have older people to protect them and look after them or they will die.

As Jack hopped home backwards he may well have been testing my relationship with him: how much could he trust me to keep him safe and/or let him do what he wanted. A child's previous experience of relationship affects what they will need, or want, to explore. Within their need to manipulate in order to survive, children also begin to explore a range of different kinds of relationship in safe play situations. Chapter 7 looked at Veronica Sherbourne's three types of relationship - caring, sharing and against. As we watch children move we can try to discern which a child is most eager to explore.

> At the end of a day of tantrums and arguments with his mother Angus (3) was in tears after a firm ticking off. 'You're mean!', he said and retreated, head down, bum up, into the big cushion on the floor. His mum got on with making the tea. Later, Angus strolled into the kitchen. 'Hold my hands', he ordered. 'Like this.' He held out both his hands and took hers. 'Hold me up', he said and leant back so that she had all his weight. 'Have you got me?', he asked, and, reassured, leant his head back and tipped up onto his toes, so she was holding all his weight. 'I knew I could do it', he said and returned to the cushion.
>
> Angus, through the Movement Play, reaffirms that his mother will continue to look after him - directly, but not consciously. He follows his body-thought; by making her take all of his weight he discovers that she is still prepared to support him even though they have argued and she has been cross.

Caring

Merline (3) and Hannah (3) are in the Movement Corner. They are getting out all the props, one after the other (ribbon sticks, lycra square, sponge balls, koosh balls, wafty flags, elastic rings) and placing them in the centre of the space. 'Let's get them all out', says Merline. When there's nothing left in the bag they hover, looking at them, wondering what to do. 'You lie down Hannah and I'll do this thing.' Obligingly, Hannah lies on her back on the floor. 'No. This way', and Merline shows her what she means. Hannah turns over and lies on her tummy. For the next five minutes Merline collects each prop and drapes it over and around Hannah. She is careful to leave her head out, but wraps and folds all the fabrics and ribbon sticks around the whole of the rest of her body. At the end she says, 'There! You're my baby and I've put you to bed'.

Sharing

Tilly (4) and Isabella (4) are standing inside a big hoola hoop, both holding onto the sides. They are talking about this and that, swaying effortlessly from side to side. Then there is a shift from talking to moving. They start to rock backwards and forwards, gently at first and then with more energy. Then Tilly tugs and runs backwards a little way pulling Isabella with her. Isabella responds by running backwards and pulling Tilly. They pause. Tilly jumps. Isabella jumps. They jump together, jump, jump, jump, laughing and squealing as they go. They sit down still in the hoop. They rock from side to side while they catch their breath, then Isabella pulls them up for another go.

Against

Emanuel (2) is out of sorts. 'No', he screams at his mum. 'No. No. NO.' She is trying to put his coat on before they go out from playgroup into the cold, wet Yorkshire day. Everything she suggests brings fresh screams of No. He is very clear - he has set himself against her and won't budge. 'Do you want a push?', she asks when it is clear that nothing will move him. This is a structure we have used in Movement Play. The expression on his face changes. A tiny grin plays around his lips though he tries to stay *angry. His Mum kneels down and puts out her hands.*

He reaches out and grabs them and starts to wrestle. 'Wait for it!', she says. 'The rules. We have 10 seconds. No kicking or biting. No trying to hurt. At the end we stop pushing. OK?' He nods. 'OK. Here we go then.' Emanuel slaps his palms against hers and pushes with all his might. He tries to push her over. She resists carefully and pushes back, just enough to give him a real struggle. She counts all the time. '1-2-3-4-5-6-7-8-9-10 Stop.' He tries to go on but she simply releases all pressure and he tips forwards, catching himself before he falls. 'Again, again!', he demands. They repeat it four times and although he pleads for a fifth, the force has gone out of it. Somehow, the direct experience of physically pushing, as opposed to the indirect experience of verbally resisting has settled something in him. He puts his coat on with minimum resistance.

NOTES FOR LEADERS:

EXPLORING RELATIONSHIPS: watch out for ...

A child who is eager to play in movement with another person, adult or child.

A child who sets rules that include relationship in their play.

A child who asks about the relationship element of the Movement Play rather than any other aspect of the experience.

A child who is drawn to pushing, pulling, tussling movements (Against).

A child who is drawn to playing exact mirroring games (Sharing.)

A child who is drawn to games that include weight taking or trust (Sharing).

A child who seeks opportunities to take care of, or look after, others (Caring).

In whole group work children who take up, and get to know, particular positions in the group - outsider, central figure, leader, co-leader, saboteur, rescuer, persecutor, victim and so on.

FEELINGS
Being Seen: affirmation

In this Landscape a child is actively meeting their need to be seen and acknowledged. This is an important foundation for their emotional well-being.

In Movement Play children can seek affirmation for many different aspects of their experience and themselves. They might need you to witness a new skill, either for the pleasure of the praise or because it doesn't feel quite real until it has been seen and acknowledged. They might need to display a particular piece of behaviour, so they can learn more about its effect. They may need to have a particular aspect of themselves acknowledged (real or fantasy) so that they can feel that it is truly a part of them. They may simply need to affirm their existence and their worth - and undivided attention goes a long way towards this. Being seen is one aspect of learning in relationship, or in community.

Chi Yen (4) stood in front of the community dance worker with her legs wide apart and her arms thrown out to her sides. 'Hullo', she crooned. 'What are we doing today?' Her head inclined to the side and she swung vigorously from side to side on her wide stance. 'Can I sit next to you in the circle?' She held her hands in front of her and jumped up and down a lot. 'Please!' She spread her arms again and swung some more. The dancer threw her arms wide in a mirroring gesture, jumped into a wide stance and said, 'Hullo, Chi Yen'. Chi Yen laughed and jumped her feet together. The dancer followed suit. For two minutes they jumped and swung, swung and jumped in their own dance of greeting. 'I must get my tapes ready now', said the dancer. And Chi Yen ran off happily to play with her friends and wait for the movement session.

Brian (4) bites his nursery worker from time to time. She is understandably wary, never quite sure when he might become aggressive enough to take a lunge at her, to kick her, to bite. She knows that she has become tentative in her approach and feels that this may only serve to make matters worse. She wants robust contact with him, feels that he, more than most children, needs and deserves a warm and loving relationship at nursery - but her wariness is real. She throws me a challenge. 'You say you work with

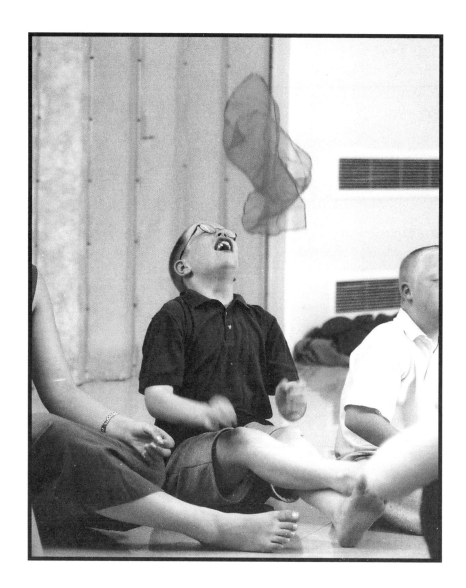

whatever a child offers ... what if that happens to be biting and kicking?'

The next time I see Brian he appears to be pretty unhappy with himself and the world. He looks uncomfortable in his skin - scratchy and constantly on the move. He wants to run and bounce off the walls, kick his legs in the air and shout. I join him, running, and then, instead of bouncing my body off the wall, I slap it quite hard ... a quick, loud slap ... and then run on again. Brian laughs. He has a go ... slap. I urge him to enjoy the sound but to take care of his hand ... not to hit so hard that he hurts himself. Then I slap the floor ... he ducks down and slaps it too. We slap with both hands, then I clap my hands together sharply with a loud crack. (I know that I am grinning madly as I do it ... it is fun, a bit startling and somehow energising). We make more cracks and slaps and then I make my thumb and forefinger into a biting, snapping mouth, snapping away in front of my face. Brian joins in and our snapping fingers have a snappy conversation as we giggle and laugh with wicked delight. Snap, slap, crack ... we vary the biting movements we make. Then Brian moves in too close and suddenly I feel as if he is lining up to wallop me. 'No!', I say with as much cool determination as I can muster, and I put both hands palm down on the carpet and keep quite still.

We return to this game often. We make rules together, like the very clear 'time out' call that either of us can use. And we make mistakes too. Sometimes Brian does give me a wallop (and earnestly apologises) and sometimes I frighten him by being too exuberant (and earnestly apologise). We make mistakes, own up to them and especially ... find appropriate ways of acknowledging and using this snapping energy that we both enjoy.

Lindsey went into the circle with exaggeratedly drooping shoulders, scuffling her feet along the carpet. When she got to the middle she curled up in a little ball on the floor and covered her eyes. After a bit she turned on her other side and curled up in the same ball, hands over eyes. Then she stood up and plodded back to the place where she had entered the circle and repeated this little phrase all over again. 'Do you know what I was being?', she said at the end. 'I was sad because my Daddy's left and I miss him.'

Here there is some specific aspect of her life that Lindsey wants to be seen - the fact that her Dad has moved out recently.

NOTES FOR LEADERS:

BEING SEEN: watch out for ...

A child who makes verbal requests for you to watch them.

A child making non-verbal requests for you to watch them: big movements, or restless movement in front of you; sitting very close.

Accidents, injuries and grumbling physical complaints.

A child who watches you as you watch them.

Challenging behaviour: a request to be seen more fully.

MOVEMENT AND THE BODY
DEVELOPMENTAL MOVEMENT PATTERNS

In this Landscape babies and young children are discovering and practising the patterns that will allow them to become fully functioning, independent people. (See Chapter 1, page 13 for further detail.) As non-specialists we can look for some obvious gaps and support children's development through everyday movements. The chart opposite outlines movements you may see that belong to this Landscape.

NOTES FOR LEADERS:

DEVELOPMENTAL MOVEMENT PATTERNS: watch out for ...

Babies lying on their backs and watching the fingers on the extended arm, then swapping to the other arm and looking at the other finger.

Babies grabbing at their toes as they lie on their backs.

Babies and young children who want to spend time on their tummies.

Babies lying on their tummies, arm and leg bent ... then swapping over sides. Many babies (and adults) will do this in their sleep when on their tummies, but will also need to do it during the day.

Babies, when lying on their tummies, tucking their toes underneath, ready to push themselves forward with that leg.

Babies belly-crawling to get away from, or towards, things.

Babies who are getting ready to crawl, rocking backwards and forward on their knees.

Babies and young children who like to belly-crawl, or crawl on all fours, even when they can walk.

Focused practice of major travelling actions: belly-crawling, crawling, walking, running, hopping, skipping (and even swinging on the monkey bars which can be a support for walking patterns).

Children who like to spin until they are dizzy, or tip themselves about - upside down, head off centre, rolling and so on.

MOVEMENT AND THE BODY
Physical Mastery

In this Landscape a child is actively seeking to develop their ability to increase their physical skill. All the Landscapes looked at so far contribute to the acquisition of physical skill in some way, but here the child has a particular motivation towards, or takes particular delight in, developing mastery of their body for its own sake. This is the child who comes home from nursery and spends an hour kicking a ball around the back garden; who would rather balance a book on their head than read it.

NOTES FOR LEADERS:

PHYSICAL MASTERY: watch out for ...

A child practising an action, skill, or part of an action, over and over again.

A child who enjoys learning steps, or making up and remembering dances.

A child setting themselves physical challenges as part of other activities (or in spite of other activities).

A child unconsciously practising physical actions when their main attention is elsewhere.

A child repeating an action, or series of actions for the sheer pleasure of it.

A child who makes the movements bigger and more elaborate than they need to be (including flourishes and dives whilst catching a ball for instance).

MOVEMENT AND THE BODY
Knowledge of the body

In this Landscape the child is interested in both the physical fact of the body and the felt fact of the body (what it is made up of, what's inside it, what it looks and feels like, how it changes when it moves vigorously or relaxes) and the felt fact (building up an internal body image).

Some children show no curiosity about this, but others are eager to find out what's in their body, and how it works, from a very early age. Some have a very clear internal sense of their body, and some have a very distant sense of it.

'There's something in here', (pointing to his chest) 'that goes bump. What is it?', said Jogi (3).

At the start of the session, as we sat wriggling our feet in the centre of the circle, Jenner (4) noticed that Daniel (4) had new, red boots on. We all admired them and then looked at each person's shoes in turn (there are only six children in this group). We noticed similarities and differences, and heard likes and dislikes. Then Daniel said, 'My sister says I'm funny because this toe is bigger than this one, and it shouldn't be'. Boots and shoes came flying off and everyone examined their toes with great interest. We noticed similarities and differences and the fact that several people's toes would not have met with Daniel's sister's approval. Then we looked at our fingers in the same way.

The next week Daniel arrived first. 'Can we look at our heads today', he said, 'because my sister says mine's a funny shape.'

Although body image is harder to pin down, it is no less real or important as an aspect of our physicality.

'Several years ago I (then 31) was moving in the studio with the instruction from the tutor to 'start off with a part of the body that you don't usually start with'. Hmmm, what

could that be? I simply didn't know. I had a sort of smug feeling that I was very much in touch with all the bits of my body, thank you very much. But I knew that something might occur to me if I waited and watched. So I just moved as I wanted, and waited. About three-quarters of an hour later I had got myself into a pleasant knot - head down, bum up, legs tangled round one another - when suddenly one of my feet came into my vision and for a few seconds I didn't recognise it! How can this be! I'd had them for thirty-odd years ... how could I not recognise my own foot? And then in a rush I realised that I was often unaware of my feet. In fact, only that day I had come to the studio in a pair of little pink, flat sandals even though the pouring rain outside was bound to soak my socks, because ... well ... I just hadn't thought about it.

For the rest of that morning my attention was completely taken up with my feet ... and by the end of the day I had built up all sorts of new information. I realised that usually my attention was all skyward. Ask me to fly and I am happy with the challenge. Ask me to tread purposefully and carefully and to feel the ground beneath my feet and a sense of boredom hits the pit of my stomach. I realised that I possessed only two pairs of shoes, each as ancient and unsuitable as the other, and that I never look down to notice them. I realised that the only broken bones I have ever had have been in my feet and (shock upon shock) that I have large bunions on both big toes. How could this be? Why hadn't I noticed before?

That day, I realised that my feet were not included within my internal image of my body. They could learn steps and point quite prettily (heck ... I'd been a professional dancer no less), but I didn't really know they were there! I bought walking boots the next week (I think of them as my hooves) and wear them if I need to remind myself of the ground beneath my feet. Come to think of it, I wear walking boots most of the time now.

NOTES FOR LEADERS:

KNOWLEDGE OF THE BODY: watch out for ...

A child who asks questions about their body, or the body in general.

A child who moves with a sense of inquiry - what will happen if.....

A child who utilises their ability to listen to the inner body and their visual skills in a combined fashion to arrive at answers or observations.

A child who works with eyes shut and eyes open, between words and bodily-felt experience.

IMAGE
Active Imagination

In this Landscape a child is exploring the internal visual experiences that movement can prompt. Some of these might be images or pictures that appear when they have their eyes shut as they move, and some may be images that are prompted by the kind of movement they have been doing. 'That was like blue dolphins in the sea.' Some children have a very strong connection with visual images or inner sounds; it is a simple way that they augment their experience and understanding. Others have no idea what it is to have an image behind their eyes in the dark, or an image stimulated by a movement.

It was Iqbal's (5) longed-for turn in the centre today. He seemed to have an idea of what he wanted to do right from the start. He went to the centre and stiffened his arms by his side, then turned small circles with his hands. After a while he started to jog along meandering pathways around the circle, first this way, then that. As he went his trunk stiffened also, so that it became one unit with no flexibility in the middle. Gradually, Iqbal's head tilted backwards and the circling of his hands stopped. His jog slowed until he stood in the middle quite still before sinking onto the carpet and rolling gently from side to side - still stiff all along his body.

When the watchers responded using the I Saw, I Felt, I Imagined structure (see page 193) Selma said, 'I imagined one of those things in the bank'. It turned out to be the pen in a swivel-holder on the counter. Gavin had imagined a toy belonging to his baby brother, a wobbly-man, and I had imagined a food processor at work.

Iqbal told us his story. 'I was in the blue sea ... and I was a dolphin. It was warm and I was warm and grey. And I wanted to catch a fish to eat but I didn't. I swam about and then I lay down on the bottom. It was muddy and warm and I liked it. And I watched everything go by.'

NOTES FOR LEADERS:

ACTIVE IMAGINATION: watch out for ...

A child who readily offers visual images whilst moving, or in discussion after moving.

A child who moves with their eyes shut and comments on what they *see* in their 'mind's eye'. This can *be* complete fantasy, drawn from reality or a visual memory.

A child who may move with their eyes shut and their hands over the eyes to intensify the focus on the pictures in their 'mind's eye.'

SENSATION, FEELING AND MOVEMENT
Listening to the body

Our brains receive constant feedback, through the proprioceptive nerves, about our bodily-felt experience. Kinesthetic awareness is a term used to describe our awareness of all this bodily-felt experience. The more developed our capacity to receive, and respond to, this information the better able we are to monitor our own physicality (heath and wellbeing), the more open and alive we are to our senses.

The activity of listening to the body is governed by the autonomic nervous system which is concerned with our inner attention. It has two aspects, the sympathetic and the parasympathetic and a child needs to develop good feedback from both if they are to achieve good body listening. The sympathetic system is activated when the body needs to be alert, and focused on activity and survival (the demands of the outside world). The parasympathetic system is activated in rest, relaxation and integration (attention to our inner nourishment). Both are vital to a healthy life. In this landscape a child needs to play in both modes.

Liam (5) is siting under the kitchen table clutching his leg, looking pained. He is grimacing from ear to ear and saying 'Ooof' a lot.
'What's wrong?', says his Dad putting the cornflakes on the table. 'Can I help?'
'No', gulps Liam between 'Ooofs'. 'I've got to do this on my own.'
He lies back on the floor and shuts his eyes. ('Ooooof') Then he starts to rotate his thigh gently, which produces a profusion of 'Arghhhhs'. After a while he turns over onto his hands and knees and moves his leg backwards and forwards over and over again. (Silence)
'Nothing I can do?', asks his Dad again.
'Shut up!'
Liam slides his leg away from him along the floor until it is straight and taut. He stays still for a long time.

Emerging from under the table he says, 'That's got it. That thing here (pointing at his groin) had gone in a knot and I was undoing it'.

Bella (3) is on the swing. She doesn't want a push, just to sway gently back and forwards, side to side, propelled only by the tiny motions of her body and legs. She is singing to herself. After a while she shuts her eyes and, holding onto the chains, leans back until her arms are straight. Her head lolls backwards. Occasionally she gives a little jiggle, which makes the swing move. Mostly she is just still. 'Do you think she's falling asleep?', says a worried passer-by to Bella's Mum. 'I'm not asleep ... I'm looking', says a voice from the swing. 'I'm looking at in here.'

NOTES FOR LEADERS:

LISTENING: watch out for ...

Inner focus

- A child with an inner focus - drifting, dreaming, staring vacantly - with a concentrated inner focus.
- Lots of repeated movement, with an inner focus, that might be deemed to be boring, or uncreative in a dance situation, but within Movement Play affords an opportunity to explore how things feel in the body.
- A child moving with their eyes shut.
- Slower movements with a careful, reflective quality about them.

External focus

- A child moving in response to an external focus; testing its ability to respond and react.
- A child getting to know about its alertness - quick movements, sudden movements, sparky movements.
- A child exploring ways to respond in a variety of conditions - being upside down, off-balance and so on.

SENSATION, FEELING AND MOVEMENT
Understanding the world outside

In this Landscape a child is using their direct perception to help them understand things beyond the grasp of their intellectual reasoning.

Polly (4) was sitting at the table eating ice-cream when she suddenly dropped her spoon with a clatter, stretched one arm diagonally above her head and the other across her chest and up to meet it. Then, with an intense and puzzled look on her face, she opened and closed her arms several times. Seemingly satisfied, she picked up her spoon again and continued with the ice-cream.

Her father was agog. 'What are you doing, Polly?', he asked.
'I was being the ironing board', she said.

Polly had spent several frustrating minutes the previous morning trying to put up the ironing board. With no success. Now she was rehearsing the procedure using information from her body to supplement the thoughts in her head.

Adults return to the body as well, of course. I watched a woman at the ticket barrier at Liverpool St tube station the other day, rehearsing how to put her ticket in the barrier and collect it at the other side. She had noticed that it is snapped up and then delivered back with alarming force. Clearly unfamiliar with the procedure, it wasn't enough to go over it in her mind, she did all the actions as well - without realising it.

Developing the capacity to use our body intelligence means that we can make this process more conscious. We can choose to work things out through direct perception. Young children play in this Landscape both consciously and unconsciously.

Page 229

NOTES FOR LEADERS:

UNDERSTANDING THE WORLD: watch out for ...

A child setting itself a problem, then addressing it in movement.

A child using direct perception to augment intellectual ideas or concepts eg. getting to know the letters of the alphabet by trying to make the shapes in their body ...

Or trying to understand what it would be like to be tall, by trying it out it in a variety of ways.

A child trying on the physical characteristics of an emotional state they have seen displayed, or a role they have read about (queen, pauper, clown).

A child exploring the experience of someone or something else.

SENSATION, FEELING AND MOVEMENT
Integrating experience and learning in the body

If you've ever edited a video on a computer you will know that you create it in many separate layers - sound on one layer, this special effect on another, sub-titles on another and all the actual footage on a fourth. When you've finished there are many layers of information all running parallel to one another. If you then want a proper copy of your video on a single tape you have to 'render' it - a tediously long process during which your computer chunters and whirs a lot whilst it joins all the separate layers of information into one integrated thing.

There is a similar process involved in human learning - somehow we have to 'render' all the layers of our learning, from the different areas of our intelligences and different kinds of experience, into deeply held knowledge and understanding. Learning begins in our body, in the sensing, intending, moving progression, and it returns to the body as well. If we have the opportunity to 'render' after we have acquired a lot of new information, we can settle in that learning so that it is truly ours, deep seated within us.

Perhaps this is one explanation for the wriggles and writhings with which young children accompany many activities - it's a kind of shuffling-down of the day's learning. I have no proof for this, expect what I see over and over again, and my own experience. I have to shuffle information down into my body before it is truly useful to me. I have to try things out in movement or sensation before I can really solve a problem, or believe what I am reading.

A friend recently described her children's relationship with the trampoline to me. As soon as these three (twins of 6 and one of 9) get home from school they go straight to the trampoline and bounce and flop about on it for ages before they are ready to do anything else. All their games centre around it, and the movement it supports. It is as if they are bouncing the day's experiences into the flesh and bones and cells of their bodies - 'rendering' it into an integrated, fully available whole.

This is a separate Landscape that children must visit as well - a wholly body-led activity that seems to serve no functional or aesthetic purpose whatsoever. An educational psychologist told me recently that she is alarmed at the number of older children she sees for whom her best advice is - 'Chill out. Do nothing sometimes. Slob about'. As our culture becomes increasingly target-oriented and speeds up, children need time in which to bed-in all the experiences that bombard them. Movement Play must allow for this as well.

And Now...

Back to the body...
As you have read, have you recognised any of the Landscapes as being 'places' or states that are familiar to you? Are there other Landscapes, not included here, that you would put on a list of your own?

If reading about them doesn't bring about any intellectual or 'bodily stir', try considering them with a body-focus uppermost. Shut your eyes, settle into a heightened focus on sensation, feeling, movement and all the accompanying visual, aural and memory layers of experience, and float the notion of a particular Landscape into your awareness. Then just notice what comes up. Sometimes, this might relate to your own bodily experience - especially when the Landscape in question is one that is particularly familiar - and at other times, you may be more aware of things you have seen in other people.

Note any Landscapes that you want to add to this list, or changes you would make to how these are described, as you build up your own physical understanding of this structure.

Back to the body...
As you watch children, or any people, moving, get curious about how they are engaging with their physicality. Can you see fleeting moments, or longer play activities, that fit within any of these Landscapes. Or, as you watch, can you simply get curious about how children are engaging with their physicality, especially at times when their physicality takes your attention. Can you identify which Landscape (from the list overleaf or one of your own) they seem to be engaged with?

Movement observation isn't easy. Spontaneous movement isn't neat, logical or linear; children don't explore one aspect of their bodily-felt experience, stop, then move onto another. One experience invites another, overlaps with the next and so on; different experiences and different kinds of learning interweave with one another. To make matters worse, most of us have become very good at not seeing movement and the ways in which we embody our experience. It takes time to start seeing it again. Give yourself time. Get interested in movement. Adopt a new frame of mind.

NOTES FOR LEADERS:

THE LANDSCAPES

SENSATION	Touch as food	Seeking essential contact -the foundation for an alive, open body
SENSATION	Sensual delight	Pleasure. Sensory awareness
SENSATION	'This is me'	Discovering where we begin & end
FEELING	Exploring feelings	Building emotional intelligence & literacy
FEELING	Exploring relationship	Feeling our effect on others
FEELING	Being Seen	Affirmation
MOVEMENT	Developmental patterns	Fulfilling innate patterns
MOVEMENT	Physical mastery	Developing physical skill
MOVEMENT	Knowledge of the body	What, where, how
IMAGE	Active imagination	Pictures and sounds prompted by movement
SENSATION, FEELING, MOVEMENT	Listening to the body	Tuning in to bodily-felt experience
SENSATION, FEELING, MOVEMENT	Understanding the world	Using direct perception to augment understanding
SENSATION, FEELING, MOVEMENT	Embodying learning	Settling in new knowledge and skills
	Many others ...	

Hopping Home Backwards

Watching Movement Play

Charts

SAY WHAT YOU SEE

NAME _____ DATE _____

GROUP_____

COMMENTS

WATCHING MOVEMENT PLAY
THREE QUESTIONS

NAME _____ DATE _____

WHAT IS HAPPENING

WHAT ISN'T HAPPENING

WHAT IS TRYING TO HAPPEN

OTHER COMMENTS

I SAW... I FELT...
I IMAGINED...

NAME _____ DATE _____

I SAW

I FELT

I IMAGINED

I THOUGHT

LANDSCAPES

NAME _____ DATE _____

SENSATION
○ Touch as food
○ Sensing into learning
○ Sensual delight
○ This is me

FEELING
○ Exploring feelings
○ Exploring relationship
○ Self worth

MOVEMENT & BODY
○ Developmental movement
○ Physical mastery
○ Knowledge of the body

IMAGE
○ Active imagination

SENSATION, FEELING, MOVEMENT
○ Listening to the body
○ Understanding the world
○ Embodying learning

COMMENTS

WATCHING MOVEMENT PLAY
ROUND UP CHART

SAY WHAT YOU SEE

WHAT IS HAPPENING

WHAT ISN'T HAPPENING

WHAT IS TRYING TO HAPPEN

I SAW

I FELT

I IMAGINED

I THOUGHT

LANDSCAPES

SENSATION
- ○ Touch as food
- ○ Sensing into learning
- ○ Sensual delight
- ○ This is me

FEELING
- ○ Exploring feelings
- ○ Exploring relationship
- ○ Self worth

MOVEMENT & BODY
- ○ Developmental movement
- ○ Physical mastery
- ○ Knowledge of the body

IMAGE
- ○ Active imagination

SENSATION, FEELING, MOVEMENT
- ○ Listening to the body
- ○ Understanding the world
- ○ Embodying learning

Hopping Home Backwards

10

Mapping the Journey

'It's all so clear ... you can *see* so much if you look.'

Reception teacher

Having established a clear understanding about what we hope children will learn in Movement Play, a framework within which to develop this learning, and tools to help us observe and record what we see - it is a short step to the creation of attainment targets against which to assess what children *actually* learn. This approach would fit with the prevailing culture, and it would be easy to write them for each of the attitudes and skills outlined in Chapter 6. Attainment targets (or the Stepping Stones of the curriculum guidance for the foundation stage) provide an excellent means by which adults can clarify their aims and measure children's success; however, as soon as we have targets by which we measure *success*, we are bound to measure (or at least consider) *failure* as well. But Movement Play is not about success or failure; it is concerned with developing self-awareness - about what *is*, not about what *should be*. It is also about trusting that the body will develop the systems it needs, in return for opportunities to play.

The structures for watching movement outlined in the last chapter provide us with a lot of information about how children are moving, and about what takes their interest as they indulge in spontaneous movement play. As we round up what we have seen, we need to consider two things.

Firstly, the extent to which each child is embodied - or growing in their ability to be embodied.

Embodiment is the foundation for children's ability to make use of their body intelligence. An embodied child is alive and open to their senses and comfortable in their body. They feel the 'bodily stir' weaving in and out of everything they do. They have the potential to use their direct perception to contribute to their learning.

Secondly, we need to notice which aspects of their experience they are interested in visiting in their Movement Play - which aspects of their lives they choose to embody - in order to ensure that they get the support they need.

MAPPING EMBODIMENT

Most children come into the world ready to embody their experience, ready to build the foundations that will enable them to be alive to sensation, feeling and movement. (Where children have sensory challenges it simply makes it more important for us to do this Movement Play work.) Movement Play is the way in which we help children to maintain and develop their ability to embody their lives. A major function for assessment is to identify what extra support we might need to offer in order to ensure that this natural process continues and deepens.

In this chapter I want to suggest that instead of creating specific targets for Movement Play, and stepping stones to work towards them, we need to create a map of each child's journey - the map of their developing relationship with their bodily-felt experience. The Embodiment Chart invites you to identify where a child is placed along a spectrum. If you repeat this chart at regular intervals it allows you to map the child's relationship with their embodiment. It is vital to note that we are not always looking for a steady, onward progression on these charts, because many things in children's lives will change the degree to which they can embody their experience. These are *maps* not *progress charts.* Of course we are keen for children to be embodied - open and alive to their bodily-felt experience, comfortable in their bodies. But these are not things that anyone can achieve all the time - nor would it be desirable to try. In mapping the learning journey we are interested in the changes and fluctuations that take place as a natural part of life. We are interested in using what we see to inform our relationships with children, not to set ever higher targets. We must expect to see the crosses on our charts flow backwards and forwards as a reflection of a changing life. If a child is stuck - if there are no fluctuations at all, or all the movement is one way across the spectrum - then we might be concerned.

Learning in the body is a spiralling process, not a steady linear progression.

NOTES FOR LEADERS:

MAPPING EMBODIMENT

Think back over the watching you have done, and the information you have collected, in the light of the question: 'Is this an embodied child?' The chart overleaf helps you to consider the specific elements that enable a child to be / become embodied. Relate your answers to how children behave in Movement Play activities as well as in other contexts. Do your answers differ in different contexts?

SENSATION
Notice the way a child responds to touch. Are they happy to touch and be touched? Do they find touch very challenging and resist it at all costs? Do they delight in sensual experience? Do they explore the world through touch?

FEELINGS
Notice the way a child responds to their feelings. Are they able to experience and express different feelings? Do they find it difficult to contain their feelings? Do they find it easy or challenging to empathise? Can they move between different feelings, or do they get stuck?

MOVEMENT
Notice the way a child looks in their body. Comfortable or uncomfortable? Do they appear to move freely and easily? Are they happy to move spontaneously? To move in front of others? To express themselves in their bodies? Do they find it very challenging to keep still?

INNER FOCUS
Is the child able to notice inner experience? Do they readily take their focus to their inner bodily-felt experience? Do they speak of images and stories prompted by their Movement Play?

EMBODIMENT

Place a cross in the appropriate place along each line

NAME _____ DATE _____

Uncomfortable in their body   Comfortable in their body

Doesn't notice sensation   Open & alive to sensation

Reluctant to focus on feelings   Open & alive to feelings

Reluctant to move   Open & alive to the 'bodily-stir'

Reluctant to focus on inner experience   Ready access to inner experience

Comments: is the child able to integrate these 'raw materials'. Does their relationship with their body change in different situations.

What next in Movement Play?

NOTES FOR LEADERS:

WHAT NEXT IN MOVEMENT PLAY? (developmental movement)

If a child consistently has many crosses at the left hand side of the Embodiment chart, it is likely that they will need as much Movement Play as you can give them. They may resist, and need, a great deal of support from you. Plan to give them maximum support for the major developmental movement patterns. (This is important for all children, but especially important if they have on-going challenges with any of these raw materials of embodiment.)

MASSAGE
Make sure that children get as much sensory stimulus as you can give them. Look at the sensory activities outlined in the Activity Section.

TIME ON THEIR TUMMIES
Ensure that they spend time on their tummies (looking at books, drawing and painting, doing puzzles and so on).

BELLY CRAWLING
Plan activities that encourage them to crawl on their tummies - belly down. on the floor. You don't have to teach them what to do; if you give them the opportunities their innate body intelligence will organise the movement patterns.

CRAWLING ON ALL FOURS
Change your environment, if necessary, to encourage children to crawl - either in pure Movement Play (see Crawling games page 354) or as they do other things. Gayle Loyd of the Seattle Developmental Movement Centre suggests that you organise activities so that children have to fetch things from one end of the room (toys, bricks, jigsaw pieces, word cards and so on) and play with them at the other. In this way, children get crawling practice without noticing.

NOTES FOR LEADERS:

WHAT NEXT IN MOVEMENT PLAY? (play activities)

Plan future activities that help children to focus on, or simply delight in, the areas you feel to be important. Your choices will be guided by:
>   children's pleasure.
>   children's choices.
>   what you feel is 'trying to happen'

Plan activities in the 'Experiencing' phase of learning.

Consider which contexts to plan for (everyday … child-led … adult led).

Decide which of the areas of bodily-felt experience you want to support - sensation, feeling, movement, inner focus - or all of them.

MAPPING WHAT CHILDREN CHOOSE TO EMBODY

Separate from children's *capacity* to embody their experience are the things they *choose* to embody - the aspects of their experience, and their learning, that they explore in their bodies. By pulling together the information we gather as we watch children's Movement Play we can identify themes, particular interests, and gaps, that will help us to plan how we support children in future. We can do this in two ways - through pure movement information and through our own interpretation of that movement.

The What *is* happening? and What *isn't* happening? charts allow you to map movement themes over a period of time - with no attempt to interpret what you see. In many ways this is the most reliable way of mapping what goes on in movement - using just its own language. We can use this information to plan further more relevant, movement activities.

Since we are working within a learning context, it is likely that we will also want to interpret the information at some points. The What's *trying* to happen? chart allows you to round up your own projections about what the child might be reaching for in their Movement Play. We can also round up our observations about the subject matter of children's Movement Play - not the movement itself, but what their moving might be 'about'. The Landscapes Round-up chart allows you to map what you think children are engaging in, over a period of time.

Mapping Chart - What is happening?

NAME _____

	MAJOR THEME
Date _____	_____
Date _____	_____
Date _____	_____
Date _____	_____
Date _____	_____
Date _____	_____
Date _____	_____
Date _____	_____

Mapping Chart - What isn't happening?

NAME _____

	MAJOR THEME
Date _____	
Date _____	
Date _____	
Date _____	
Date _____	
Date _____	
Date _____	
Date _____	

Mapping Chart - What is trying to happen?

NAME _____

	MAJOR THEME
Date _____	_____
Date _____	_____
Date _____	_____
Date _____	_____
Date _____	_____
Date _____	_____
Date _____	_____
Date _____	_____

Mapping Chart - Landscapes

Place a tick in the appropriate box along each line

	Date	Date	Date	Date	Date	Date	Date
SENSATION							
Touch as food							
Sensual delight							
This is me							
FEELING							
Exploring feelings							
Exploring relationships							
Being seen - self worth							
MOVEMENT & BODY							
Developmental Mvt							
Physical mastery							
Knowledge of the body							
IMAGE							
Active imagination							
ALL THREE							
Listening to the body							
Understanding the world							
Embodying learning							
OTHER							

Mapping embodiment - comfort

NAME _____

Place a cross in the appropriate place along each line

| Uncomfortable in their body .... Comfortable in their body |

Date _____

Date _____

Date _____

Date _____

Date _____

Date _____

Date _____

Date _____

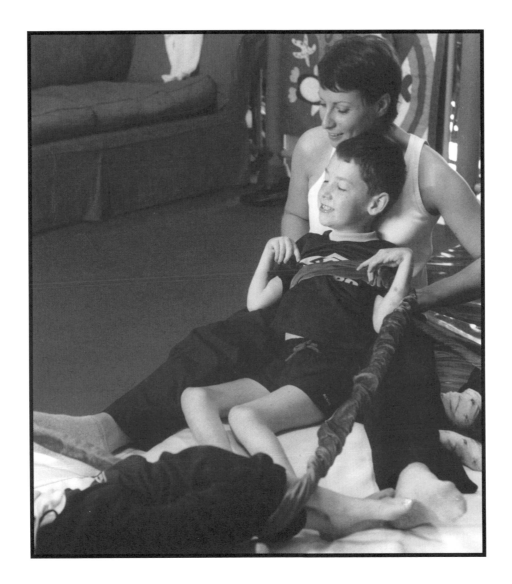

Mapping embodiment - sensation

NAME _____

Place a cross in the appropriate place along each line

	Doesn't notice sensation .... Open and alive to sensation
Date _____	
Date _____	
Date _____	
Date _____	
Date _____	
Date _____	
Date _____	
Date _____	

Mapping embodiment - feeling

NAME _____

Place a cross in the appropriate place along each line

Reluctant to focus on different feelings ..... Open and alive to feelings

Date _____

Date _____

Date _____

Date _____

Date _____

Date _____

Date _____

Date _____

Mapping embodiment - movement

NAME _____

Place a cross in the appropriate place along each line

Reluctant to move .... Open and alive to bodily-stir

Date _____

Date _____

Date _____

Date _____

Date _____

Date _____

Date _____

Date _____

Mapping embodiment - inner focus

NAME _____

Place a cross in the appropriate place along each line

Reluctant to focus on inner experience ..... Open and alive to inner experience

Date _____

Date _____

Date _____

Date _____

Date _____

Date _____

Date _____

Date _____

USING THE CHARTS TO MAP THE JOURNEY

Each of us reads movement all the time, but until we look at it in focused ways and sift what we see, the information we take in may not be particularly useful. These charts are intended to make it easy for you to clarify the information you gather from watching children engage with their bodily-felt experience and to encourage you to include that information within any record keeping you currently do.

Observation is a time consuming business; recording even more so. In busy Early Years settings it might feel like a luxury, even though we know that the information it yields will always help our planning. However, if we want Movement Play to be an integrated part of the curriculum it is essential to gather information about how and what children learn.

11
Back to the body

'If you want to move your mind, move your body

If you want to move someone, move your body

If you want to move the world, move your body'

Eiffel 65

Jack is ten now and a whiz on the football field. It's six years since I started to gather material for this book and in that time Jack has stopped hopping home backwards and started earnestly practising to become the next David Beckham. He is fearless in goal, a scale model of Jaap Stam in defence and a disciple of Ryan Giggs when he takes on opponents in mid-field. After school he is to be found swinging from the monkey bars, taking shots on goal, practising his keepy-uppies or perfecting a slicing backhand on the tennis court. Physical mastery is his thing.

That bunch of kids who dawdled and hopped home with me all those years ago were sitting round the tea table recently talking about school. Jack's sister spoke of a boy in her class at High School who is persistently rude, disruptive and wild. He is a martial arts champion, a wicked dancer, full of physical and verbal humour ... and a real handful. With no time for the requirements of Key Stage 3 he regularly incurs the wrath of his teachers. 'But he's brilliant at sport', shrieked Jack. 'Why does sport always come second? If we have a busy week at school it's always PE that's cancelled, never literacy hour. And it's PE that I'm good at. Why is it always second best?'

The beginning of the twenty first century is a truly challenging time in which to develop learning environments for children. We must ensure that they are equipped for what lies ahead, yet the pace of change is so rapid we can barely imagine what that might be. As we struggle with the

Page 265

implications of information and communication technology, as we educate a population to compete successfully within world markets, we are losing sight of the body as our first home, and direct perception as a robust way of learning.

Jack's right. Physical education is second best in school. The body is second best in our society. The age at which children must stop rolling down hills and start developing their intellectual intelligence is getting lower. The pressure on teachers and pupils to reach academic targets is increasing. Even 'creative' subjects like music, art and dance, which used to deal more with inner experience and feeling, now increasingly deal with intellectual aspects such as history, criticism and appreciation.

At the same time there is rising concern about young coach potatoes - children who ride to school in cars, sit in front of computer and television screens, and exercise only rarely. Children who have increasingly tenuous relationships with their bodies.

I'm pretty sure that the boy of whom Jack's sister spoke has missed some developmental movement patterns. There are lots of bright, intelligent, challenging kids in High Schools who are missing some neurological wiring, which makes it difficult for them, for many reasons, to engage with intellectual material. This is going to happen increasingly often if we pass over ordinary movement play in the early years, in favour of making babies more manageable - condemning them to baby chairs of all shapes and sizes and sophisticated toys that engage the intellect, but restrict Movement Play.

My brother, a serious cricket fan, tells me that sports people describe moments of total connection between intention and action as 'in the zone'. When they are 'in the zone' they simply know they will catch that ball, or hit it for six. He tells me that he was 'in the zone' just once; took four impossible catches, when playing in-door cricket, at silly mid-on one after the other, at amazing pace. Being 'in the zone' requires, I suspect, the ability to operate from our direct perception without our mental reasoning overriding it, or getting in our way. I suppose we can't expect to be 'in the zone' all the time, just as we can't expect to be inspired to write the perfect poem every time we sit down to try, but I'd like to think we can inch our way towards it by developing our body intelligence. Ultimately, the complete dominance of intellectual and academic pursuits does us no service. We are not only way out of the zone, the zone isn't really even in view. We human beings, with our increasingly sophisticated powers of thought, are getting in our own way. Our culture, and its institutions, are tipping further out of balance, further towards the intellect and away from the body. Further towards mental reasoning and away from direct perception. But as a species we need to draw on both.

In examining body intelligence in detail, this book has put the spotlight on learning in the body. Story after story has pulled out, and separated, the learning we do through participation with our senses ... often as if it really is separate from intellectual activity. But the thinking we do in our bodies, and the thinking we do in our intellects, support one another, interweave and become inseparable for much of the time. Each of us, given the chance, will find our own balance, our own ways of drawing on these two aspects of ourselves. Movement Play is a small contribution towards giving future generations of children the chance to drawn on both.

In his last school report Jack wrote this: 'I like PE best because it's the only subject I don't feel cramped up in.' So at the end of all these words we must come back to the body so we too are not 'cramped up' by them.

Back to the body

Shut your eyes. Listen in. Let your attention roll around the sensations, feelings, movements and images at the edge of you awareness. Bring them into the centre.Take your attention back over all the words and ideas and suggestions in this book and let your body do the thinking ... in wriggles and jiggles, pictures and sounds, sensations and feelings. Before you decide to do anything with these ideas, consult your body intelligence: sensing ... before intention ... before action. At any time you plan to move with children, consult your body intelligence: listen into your body-thoughts as well as your rational thoughts. At any time you become confused or unsure, you can consult your body intelligence.

Go back to the body ...

SECTION 3

Movement Play Activities

The following activities offer practical suggestions for ways in which adults can help babies and children to develop, and make use of, their body intelligence.

THE ACTIVITIES
Chapter 12 is about Noticing Movement - ways to make movement an ordinary part of everyday life. The next 6 chapters offer practical suggestions.

> Activities focusing on Sensation.
> Activities focusing on Feelings.
> Activities focusing on Movement.
> Circle Time Activities.
> Activities focusing on Image.
> Endings.

The Chapter heading gives an indication of the area of learning each activity _best_ serves - but the activities can often _be_ used in a variety of ways. Adapt and change them to suit your purposes.

Many of the activities will be very familiar to you - a part of everyday life with babies and young children. They are included here in order to refresh your confidence in their worth, to encourage you to return to movement with a different frame of mind, and to help you to focus on movement even more.

AGE INDICATIONS
Only you will know what is appropriate for your children. I am reluctant to pin activities to specific ages. However, broadly speaking.

> BABIES indicates 0 to about 2 years old.
> YOUNG CHILDREN indicates 2 and 3 year olds.
> CHILDREN indicates about 4 to 8 year olds.

12
Noticing Movement

This section is about Noticing Movement - ways to make movement an ordinary part of everyday life. The practical suggestions are divided into three sections

Noticing Movement
Starting to look

Aim: Preparation for adults prior to working with children

Suggestion:

This is about noticing the everyday movement that accompanies every activity human beings do. Curiously, movement mostly goes by unnoticed. We notice the movement that annoys us, or disrupts us or our intentions, but miss the rest. To bring it to your attention can be harder than it sounds because we have become so adept at shutting it out. Here are some suggestions for beginning to notice it again.

○ watch the television with the sound turned down. Notice all that you can through the movement alone. You will probably find that you try to interpret what is going on. Resist this for the moment and just watch the movement. The more you practice, the more you will notice.

○ watch out of the car / bus / train window as you are travelling. Notice the movements people do as they are engaged in conversation; notice all you can about the way people walk, or look before they cross the road ... and so on.

○ watch children at play. Watch through a window so that they won't be disturbed by you, and you are uninterrupted.

○ if possible, watch children from the sidelines as they go about their usual activities. Try to shut out the words and just see the movement. Notice how much is going on separate from the words.

○ finally, practice seeing movement and hearing the words at the same time.

Noticing Movement

Talking about movement

Aim: To make everyday movement visible

Suggestion:

Help children to notice the movement that happens as part of their everyday lives. When you are gathered together, draw their attention to their movement, as well as their words. It is crucial to do this in a non-judgmental, simple way that enables them to take the movement at face value. So often when we talk about movement, we undermine it rather than valuing it.

Draw attention to movement by pointing it out and talking about particular aspects. These might be drawn from: the shape of the whole body, the placing of particular limbs, how the child is taking their weight, small movements or bigger movements, balances, body actions - like stretching, bouncing, jumping and so on. ('Look at the shape that Joe's body is making. His hands are tucked under his knees and and his fingers are doing a little wriggle on the floor'.)

Look particularly at:
- ○ the shapes, and small movements, of all the bodies as children sit on the carpet, or gather for a snack.
- ○ the different ways that children put their hands up to answer questions.
- ○ the wriggles and jiggles that accompany listening or waiting.

Make clear boundaries between times when you encourage them to move and times when you need them to be still.

Noticing Movement
Mirroring and Reflecting Children's Movement

Aim: To notice movement in everyday life

Suggestion:
Draw attention to the movement that individual children do - either as they are getting on with something else, or when they break into movement because they can't stop themselves. As well as talking with them, move with them. Perhaps a child is painting and you notice that they are standing on one leg with a foot wiggling behind them. Draw their attention to it by standing beside them in the same way - not mimicking to make fun of them, but sharing something of their body experience as well as what they have to say to you. See Mirroring and Reflecting on pages 168 - 170.

There are many reasons you might want to do this
- ○ simply to put movement on the agenda.
- ○ to emphasise your full attention for them.
- ○ to show your empathy with them at this point.
- ○ to show them that this is a recurring theme - that they often stand like this - so that they begin to notice more about themselves.
- ○ to remind them of something you have asked them *not* to do.

Noticing Movement
Everyday Dancing - marking events

Aim: To use movement and simple dances as an ordinary part of the day; to show that dance is a way we can mark events

Suggestion:

Find places in the day where you can use dance to mark what you are doing. Base these on social dance forms where steps are not important, but the shape and structure are.

- a conga of children and adults from the cloakroom to the classroom ... into dinner ... out to the playground.
- a line dance when children and parents meet again at the end of the day. Each line goes in towards each other and out again, before meeting, hugging and going home.
- a circle dance when everyone first arrives on the carpet. Nothing complicated, just holding hands and going one way, and then the other. A chance to notice all the faces and 'arrive' before starting the first activity.
- a huge circle dance, gradually gathered, to mark the end of play time and the need to go inside again.

Don't worry about the steps as this takes all the fun and purpose out of it. It doesn't matter about right and left legs. It does matter that the children feel the shape of the dance, and that this shape emphasises the atmosphere or event that you are marking. Circles for gathering and community feeling; opposing lines for meeting, parting or being on opposite sides; long lines for travelling.

Noticing Movement
Everyday Dancing - celebrating events

Aim: To use movement and simple dances as an ordinary part of the day; to
        show that dance is a way we can celebrate events

Suggestion:
Using the same kinds of dance as in the last suggestion, celebrate special events in
your lives.

○ a conga into the kitchen to fetch the dinner lady who has cooked for a generation
    of children. Invite her to go at the head of the line and conga around all the
    dinner tables.

○ a joyous circle dance around the birthday girl or boy; or a very quite circle around
    a mum, child and their new baby.

○ a line dance under the arches to say farewell to the children who are leaving
    playgroup and going to school; carry the babies under the arches when they
    become big enough to go up into the next room.

○ line dance around the nursery, or the playgroup hall, to say farewell to all the
    nooks and crannies that the children know so well, before they move on.

13
Activities Focusing
On
Sensation

These activities are designed to provide opportunities for babies and children to build their sensory feedback systems, indulge in SENSORY EXPLORATION, to wallow in SENSORY DELIGHT and satisfy their basic need for TOUCH AS FOOD. In these activities, children learn to LISTEN IN to the sensations in their bodies.

Movement Play Activities

Massage

Age: BABIES, YOUNG CHILDREN AND CHILDREN
Aims: To focus on sensation; to use a variety of different kinds of touch
Props: None
Music: Optional. Something varied like a collection of piano variations
Numbers: One to one. And one to one in a group

Activity:

Get comfortable together in a way that suits you both. Create as much bare skin on your legs and arms as you feel is appropriate. If possible, let the baby or child have some areas of bare skin other than just hands - legs and arms, or more, if appropriate to your relationship. Massage different parts of their body, and in different ways.

Your hands have expressive power and can convey anything you wish. Offer one clear touching message at once and leave spaces for the child's reaction. Start gradually. Start with extremities and work inwards towards their centre. Later, work from the centre outwards as well. Try different touch qualities: soothing, playful, rhythmic, pushy, liquid, bubbly, firm glancing and so on.

What do you feel from the child? How do you feel you want to respond? Work from your direct perception, the feedback from your sensations, feelings and movement, rather than thinking out what you will do.

Movement Play Activities
Three-in-one massage

Age: BABIES, YOUNG CHILDREN AND CHILDREN
Aims: To focus on sensation using three kinds of touch
Props: None
Music: Optional. Gentle and lively
Numbers: One to one. And one to one in a group

Activity:
As always, begin by tuning in. Lay your baby or child on the floor and join them. Make sure you are both warm and comfortable. Have cushions available to prop you up if necessary. Explore three simple ways to massage your baby or child. If they want to watch your face, lay them on their back. If they are happy to focus on the feeling sensations alone, lay them on their tummy.

Give the child firm smooth strokes from their head, down over their shoulders and down their back. Use the palms of your hands in long, calm strokes. Then give fast and softly invigorating finger tapping 'rain' from head to his toes. Finish with firm, soft kneading over their shoulders and back. If your child doesn't enjoy a particular touch, stop straight away.

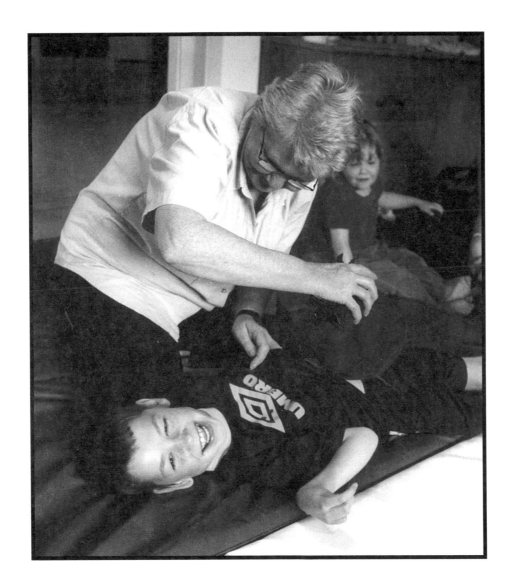

Page 283

Movement Play Activities

Pizza massage

Age: BABIES, YOUNG CHILDREN AND CHILDREN
Aims: To focus on sensation in a playful atmosphere
Props: None
Music: Optional. Bright and lively
Numbers: One to one. And one to one in a group

Activity:
This can follow on from another kind of massage, or be a game in its own right.

Imagine you are going to make a pizza on the baby's tummy, or their back. Start by rolling out the pizza dough into a flat circle. Next, spread the tomato all over the dough. Then, lightly chop up the toppings - using other areas of their body to chop on. Dab the toppings all over the dough - different dabs for different sorts of topping. Finish by sprinkling cheese all over ...

Develop the ideas each time you do this activity. Invite older children to make suggestions and see if your 'baking' matches their exacting standards.

Movement Play Activities
Cook book massage

Age: BABIES, YOUNG CHILDREN AND CHILDREN
Aims: To focus on sensation in a playful atmosphere
Props: None
Music: Optional. Bright and lively
Numbers: One to one. And one to one in a group

Activity:

Challenge other masseurs to see how many different kinds of food you can 'prepare' and 'bake' on the babies' bodies - biscuit dough cut into little shapes; bread-dough kneading and proving; decorating fancy cakes with cherries and hundreds and thousands; cucumber slicing ...

Ask older children to give you suggestions and respond to the way you 'prepare' and 'bake' them. If you're passing ideas around amongst the adults, make sure that the talking doesn't take over. Keep your attention firmly tuned in to your baby or child.

Movement Play Activities

Blowing

Age: BABIES, YOUNG CHILDREN
Aims: To focus on sensation using a very light touch ...
Props: Straws
Music: Optional. Very quiet and flowing
Numbers: One to one. And one to one in a group

Activity:

Start by bringing your baby's attention to different parts of their body, by placing your hands on the different bits and giving a stroke, or a rub, or a pat. Wake up as much of the baby's body as you feel is appropriate.

Then use your breath instead of your hands. Blow gently over the child's skin. Blow softly; blow in straight lines; blow in circles; blow in starts and stops; blow raspberries on their toes and fists.

Then, to give a different feel, blow through a straw which directs a pin-point of air rather than the more general blow from your lips. Make patterns along their body.

Movement Play Activities
Roller massage

Age: BABIES, YOUNG CHILDREN AND CHILDREN
Aims: Using props to focus on sensation
Props: Balls and balloons
Music: Optional. Gentle but upbeat
Numbers: One to one. And one to one in a group

Activity:

Lay your baby on the floor, or a safe surface that is more comfortable for your back. Begin by awakening the baby's body to touch. Use soft balls of different sizes and textures to roll over their body. Try a small beach ball, a soft balloon, a koosh ball, a small sponge ball, a ping pong ball, a water ball. Roll around the child's body to outline her shape. Use firm, but not hard, pressure. Find routes that you can repeat again and again until you both know them. Then make surprises along the way.

Movement Play Activities
Different strokes

Age: BABIES, YOUNG CHILDREN AND CHILDREN

Aims: To introduce different sensations; to work with a child who doesn't like physical contact

Props: A range of items with different textures

Music: Optional. Lively rather than relaxing

Numbers: One to one. And one to one in a group

Activity:

When your baby has become familiar with massage activities, try using a range of different textures - some soft and comforting and some surprising. Go very gently, watching closely for what the baby does and doesn't like. Continue to use as much of their body as you can.

Use soft, furry fabric and silky scarves; cool, smooth stones, make-up brushes of all sizes, something a little bit scratchy like a comb, or a pumice stone. As you use different things, mirror your expectations of what it might feel like with your facial expression and the words or sounds you use.

Movement Play Activities
Different scents

Age: BABIES, YOUNG CHILDREN AND CHILDREN
Aims: To introduce different scents alongside the sensations
Props: Different scents - as many natural ones as possible
Music: Optional. Gentle but lively
Numbers: One to one. And one to one in a group

Activity:

As you massage your baby introduce different scents with different kinds of massage. Put the scents on light, silky scarves and waft them around close to the baby. Don't use creams and oils on their skin in case they cause an allergic reaction.

Don't use essential oils unless you have advice from a specialist; they too can cause strong reactions. Instead, use light perfumes or fruits and flowers. Link one smell with one kind of sensation by always using them together.

Movement Play Activities

Massage and munch

Age: BABIES, YOUNG CHILDREN AND CHILDREN
Aims: To introduce smell and taste alongside touch
Props: Fruits
Music: Optional. Gentle but lively
Numbers: One to one. And one to one in a group

Activity:

Use fruit, of different sizes and shapes, as a massage ball. Use it gently so you don't squash it. Trace the child's outline; make connections along the child's body - leg to hip, hand to arm, fingers to palm and so on. Try apples (take off the scratchy stalk first), oranges, grapes, peaches, kiwi, kumquats, cherry tomatoes, apricots, plums and cherries.

Then, cut up the fruits and explore the smell, and taste anything that is safe for the child to try.

Movement Play Activities

Tummy games

Age:	BABIES, YOUNG CHILDREN AND CHILDREN
Aims:	To encourage babies to find and feel their centre
Props:	None
Music:	Optional. Gentle but lively
Numbers:	Small groups of 6 - 8. Bigger groups where necessary

Activity:

Babies need to be on their tummies for a good proportion of the day. From the time they first roll over, having their tummy in contact with the floor is important. Through this simple contact they develop a firm sense of their centre - which is an important aspect of future self esteem. (And seems to help them come out of nappies earlier than babies who spend very little time on their tummies.) Keep them out of baby chairs and join them on the floor to make sure they don't skimp on this important stage.

Find other ways of letting them play with their tummies in contact with a surface - over your knees, over your shoulder or rolling them very gently on a big gymnastic ball.

Encourage older children to spend time on their tummies as they play or look at books.

Movement Play Activities
Toe flicking

Age:	BABIES and older children who need sensory stimulation
Aims:	To encourage babies to find their toes and prepare for future movements
Props:	None
Music:	None
Numbers:	One to one

Activity:

Most babies find their toes early in their lives and lie happily on their backs catching their toes and letting go of them ... catching them and letting go again ... over and over. This is an important activity that enables them to get to know the end of their body (This is Me) and prepares their toes for the important pushing they will do (Developmental Movement) when they first start to move of their own free will, in the belly-crawling position. Then, the toes must curl under and push ...

Support your babies toe flicking games whenever they indulge. Don't take over - let baby do this piece of work for themselves. Make sure that your baby's feet are uncovered whenever possible. Work on the rule of thumb that if they don't need gloves they don't need socks ... if you are anxious, uncover their feet, encourage toe flicking games, and then cover them again. But babies feet don't get cold like ours might and it is very important that they have maximum opportunity to feel, and use, their toes.

If for some reason your baby can't, or won't, play with their toes, give them lots of toe and foot massage, and in particular, do short, light pulling actions on their toes - flicks - working towards their body, as they would if they were doing it.

Movement Play Activities
Satisfying the wriggles

Age: YOUNG CHILDREN AND CHILDREN
Aims: To help children to be still by giving them a strong sense of their body
Props: None
Music: None
Numbers: One to one

Activity:

If you have a compulsive wriggler, a child who cannot sit still during a story, or a quiet activity, find out if they can tolerate touch. If they enjoy a massage, let them curl up next to an available adult and drape their legs, or body, over their knee as they sit on the floor, or in a chair. Ask the adult to massage them in a firm way. There is no particular expertise required here. The wriggling may well be an unconscious strategy for getting the affirming tactile feedback they need in order to settle. If you help them to feel their boundaries, by touching them firmly, it may help them to be still.

Movement Play Activities

Moving with eyes shut

Age: CHILDREN
Aims: To help children to focus on the felt experience of their body as they move
Props: None
Music: Optional. Something that will encourage them to work slowly
Numbers: Small groups of 6 - 8. Bigger groups where necessary

Activity:

Children start by finding somewhere comfortable on the floor, lying down, settling in, shutting their eyes and listening in to the sensations, feelings, movements and images that are happening inside their bodies. They are going to move lying down.

Invite them to move just their arms, following their felt-sense of how they want to move. Keep talking, and prompting, as they move - so they feel safe in your presence. Tell them they can crack their eyes open if they need to. (And if some children don't want to move with their eyes shut at all, let them move with their eyes open.) Encourage them to notice sensation, feelings, movements and any pictures or sounds, memories or stories that float into their thoughts as they move.

As they become familiar with the activity, gradually introduce more movement - they can move sitting up, kneeling up, and perhaps even standing (in small numbers and with everyone watching out for their safety).

Movement Play Activities
Listening in

Age: CHILDREN
Aims: To help children to focus on the felt experience of their body in stillness
Props: None
Music: Optional. Quiet and unimposing
Numbers: Small groups of 6 - 8. Bigger groups where necessary

Activity:

It is easier for children to move than to be still. Once they are used to moving with their eyes shut, invite them to listen in to the sensations and feelings inside their body as they are still. Ask them to see if they know how they would move ... if they were going to. Their answers might be fantasy, as well as real.

Encourage children to draw after they have 'listened in' - to focus their experience.

Hopping Home Backwards

14
Activities Focusing
On
Feelings

These activities are designed to provide opportunities for babies and children to build their emotional intelligence, to EXPLORE FEELINGS and to EXPLORE RELATIONSHIPS. In these activities, children learn to LISTEN IN to, and begin to express, their feelings

Hopping Home Backwards

Movement Play Activities

Coracle

Age: BABIES AND YOUNG CHILDREN
Aims: To experience a caring, then a sharing, relationship
Props: None
Music: Optional. Calm and gentle
Numbers: One to one. And one to one in a group

Activity:

A coracle is a light, round boat. Sit down with your baby, on an armless chair or on the floor. You are the coracle - cradle the baby in the 'boat'. The baby can face you, or face the same way as you with her back against your tummy. (A young baby will need to face you so that they can see your face, and begin to match your intentions with your facial expressions and your actions. An older baby, who knows the game and trusts it, may be more interested in the physical sensations and happy, therefore, to face away from you. Watch carefully and place the baby accordingly.)

The coracle rocks front and back, side to side, in a figure of eight ... any way. You make all the decisions about where, when and how to rock. Emphasise the care you take of the baby as you do it.

Then encourage them to rock the coracle themself. Follow any signals they give you about when to start and stop, and where and how to rock. Let them rock fast and furiously or gently. Emphasise the fact that it is the baby that is deciding how to move.

Movement Play Activities

Cage

Age: BABIES AND YOUNG CHILDREN
Aims: To experience an against relationship
Props: None
Music: Optional. Nothing too imposing or rhythmic
Numbers: One to one. And one to one in a group

Activity:

Cage is the 'against' version of coracle. The baby is encouraged to push against you. You are the cage. Sit down with them in your lap 'trapping' them securely. Put your arms around them so that they cannot move. As soon as they resist, let them go and allow them to crawl free of your embrace immediately.

Keep it playful and let them see this on your face. Encourage them to break out of your cage and always let them get free. Welcome them back and congratulate them on their strength and determination. As they grow in confidence, make it harder work for them to gain their freedom. Use all your body, not just your arms.

Let older children cage part of you - a leg, an arm, your head - and in turn make your escape. The way you escape, gently but determinedly, will also give the child an example of appropriate force.

Movement Play Activities
Paperweight

Age: BABIES AND YOUNG CHILDREN
Aims: To focus attention on giving and taking weight; to experience a sharing
            relationship
Props: None
Music: Optional. Relaxing music may help you to focus
Numbers: One to one

Activity:

Giving your weight to someone is a very direct expression of trust equivalent to 'Here
am I - look after me'. Very young babies have to rely on adults to carry them about all
the time. As children get older, this happens less and less, but the importance of the
giving and taking of weight doesn't diminish.

Let your baby lie on you, resting their whole weight on your body. Work with your
whole body to heighten the nature of the relationship between you. Let your baby lie
on your tummy, on your back as you lie on the floor, or across your legs. You may put
the baby on yourself, or ask someone else to place her gently on. Gently and firmly
press your baby's weight into yours so the contact between you is very clear.

Once babies and children have become used to resting on you, rest bits of your body
gently on them. Start with your head on their tummy or back. Gently press your weight
(to an acceptable level) into the baby's body.

Movement Play Activities

Stillness

Age: BABIES, YOUNG CHILDREN AND CHILDREN
Aims: To support stillness as well as movement; to focus a quiet relationship
Props: None
Music: Optional. Relaxing music may help you to focus
Numbers: One to one

Activity:

Don't feel that because this is Movement Play, you have to move all the time. Stillness is an important part of this work.

When your baby or child chooses to be still, rest with them, creating as much contact between you as you can. Curl your body around theirs, or gently lay a hand across their back, or legs ... to let them know that stillness is something you can share.

Older children may enjoy the sensation of making a still shape as they are standing or sitting, along or in the centre of the group. Draw their attention to the stillness through words, or by placing a hand in the small of their back and adopting your own very still stance. Give them a verbal structure to focus it further: 'Can you hold it for 5 seconds?' 'Can you find a way of moving on to another still shape?'

The important thing is that you give value to stillness as well as movement.

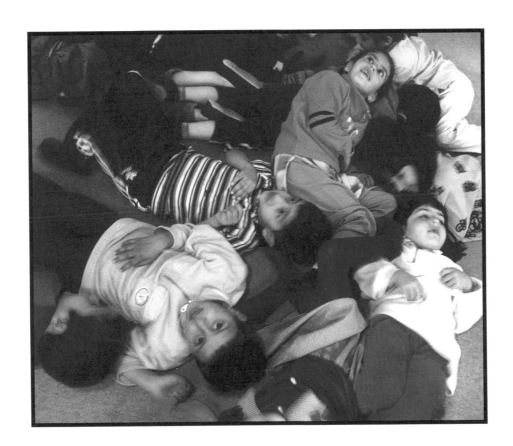

Movement Play Activities

Up in a lift

Age: BABIES AND YOUNG CHILDREN
Aims: To experience and explore a feeling of anticipation
Props: None
Music: Optional. Something bright and jolly
Numbers: One to one. And one to one in a group

Activity:

Do this when your baby indicates that they will enjoy it. Only continue as long as they display interest and enjoyment, and stop immediately if they show distress. The baby has to feel very comfortable or there will be no possibility of learning - only defending. Do it with them, not to them.

Stand with your baby or child facing you. Hold them under their arms, legs hanging free. Start low down and lift them slowly until their face is higher than yours. Chatter away to them as you do it. Hold the child at the top then bring them slowly down again. If they are comfortable, try coming down more quickly, building up the speed as the child's enjoyment or curiosity dictates. Do a quick whiz down and go up slowly each time. Give lots of verbal feedback and lots of support around the whizzing bits.

As you both become familiar with the activity, really play with the anticipation - just when is that whiz going to happen? Let the baby indulge in the experience of anticipating.

Movement Play Activities

Risks

Age: BABIES AND YOUNG CHILDREN
Aims: To experience and explore the feeling of risk
Props: None
Music: Optional. Nothing too imposing or rhythmic
Numbers: One to one. And one to one in a group

Activity:

This is a continuation from the last activity and is only appropriate if your baby is really enjoying the downwards whiz. Hold your baby above your head with arms straight. Make sure that they can see around as well as down at your face. Let them get used to being up so high. If they are comfortable, and you feel strong enough, thrown them into the air a little, and catch them again. Repeat until they have had enough or you are exhausted. Always finish with a close cuddle and masses of praise and attention.

Take care of yourself: bend your knees as you catch her and take plenty of rests. Stop before you get too tired.

This activity allows the baby to experience risk taking, and to build their trust in you as you keep them safe. The baby will only be able to experience and explore the feelings around risk if they feel safe enough - and not frightened.

Movement Play Activities

Conversations

Age: BABIES AND YOUNG CHILDREN
Aims: To chat in movement; to let the child know they are seen
Props: None
Music: Lively songs you know may help to give you confidence
Numbers: One to one. And one to one in a group

Activity:

Let your baby know that you can hold conversations with her in movement as well as in babble and words. Start by tuning in and noticing more about the way the baby is moving. Join them on the floor, or beside their chair, and mirror their position - making sure that they can see you. Use mirroring, reflecting, patterning and so on (pages 168 - 174) as your way of responding to what you see.

As you settle in together, try to establish a flow bond (page 174) so that your movement affirms your relationship with your baby.

When you have established the 'rules' - that you are following the babies movements - you can introduce movement of your own and tempt your baby to follow you.

Movement Play Activities
Feeling and a movement

Age: CHILDREN
Aims: To encourage children to express and share feelings through
            movement; to watch others do the same
Props: None
Music: Only as a background accompaniment
Numbers: Small groups of 6 - 8. Bigger groups where necessary

Activity:

Start by talking about how our movement, our bodies, mirror how we feel. You might like to give some obvious examples - happy and lifted; sad and slumped and so on. Talk about how all our movements, however tiny, show how we feel. Invite each child to do a movement that speaks of how they feel today. Invite them to show their movement to the group and ask everyone to do it with them. (Always let a child pass if they don't want to do it.)

You may want to add words. Each child can name the feeling (or the movement) for themselves. This often provides unusual, sometimes made up, words. Allow children to be in control of this, and take pleasure in their ability to invent.

Words gathered in this way can be a good starting point for young children's poems. Gather the words from a whole group and arrange them together.

Movement Play Activities
Back to back: caring

Age: CHILDREN
Aims: Listening to another body
Props: None
Music: Optional. Slow and gentle
Numbers: Small groups of 6 - 8. Bigger groups where necessary

Activity:

Invite children to sit back to back in pairs. Encourage them to settle in together, to shut their eyes, and to feel the warmth of their partner's back. Ask them to listen in, to see how much they can feel through their backs. Can they pick up tiny movements that their partner makes?

Watch out for children who quickly want to push, or do very big movements. The next two activities might suit their interests better.

Movement Play Activities
Back to back: sharing

Age: CHILDREN
Aims: Listening in and working together
Props: None
Music: Optional. Slow and gentle
Numbers: Small groups of 6 - 8. Bigger groups where necessary

Activity:

This time, invite children to see if they can move along together, with their backs touching - first towards one partner and then towards the other. They have to do a great deal of working together, as one has to push and walk backwards on their bottom, while the other walks forward on their bottom but not so fast that they lose touch with their partner's back. Both have to press into each other, whilst negotiating the travelling. Swap directions.

Invite them to try it with eyes open and with eyes shut, making sure that they won't bump into each other.

Movement Play Activities
Back to back: against

Age: CHILDREN
Aims: Listening in and taking care of a partner
Props: None
Music: Optional. Firm and calm
Numbers: Small groups of 6 - 8. Bigger groups where necessary

Activity:

Children sit back to back in pairs. Invite one child to push against their partner - gently.
The other child must dig in and resist. Can they plant themselves so firmly that they
cannot be moved?

If children are very boisterous with this activity, give a short time limit. Something like
a count from one to ten. Establish safety guidelines first. If one child is particularly
committed and strong, let them work with you rather than another child.

Invite children to work with their eyes shut as well as open. Encourage them to notice
as much as they can about what it is like to push with their eyes shut: can they notice
sensation, feeling, movement and images?

Movement Play Activities

Bridges

Age: CHILDREN
Aims: Listening in and working together
Props: None
Music: Optional. Steady and firm
Numbers: Small groups of 6 - 8. Bigger groups where necessary

Activity:

Show children how to make a strong bridge on all fours - knees and hands quite wide so that the bridge is strong. Working in pairs, let one child make a bridge and the other crawl under, around, squeeze through the legs, climb over and so on ... then swap over. Invite them both to do the same thing with their eyes shut, carefully feeling their partner and taking great care of them as they feel their way around.

If one child can make a strong bridge, invite the other to balance against it - sitting and leaning, lying over the top and so on. Invite children to work slowly with eyes closed, as well as with eyes open.

Invite pairs to join up so that two children make a bridge and the other two play on, over and around it. Perhaps you could get the whole group to join up to make a huge bridge that children can play on.

Movement Play Activities
Sticky hands

Age: CHILDREN
Aims: Listening in and working together
Props: None
Music: This doesn't need music but you may like some in the background
Numbers: Small groups of 6 - 8. Or big groups where necessary

Activity:
Invite children to work in pairs, putting the palms of their hands together and, without the hands parting at all, seeing where they can move. Ask them to keep their feet in one place at first; travelling may follow. Encourage them to work with eyes open and with eyes shut to see what each is like.

Talk as they move, helping them to negotiate an ending together. Give them time to do this, rather than asking for an instant ending. Encourage them to finish with complete stillness.

Movement Play Activities
Hedgehogs

Age: CHILDREN
Aims: To explore a particular kind of relationship; to practice self protection
Props: None
Music: Optional. Firm and calm
Numbers: Small groups of 6 - 8. Bigger groups where necessary

Activity:

Hedgehogs curl up to protect themselves. In this activity, children work in pairs. One child curls up in a tight ball, and stays curled even when a friend tries to open them up. Encourage children to try hard to open up their hedgehog, but at the same time to make sure that they are not hurt.

If children do not want to be the hedgehog, or the puller, make a safe watching space and support their choice to be a watcher, rather than a mover.

Encourage the hedgehog to tell their partner if anything hurts. Support conversations about how it feels to be pulled open and how it feels to protect yourself.

Watch out for over-enthusiastic pulling and tugging. Talk with children about taking care of each other and still having good physical fun.

If you have the energy, see if the hedgehogs can stay curled up while you pick them up around their chest and waist.

Can the hedgehogs roll around while they are curled up? They will need friends to sit round in a circle and keep them safe.

15

Activities Focusing
On
Movement

These activities are designed to provide opportunities for babies and children to practice significant DEVELOPMENTAL MOVEMENT ACTIVITIES, to develop their KNOWLEDGE OF THEIR BODY to develop PHYSICAL MASTERY as they play. In these activities, children learn to LISTEN IN to the layers of experience prompted by movement, and to EMBODY THEIR LEARNING in their bodies, as well as in their intellects

Movement Play Activities
Floor gym

Age: BABIES, YOUNG CHILDREN AND CHILDREN
Aims: To establish the floor as an important playing ground; to provide developmental movement practice
Props: None
Music: Optional. A varied tape of fast and slow, lively and lilting
Numbers: Small groups of 6 - 8. Or big groups where necessary

Activity:

Make sure the floor is comfortable, warm, clean and clear. You may choose to put down a special floor mat, partly to establish a ritual for Movement Play time and partly to provide the optimum conditions for the developmental movement patterns. A large square of vinyl flooring is ideal (taped on the reverse side down the lengths). This can be kept clean especially for Movement Play and provides the right amount of slip and resistance for belly-crawling. (If babies find that they enjoy sliding on their knees instead of crawling, make sure you take it away and encourage them to crawl on all fours as well.)

Join your babies on the floor and support the movements that they choose to do. Encourage them to play in a variety of ways - on their backs, their tummies, belly-crawling and crawling on all fours in particular. Invent games together to keep children interested in staying down on the floor.

(Whenever you join in with crawling on all fours, wear knee-pads - the soft variety used in some sporting activities, not the hard plastic protectors used in roller skating. Babies and young children have extra padding on their knees that adults lose as they grow older. They can crawl as much as they like without damaging their knees; we can't.)

Movement Play Activities

Human play frame

Age: BABIES AND YOUNG CHILDREN
Aims: To show that bodies are the best toys; to build trust and pleasure in
            paired Movement Play
Props: None
Music: Optional. Calm and steady
Numbers: One to one

Activity:

Get down on the floor with the babies. Your body is the play frame and your baby
climbs through the shapes, obstacles and gaps. Invite your baby to climb on; make
shapes that they can crawl through, slither through, around and over. As you both get
used to the game, you can move to create surprises for her - cracks to squeeze
through, bits that 'collapse' and so on.

You can alter the activities you offer to meet aims that you want to meet with each
child - games that emphasise sensation, feeling or movement and address different
Landscapes. (See pages 196 - 233)

Movement Play Activities

Rocking

Age:	BABIES AND YOUNG CHILDREN
Aims:	To experience and explore a particular kind of moving
Props:	None
Music:	Optional. Waltz or swing time music
Numbers:	One to one. And one to one in a group

Activity:

Everyone does a version of this with babies. First, make sure at all stages that the baby really wants to do this. (We have all mindlessly rocked babies whilst thinking of other things.) Start by tuning in so that you are fully focused on the baby, watching for all the tiny movement signals and cues. Hold the baby securely, make sure you are both comfy. Rock the baby, gently at first, with more abandon if you feel that the baby is interested in this.

This is not just a standing or sitting activity: think of your whole body as a plaything and a resource. Rock standing, sitting, lying down, side to side, backwards and forwards. Rock the baby in your arms, on your legs, over your shoulder, on your tummy.

The more adventurous and involved you are in different kinds of movement at this stage, the more you will transmit the message - Movement Play is important, fun and valued.

Movement Play Activities

Swinging

Age: BABIES AND YOUNG CHILDREN
Aims: To experience and explore a particular kind of moving
Props: None
Music: Optional. Waltz or swing time music
Numbers: One to one. And one to one in a group

Activity:

Start by tuning-in and making sure that the babies really want to join in. Hold the baby securely on their back, supporting head and spine. Stand in a clear space. Start by rocking gently and develop the movement. Rocking will keep the babys' body close to yours. Swinging gives them the experience of leaving you and coming back - an important feeling. This activity also gives experience of rhythm.

As babies grow and become comfortable with this activity try:
   ○ swinging low through wide-apart legs
   ○ swinging high like swing boats over your head
   ○ swinging round and back the other way
   ○ swing slow, then fast, then slow again

If you swing fast, it can be developmentally useful - like spinning activities that help babies and young children to develop an internal understanding of the position of their body in space, assist in the development of balance and help eye convergence.

Page 325

Movement Play Activities
Rocking the boat

Age: BABIES AND YOUNG CHILDREN
Aims: To experience and explore a particular kind of moving
Props: None
Music: Optional. Waltz or swing time music
Numbers: One to one. And one to one in a group

Activity:
Sit on the floor with your baby cuddled in your lap. Get comfy yourself, either cross-legged or with your knees bent and legs apart. Settle the baby comfortably in your lap. Rock side to side like a boat on the waves. Start small, grow the movement as your baby dictates. Support yourself with your arms as you rock further over.

When you are both ready, rock right off balance and roll the baby gently out of the boat. Stay very focused on as they climb back in for another turn.

As an alternative, try rocking backwards so that your legs, and the baby's, can kick in the air.

Movement Play Activities

Slide

Age: BABIES, YOUNG CHILDREN AND CHILDREN

Aims: To experience and explore a particular kind of moving

Props: A play parachute or strong cloth (quilt, sheet or blanket). Another adult

Music: Optional. Bright and lively

Numbers: One to one. And one to one in a group

Activity:

You need a smooth, wooden or lino floor surface. Spread a cloth, lycra-square or quilt on the floor. Sit on the cloth and lay the baby or child on your tummy, or sit them in your lap. Ask the other adult to gather up the cloth behind you and pull you both along. Start with a very gentle pull. Remain totally focused on the baby, ensuring that you have their 'permission' to go on. As the baby becomes familiar with the activity, you can slide faster and in a more risky fashion.

Finish by cuddling in the cloth.

If the baby is very confident, they may be happy to have a turn without you. Take it very carefully and check the 'permission' at all stages.

Movement Play Activities
Bumps and lumps

Age: BABIES AND YOUNG CHILDREN
Aims: To experience and explore a particular kind of moving
Props: None
Music: Optional. Gentle and rhythmically varied
Numbers: One to one. And one to one in a group

Activity:
Start by cradling your baby or child in your arms. When you feel that they would enjoy this, send a wave through your arms, lifting and lowering the baby as you do. When you are both comfortable with this kind of movement, place the baby on a different part of your body - across your legs, on your chest, on your back, round your neck - and send the ripple through that part of your body so that it moves the baby. The wave can be strong or gentle, regular and sure, or intermittent and playful.

Further Guidance:
Choose carefully whether the baby can see your face or not. A young baby will need to watch, an older baby may be more interested in the movement sensation, or the relationship games, ie. anticipating the unpredictability of when the wave will happen.

Movement Play Activities
Rolling

Age: **BABIES AND YOUNG CHILDREN**
Aims: To experience and explore a particular kind of moving
Props: None
Music: Optional. Gentle
Numbers: One to one. And one to one in a group

Activity:
Work on a vinyl floor square, carpet or soft floor covering. Lay your baby on the floor. Put your hands on their tummy or back and gently begin to push so that they rock onto their side. Let them come back to centre and repeat. Notice if your baby resists or goes with the push. It they resist, work very slowly, or wait until another time.

Work gradually until the baby goes right onto their side. Support them so that don't flop right over. The baby may use their body like a rolling pin - in one piece - or roll with a twist in their spine. Different age babies will respond differently.

If they enjoy rolling, roll them right over. Roll them on the floor, or up your legs. (Take care of your back.) If they roll on their own, roll with them. Roll lots of young children together in a line. This, too, offers developmentally useful activity supporting the development of balance and eye convergence. Find lots of different ways to roll in which the head is tipped and tilted in different ways.

Movement Play Activities

Reach

Age: BABIES
Aims: To encourage relationship to the wider environment
Props: None
Music: Optional
Numbers: One to one. And one to one in a group

Activity:

Support this activity when you start to see your baby begin to make the transition from an inward focus on its own body sensations, to an outward focus on the outside world. This is the time to play games that focus on the transition.

Start with a massage to establish the baby's own body. Finish the massage with strokes that go from the babys' centre to their edges - fingers and toes. Gradually change the spatial relationship between you and the baby by introducing objects for them to focus upon. Offer them at a distance of about a baby's arm's length form their eyes. Offer exciting looking textures - just out of reach so that the baby has to reach for them. A glittery scarf, a koosh ball ... anything that takes their fancy. Tempt them to reach for it with their hands. Let them catch it and give them lots of encouragement and praise.

Swap sides so that the baby has to turn its head from one side to the other (their arms and legs will probably swap about as well). This is developmentally useful as well as being a good game.

Watch carefully to make sure you play this when it is relevant and respond to the particular reaction you get. Develop the activity into caring, sharing or against games with the scarf that the baby has caught. Give a gently tug; wrap the baby in it; waft it gently to and fro between you.

Movement Play Activities
Jiggle and jump

Age: BABIES
Aims: To delight in movement
Props: None
Music: Optional. Lively jigs
Numbers: One to one. And one to one in a group

Activity:
Sit on an armless chair and stand the baby on your knee. Hold their hands, wrists and elbows. Jiggle, bounce and jump them on your knees. Let them dance, small at first and then ever more extravagantly as their delight grows. As you come to the end, slow down and signal that you will be stopping. Bring them to sitting before you stop.

Take rests when you need to and let her enjoy the anticipation of when the activity is going to start again. Because of the stop-start nature of this activity, you need to signal the final ending really clearly so that they can get ready for it to stop.

You've probably done this a million times before. This time, really watch what your baby does. Use any of the observation structures to increase the amount you see, and, therefore, the amount you can support. Pick out some aspect that the baby seems particularly interested in and find another way of supporting just that aspect of their movement.

Movement Play Activities

Body music

Age: BABIES AND YOUNG CHILDREN
Aims: To make exploration of the body ordinary
Props: None
Music: Optional
Numbers: One to one. And one to one in a group

Activity:

Your body and your baby's body are the whole band. Use your whole body to make different sounds: patting, knocking, rubbing, stroking different parts of your body together. Encourage young children to explore the sounds they can make with their own body. Let it grow into a conversation or play follow my leader.

Sometimes the sounds will be interesting, but sometimes the movements that you discover will be more interesting - either the look of them, or the feel of them. Notice and explore the sensations that go along with the sounds and movements.

Movement Play Activities
How do you want to move today?

Age: YOUNG CHILDREN AND CHILDREN
Aims: To encourage attention to bodily-felt experience
Props: None
Music: Optional. You will need to offer an alternative - fast or slow
Numbers: Small groups of 6 - 8. Or big groups where necessary

Activity:
Invite children to discover how they want to move at this moment. Show them what you mean. Take a moment to feel what you want to do (listen in) then move across the room. If you're not comfortable with moving ask a confident child to demonstrate for you. Talk them through, helping them feel what they want to do rather than think about it.

Give verbal support throughout the activity at first, encouraging children to keep themselves and each other safe as they explore. If a child doesn't want to move, support their choice to keep still. Invite children to find as many different ways to move across the circle as they can. Encourage them to feel these out, not to think them out. If they get stuck, take them back to listening in to their bodies before they move. Sensing ... intending ... action.

(You may want to make a special place in the room that children can go to if they don't want to join in any particular activity - a place to be still, to listen in and to watch. When children use this, give verbal support to ensure that they know they are making an active choice and are still part of the activity.)

Movement Play Activities
This is my ... and it wants to ...

Age: CHILDREN
Aims: To encourage attention to bodily-felt experience in a detailed way
Props: None
Music: Optional. You will need to offer an alternative - fast or slow
Numbers: Small groups of 6 - 8. Or big groups where necessary

Activity:

Working in a circle, ask children to make sure there is a space between them and the next child on either side. Invite each child to say which bit of the body they want to move and what it wants to do. 'This is my ... and it wants to ...' Encourage the other children to join in with each movement. Encourage children to take responsibility for finishing their turn and passing on to the next person.

Bring children's attention to the available space and safety issues. If you are working in a small space, encourage them to choose movements that won't bash the person next to them over the head.

Movement Play Activities
Body greeting

Age: CHILDREN
Aims: To develop the ability to notice, and work, with others
Props: None
Music: Optional. Gentle background
Numbers: Small groups of 6 - 8. Or big groups where necessary

Activity:

Ask the children to move around the space as they choose, invite them to look around and notice each other. Invite them to greet each other with different parts of their bodies - shake hands, rub noses, touch elbows, link arms, bounce bums. Give careful support to ensure they take care of each other. As they get to know the activity, ask them to find their own ways of meeting and greeting.

If you want to give this activity more focus, bring it back into the circle and have each pair working separately - crossing the circle - while the others watch.

Invite children to choose a friend with whom they would like to make a body greeting. Let one lead and the other fit in; or let them find it between them.

Movement Play Activities
Elastic circle

Age: YOUNG CHILDREN AND CHILDREN
Aims: To introduce spontaneous movement gently and comfortably
Props: A soft elastic
Music: Optional. A varied tape of fast and slow, lively and lilting
Numbers: Small groups of 6 - 8. Or big groups where necessary

Activity:

Start with the children sitting in a circle - they stay sitting throughout. Take a circle of wide elastic into the middle of the circle and hand it to the children, so that each one is holding on to it. Return to your place in the circle and invite the children to explore the elastic - to look at it and to feel it. Gather anything they want to say about it. When they are ready, move on to the main activity.

Without music to begin with (as it raises excitement), do a clear movement with the elastic and invite everyone to join in with you - something very simple, clear and repetitive, swaying from side to side, moving the elastic in and out of the circle in front of you, slithering it backwards and forwards along the ground and so on. Offer lots of verbal encouragement so that as many children as possible join in. Acknowledge anyone who really doesn't want to do it and reassure them that it is all right to watch. Encourage then to keep hold of the elastic though.

Stick with the same movement until the whole group finds your rhythm and joins in. Then find another clear movement, encouraging them to follow you again.

When children are familiar with this activity, they can lead it.

Movement Play Activities
Musical elastic

Age: YOUNG CHILDREN AND CHILDREN
Aims: To work with music and maintain focus
Props: A soft elastic
Music: Something lively and sociable
Numbers: Small groups of 6 - 8. Or big groups where necessary

Activity:
Use an elastic circle with music. Invite children to follow you as you make clear movements that they can join in with. Young children will need lots of support from adults.

Depending on the nature of your groups, music will have different effects. It can enliven a shy group, and over-excite an excitable group. Try to choose movements that will fit with the mood of the group, ie. if they are excitable, let them try a vigorous jiggle of the elastic. If they are very shy, offer small movements that leave your hands in your lap, close to your tummy. This feels less exposing than a big movement away from your centre.

If the group find it very exciting, let them have a little time to jiggle and wriggle when they first hear the music. Keep them sitting down - there is a lot they can move without standing up. Keeping them on their bottoms contains and focuses the movement. Invite them to look around at the variety of different kinds of movement in the circle.

Movement Play Activities
Noticing the differences

Age: CHILDREN
Aims: To notice movement in more depth; to take on someone else's point of
            view
Props: A soft elastic
Music: Lively. Scottish and Irish jigs for example
Numbers: Small groups of 6 - 8. Or big groups where necessary

Activity:

Start off in the same way as for Musical Elastic. As children move, taking up whatever they have suggested in their own bodies, look around and see all the different ways they are moving. There are bound to be lots of differences even though the broad shapes and movements are the same. Draw attention to the little differences; the way the elastic is held; the bounce of the shoulders; the tapping of one foot and so on. Do the movement of one child. 'This is Ben's movement.' Draw attention verbally to different aspects of this movement. 'Ben has one leg curled underneath the other as he is sitting. He is holding the elastic with his hands underneath.' Ask the other children to move as exactly like Ben as they can.

Give lots of verbal encouragement and pointers to help everyone to tackle the task as well as they can. Some children might find it difficult. It necessitates giving up their own movement (self) and taking on someone else's.

Children address a basic social skill in this activity - taking on someone else's way of being in the world. Repeat, using lots of other children's movements in turn.

Movement Play Activities
Following other leaders

Age: CHILDREN
Aims: To notice movement in more depth; to take someone else's point of
             view
Props: A soft elastic
Music: A wide variety
Numbers: Small groups of 6 - 8. Or big groups where necessary

Activity:

As the children become confident in following a leader, ask if anyone else would like to be the leader. Make sure the whole group know who is the new leader and that they watch carefully. Give each leader a minute or so.

If you have a lively group who are bursting to take control, there might be a flurry of requests. (Notice the dance of 'Me ... Me' that erupts.) Lively children often offer movements that are very difficult to follow - because they constantly change, because they involve turning outwards from the circle, or because they have flying legs and feet and might be dangerous. This is very understandable. At this age, many children, given the opportunity, want to be seen in all their glory. They need help to make it acceptable for the group as a whole. Here are some strategies to use to help them to learn how to operate in the group:

- ○ praise the movement first, before you begin to contain it. It might not be suitable for a whole group, but it is wonderful as an expression of this child
- ○ if a child clearly needs to move a lot and cannot reduce it, let them go into the centre and move first, then come back and try something that everyone can join in with

(continued overleaf)

Movement Play Activities
Following other leaders (continued)

○ if it still keeps changing, point this out saying that the others are having difficulty following it. Ask how they might change it so that it is possible for the group. Avoid telling them how to change it. Keep giving verbal feedback. If they are still unable to reduce the movements, acknowledge that this isn't how they want to move today and let them have another turn in the middle. You can ask the other children to pick up a quality from the movement that they can do sitting in their places - a wriggle in the shoulders, flapping hands and so on. 'This is how Melissa is feeling today ... lots of movements, jumps, kicks, wriggles.'

○ point out that a movement might be dangerous, and ask what could happen if we all do the movement together; ask the leader how they might change the movement so that it is less risky; help them to make the changes. Take plenty of time to talk over the consequences of the movements the children do. There is so much learning to be had from the way the group, and individual children within it, organise themselves.

Movement Play Activities
Pass

Age: CHILDREN
Aims: For everyone to have a turn moving as they wish; for others to notice
            and follow
Props: A soft elastic
Music: Optional. Lively and steady
Numbers: Small groups of 6 - 8. Or big groups where necessary

Activity:

After you have been the leader, pass the leadership around the circle so that each child
has a turn. When each child has had their turn they turn to their neighbour and say
'Pass'. Let them know that if they don't want a turn they can say 'Pass' straight away,
and it will go onto the next person.

If possible, let children be responsible for passing it on to the next person. Some
children may need help to control the length of the turn. They may look to you to say
when they should finish. Direct it back to them. 'Finish when you are ready or when
you feel you've taken your share of the time.' Some will want to go on for a long time;
others to pass almost immediately. Try not to give directions - ('Pass it on now you've
had a long turn.') but use the opportunity for learning by prompting the child ('You do
want a long turn today! How are you going to finish?'). If the length of turns is a
problem, ask the children to help solve it. They generally have lots of ideas.

Movement Play Activities

Bottoms down

Age: YOUNG CHILDREN AND CHILDREN
Aims: To contain lively energy; to support a shy group
Props: A soft elastic
Music: Something lively and sociable
Numbers: Small groups of 6 - 8. Or big groups where necessary

Activity:

This is another activity to do with an elastic. Invite children to sit holding the elastic and see how they can move keeping their bottoms on the floor. Play all the familiar elastic games (Pass, Follow the leader) within this new structure.

This can be a useful way of containing a boisterous group and a way of showing children how inventive they can be within restrictions. This may be useful learning prior to supporting children in directing their own play in a Movement Corner.

Movement Play Activities

Name and a movement

Age: CHILDREN
Aims: To practice being at the centre of attention; to choose one piece of movement from the flow
Props: None
Music: Optional. Calm and steady
Numbers: Small groups of 6 - 8. Bigger groups where necessary

Activity:
Either in a circle, or dotted around the room, suggest all the children find out how they want to move just at this moment.

In a circle, each child shows their movement to the group and everyone does it with them. Invite the leader so say their name as they do it, finding out precisely how the name fits the movement. Everyone says it with them. Repeat three or four times for every child. (Always let a child 'Pass' if they don't want to do it.) Some children will need extra support in finding and choosing their movement, and then showing it in the circle. First give them lots of time and reassurance. If they want to do it, but still can't manage it

○ try giving open prompts: 'What wants to move?'. Then wait
○ try mentioning various parts of the body, to see if that helps. Watch carefully to see if there is tiny motion, or the sense that something could move. 'Where do your elbows need to go?' 'Do your shoulders want to twist?'
○ if they can't use either of these prompts, reflect back their shape (how they are sitting) or their movement (a tapping foot; the tilt of the head; a particular stillness) - what they are already doing and encourage everyone to join them in something you see. Sometimes this might prompt another shape, and sometimes it is right just to take their turn in this way.

Movement Play Activities

Still shapes

Age: CHILDREN
Aims: To explore stillness
Props: None
Music: Optional. No fixed rhythm. When you first do this activity - no
music
Numbers: Small groups of 6 - 8. Bigger groups where necessary

Activity:
Each child makes a still shape, either in response to a sensation, feeling or their name. Here the task of the adult is to help each child to find a still shape. Small children often find it quite challenging to stop their movement flowing naturally on. This activity underpins decision making skills - deciding upon something and sticking with it - as well as practising a different way of being in their bodies.

Many children need a lot of support to come to a real stillness. Some may need a lot of practice, so think of it as a long term aim. Use a lot of verbal feedback to help them to be still. Sometimes you can offer support throughout your own body, putting a hand, or a hip, against a part of the body that keeps moving for instance. Do this with care and only if you really think that the child will find it helpful.

If they really can't be still, acknowledge that they obviously need to move today and find things to say about the movement that they do.

Movement Play Activities

Feet in

Age: YOUNG CHILDREN AND CHILDREN

Aims: To encourage children to notice bodies; to notice everyday starting points for Movement Play

Props: None

Music: None

Numbers: Small groups of 6 - 8. Bigger groups where necessary

Activity:

Invite children to look at the shapes of all the bodies as they sit round in the circle. Invite them to put their feet in the centre and look at all the shoes, and at all the different ways their feet are 'sitting'. Pick out different shapes and mirror them, inviting the children to 'try on each others feet'. How accurate can they get be?

In early sessions there may be a lot of talking and not so much moving. This will change as the children become familiar with Movement Play activities. Let them take their time making the change.

You can substitute hands, or any other bit of the body, if it fees more appropriate; or as a way of developing this structure in different sessions.

Movement Play Activities
Dancing feet

Age: **YOUNG CHILDREN AND CHILDREN**

Aims: To encourage children to notice bodies and movement; to notice everyday starting points for Movement Play

Props: None

Music: Optional. Lively

Numbers: Small groups of 6 - 8. Bigger groups where necessary

Activity:

Pick up the wriggle or jiggle that a child is doing. There will inevitably be one child who has some movement going on in their feet. Mirror the movement as accurately as you can and draw the other children's attention to it. Let them try it out. Keep bringing their attention to more of the detail to help them to mirror accurately. Try different children's movements in turn, each time picking out what someone is already doing.

There will probably always be a wealth of different kinds of moving available for you to pick up. However, if the children really are all doing exactly the same, and you don't feel there is anything interesting for the next movement, ask them to go back to their own way of moving ... and start again.

Movement Play Activities
Whose feet?

Age: YOUNG CHILDREN AND CHILDREN
Aims: To develop movement memory; to develop movement recall
Props: None
Music: None
Numbers: Small groups of 6 - 8. Bigger groups where necessary

Activity:

The next time you meet, or later in the session, replay one of the feet dances you have done before, and see if anyone can remember whose it was. Recap on several, identifying the mover and having another go at each movement. Let the child whose movement it was correct everybody - if they remember it well enough. If not, still let them be in control and change the movement if they want to. Ask the child to see if they can remember the sensations from the movement, and see if they can reproduce it that way.

At any point that you have difficulty in remembering what the movements were, dip back in to body memory by shutting your eyes and feeling your way there. Help children to change their focus from looking at bodies, to sensing inside themselves.

Movement Play Activities
Foot dances

Age: CHILDREN

Aims: To develop movement memory; to develop children's ability to work in relationship with one another

Props: None

Music: Optional. Choose according to the mood of the group

Numbers: Small groups of 6 - 8. Bigger groups where necessary

Activity:
Join three of the different foot wriggles together to make a sequence. Let the children work out which three and in which order. Help them to do this in their bodies - rather than resorting to thinking it out. Let the wriggles and jiggles arrive, rather than deciding them and then doing them.

If necessary, let each child choose their own sequence, especially if doing it as a group means that it becomes more about heads than bodies.

Develop the activity by using different parts of the body to make the three movements.

Movement Play Activities
Crawling games

Age: BABIES, YOUNG CHILDREN AND CHILDREN
Aims: To support a significant developmental pattern
Props: None
Music: Optional. Lively and steady
Numbers: Small groups of 6 - 8. Bigger groups where necessary

Activity:

This activity is designed to support the significant developmental movement patterns of belly-crawling and crawling on all fours. Working in pairs, invite one partner to find all the shapes they can make that will allow their partner to crawl through. Encourage the partners to crawl on their belly and on all fours - and then swap over.

Play crawling Tig; crawling Simon Says, crawling Follow-my-leader, crawling Grandmother's Footsteps, crawling What's the Time, Mr Wolf? Make sure you use both kinds of crawling - on their bellies and on all fours.

Movement Play Activities

Spinning

Age: YOUNG CHILDREN AND CHILDREN
Aims: To support a significant developmental pattern
Props: None
Music: Optional. Choose according to the mood of the group
Numbers: Small groups of 6 - 8. Bigger groups where necessary

Activity:

Children often like to spin until they are dizzy - which is quite hard for adults to watch, since the very idea usually makes us feel sick. It is, however, important that children spin. So if you see a child who likes to spin a lot, they are probably simply following their body intelligence. If a child doesn't like to spin, if they feel sick very quickly, they may need to practice more than anyone - let them take it slowly and at their own pace.

Encourage spinning in a variety of ways. (Our brains need variety to learn best.) Try log rolls across the floor (body held stiff). Encourage one partner to roll the other. Let children turn round and round on the spot - and talk about it afterwards. Let two children spin each other for just eight seconds one way, and then eight seconds the other. Encourage children to stop suddenly - and let the dizziness subside, before they repeat it the other way. Encourage children to spin in lots of different positions. All of this helps children to learn about balance and where their body is in space, as well as giving the eyes valuable practice in converging.

Movement Play Activities
Pushing and pulling

Age: CHILDREN
Aims: To work with a particular energy; to work with self-determination
Props: None
Music: Optional. Something slow and positive. None when you first start
Numbers: Small groups of 6 - 8. Bigger groups where necessary

Activity:

Invite the children to sit, lie or kneel on the floor and to see how they want to move down there. In particular, show them (or use a child to demonstrate) how they might pull themselves along or push themselves along in many different ways. Encourage them to use their strength to push and pull with hands, feet, shoulders, elbows, fingers, noses and so on.

Watch very carefully to see if any children resists using their strength, and if others get so excited they find it difficult to keep themselves safe. Let children watch each other and celebrate the differences amongst them. Use the I Saw, I Felt and I Imagined structure if you want children to talk about what they saw and what they felt. (Pages 193 - 196)

Movement Play Activities
Body balance

Age: CHILDREN
Aims: To explore new ways of moving
Props: Bean bags, sponges, small cushions
Music: Optional. Slow and stately
Numbers: Small groups of 6 - 8. Bigger groups where necessary

Activity:

Sitting on the floor, the children each choose a prop. Invite them to balance their chosen object on a particular part of their body - forearm, shoulder, back, tummy, head, ear and so on. Then ask them to move, in all the different ways they can, whilst balancing the beanbag in its original place.

Then try another part of the body. They will have to change the way they move for each different balance, sometimes lying down or slithering on their bellies.

Once they have done this part of the activity, ask them to put the object aside and move as if they were still balancing it.

When they have settled with this activity, see if they are willing to work with their eyes closed. Invite them to feel what the movement is like. Ask them to move lying down, sitting down or on all fours and only have a few children moving at once, to make sure that they are safe. Suggest they work slowly and crack their eyes open if they need to see.

Movement Play Activities
Dinner mat dances

Age: CHILDREN
Aims: To help children to work wholeheartedly - within restrictions
Props: None
Music: Optional. Lyrical and steady
Numbers: Small groups of 6 - 8. Bigger groups where necessary

Activity:

Use something flat, and about the same size as a dinner mat, for this activity. Each child is invited to sit, stand, kneel or lie on their dinner mat to begin. They can then move in any way thay want, as long as they don't leave the mat.

Give them time to explore, then encourage them to feel how they want to move, rather than to think it out.

Let children show each other the movement they have explored.

Hopping Home Backwards

16
Movement Activities Suitable For Circle Time

These activities all provide a focus for children to move in the centre of the circle whilst others watch. They support children's need to BE SEEN and AFFIRM SELF as well as ensuring that being watched is as ordinary as being listened to.

Hopping Home Backwards

Movement Play Activities

Circle Time
Dancing in the centre

Age: CHILDREN
Aims: To make 'being watched' as ordinary as being 'listened to'
Props: None
Music: Have one fast and one slow tape available
Numbers: The whole class or smaller groups

Activity:
Offer children the opportunity to move in the centre of the circle. Offer the following structure:

'Would you like to dance on your own or with me?' (For further guidance see pages 143 - 152.)'Would you like fast music or slow music?' Once the child has chosen, allow about three minutes for each one to move. Give a clear signal just before it is about to end. After the child has sat down, allow plenty of time to talk about the moving - letting the mover talk first, if they want to.

Encourage the watching children to focus carefully on the mover and to notice as much as they can. Let them know that they will be able to share what they have seen afterwards. Help the children to express what they have seen, noticing different types of moving and stillness, pattern, shape and body actions (jumping, hopping, skipping and so on). The more you are able to pick out different aspects of the movement, the more the children will learn about the variety of things there are to see in movement.

Movement Play Activities
Circle Time
Reasons for dancing in the centre

Age: CHILDREN
Aims: To make 'being watched' as ordinary as being 'listened to'
Props: None
Music: Have one fast and one slow tape available
Numbers: The whole class or smaller groups

Activity:

These are all suggestions for reasons children might want to dance in the centre. They are things that you can either suggest, or simply pick up on as they occur. It is exactly what you are already doing in News Time or Show and Tell. This simply acknowledges that movement is another way the children can mark and integrate life events, and let others know who they are.

Celebrating: the arrival of a new sister or brother; a new puppy; something special happening at the weekend.

Mourning: sadness for something lost, a pet perhaps.

Something particular about our bodies: a nasty splinter being removed that morning; a broken arm in a sling; a new hair cut.

Movement Play Activities
Circle Time
A structure for the watchers

Age: CHILDREN

Aims: To enable the watchers to structure what they see

             To bring attention to the ways in which people negotiate relationships

             To build emotional intelligence and maturity

Activity:

After a few 'go's when the watchers speak of anything that occurs to them, introduce them to the 'I saw, I felt, I imagined' structure. Explain that now they can speak about what they saw, what they imagined and what they felt as the child in the centre danced. When the movement is over, remind them of the structure and ask for responses. Ask three or four children for a response under each heading.

The adult's task is to keep the children focused. Encourage them to locate which bit of the movement inspired their imagination or feeling. 'When Sam spun round and round I imagined a Catherine Wheel on bonfire night' rather than just 'I imagined a Catherine Wheel'.

The hardest one is 'I Felt'. Try and encourage the children to work out how they felt as they watched, not what they thought the mover was feeling. This isn't easy but a valuable skill to acquire.

Remind movers that each watcher sees/remembers different bits, imagines different things and feels different things in response. And that none of these is necessarily what they thought about, or felt, as they moved.

Movement Play Activities
Circle Time
Ribbon sticks

Age: CHILDREN
Aims: To support different ways of moving; to support shy children who need
           a stronger focus to feel confident in the centre of the circle
Props: Two Ribbon Stick (handle and broad ribbon)
Music: Have one fast and one slow tape available
Numbers: The whole class or smaller groups

Activity:

Offer Ribbon Sticks (one or two) as a prop to move with in the centre. If possible, offer the child a choice of colour, and ask whether they would like fast or slow music. Don't offer to dance with them (the ribbon stick takes your place) unless they specifically request your presence. As always, let them dance for three or four minutes in the centre. Ask for feedback within the 'I Saw, I Felt, I Imagined' structure from the others.

Invite the mover to be in the centre; but some reticent children will only feel comfortable if they stay close to their place on the edge. They can send the ribbon fluttering into the middle, but stay near the edge themselves.

Talk about safety, as the ribbons might catch someone's face. As always, talk about the need to protect yourself if the ribbon flies near. Suggest that the watchers can hold a hand in front of their face if they feel anxious. Urge them all to be alert and take good care of themselves. Suggest the mover also notices the effect different movements have on others.

Movement Play Activities
Circle Time
Chair

Age: CHILDREN
Aims: To provide a focus for spontaneous movement in the centre
Props: A sturdy, well-balanced chair
Music: Have one fast and one slow tape available
Numbers: The whole class or smaller groups

Activity:
Put a chair in the centre of the circle. Invite children to make different shapes with the chair - lying on the seat and lifting their legs; crawling underneath; stretching out whilst holding the back and so on. Offer them fast music or slow music as a background if they want it. Let each child make three or four shapes. Invite the others to notice what they can about the shapes the mover makes. Ask for feedback at the end of the three shapes.

Encourage children to make a still shape each time so that the watchers can really see a precise shape. You may need to go into the centre to offer physical support, either if a child tries something quite risky, or if a child finds it very difficult to be still. Stress the need for careful attention to safety and be prepared to steady the chair if necessary.

Invite children to make shapes in pairs and in groups, each fitting around those who are already there.

When children are used to making still shapes, invite them to move continuously, with the chair as their focus. On, over, under, around ... as they wish.

Movement Play Activities
Circle Time
Big balloon

Age: CHILDREN
Aims: To provide a focus for spontaneous movement in the centre
Props: A large, helium strength balloon
Music: Have one fast and one slow tape available
Numbers: The whole class or smaller groups

Activity:
Offer a big balloon on a length of ribbon to move with. A balloon has a very light, airy quality and inspires particular kinds of moving. Offer fast or slow music. As always, allow three or four minutes to move and then ask for feedback from three or four watchers within the 'I Saw, I Felt, I Imagined' structure.

Be clear about the need to hold onto the balloon, otherwise the time is taken up with retrieving it from outside the circle.

Check first if anyone in the group is frightened of balloons as this can be a strong fear for some people.

Ask children not to sit or lie on the balloon or it might burst. Offer a big, soft ball as an alternative and let children choose the prop that suits their movement desires.

Movement Play Activities
Circle Time
Big ball

Age:	CHILDREN
Aims:	To provide a focus for spontaneous movement in the centre
Props:	A large physiotherapy ball or small, squashy blow-up ball
Music:	No music or slow music to begin with. If you have a child who really enjoys moving fast with the ball it would be wonderful to support it with fast music.
	You need to be sure that you can keep everyone safe first
Numbers:	Whole group, small group, or one to one

Activity:

Offer a Big Soft Ball to move with. These can be lain on, sat on and rolled over, as well as held. Offer fast or slow music. (In the early days of working with this prop you might choose to offer slow music only, to aid safety.) As always, give children three or four minutes to explore the movement possibilities of this round, squashy tough shape. Invite feedback within the 'I Saw, I Felt, I Imagined' structure.

Children respond very differently to this prop. Until you know how each might respond it is a good idea to be in the centre of the circle with each child to lend a steadying hand. Encourage them to explore what happens if they sit ... lie ... roll on it carefully, before they start moving fluently. Some children may need a lot of extra hands-on physical support from you before they feel comfortable with the ball's unpredictability. Some children will revel in the chance to take risks - to roll over, push along, bounce and so on. Talk about safety issues - the need to take care of other people and to protect yourself.

Movement Play Activities

Circle Time
Moving with a partner

Age: CHILDREN
Aims: To support learning about relationships; to celebrate friendships
Props: None
Music: Have one fast and one slow tape available
Numbers: Whole group, small group, or one to one

Activity:

When children are comfortable with moving on their own, offer them the opportunity to move with someone else in the circle. Nominate one child to be the Primary Mover. This child chooses their partner and the music - fast or slow. Make it clear that it is their dance that the other child is joining them. (This establishes a clear relationships from the start. You may wish to vary this in future by nominating two equal partners.) As always, allow the three or four minutes in the circle then ask for feedback from the watchers within the 'I Saw, I Felt, I Imagined' structure.

Children tackle this task in very different ways. Some will work closely with a partner straight away, mirroring and reflecting their movements. Others will hardly acknowledge the presence of the other person, each doing their own movements alongside one another. Some will do a bit of both.

Movement Play Activities
Circle Time
Seeing relationships

Aims: To enable the watchers to structure what they see
          To bring attention to the ways in which people negotiate relationships
          To build emotional intelligence and maturity

Activity:
This invites children to notice the way in which the movers work with one another.
Suggest they might look out for such things as who is leading?

- ○ does this person lead all the time, or does the leadership swap?
- ○ do they watch each other. and respond to each other, or are they working
  separately?
- ○ are they facing each other or are they side by side?
- ○ how do they negotiate the beginning and ending?

After a pair has moved in the centre, invite feedback.

If the children find it hard to engage with this at first, it is helpful if adults give lots of
feedback of the things they saw. This work can support young children's emerging
ability to share, lead and be led.

Movement Play Activities
Circle Time
Pair work with ribbon sticks

Age: CHILDREN
Aims: To support learning about relationships
Props: Four Ribbon Sticks
Music: Have one fast and one slow tape available
Numbers: Whole group, small group, or one to one

Activity:

Offer Ribbon Sticks as a prop to move with in the centre with a partner. Offer a choice of colour and a choice of fast or slow music. As always, give then three or four minutes to move in the centre of the circle. Invite response from the watchers.

Talk again about safety issues as now there are two sticks and ribbons to watch out for.

At the end, invite the movers to speak about their movement. Then invite watchers to say things that they have noticed, either within the 'I Saw, I Felt, I Imagined' structure, or about the way the two moved together.

Movement Play Activities

Circle Time
Pair work with a big balloon

Age: CHILDREN
Aims: To support learning about relationships; to bring attention to the centre
             of the body
Props: One big, helium strength balloon or a soft, squashy ball
Music: Have one fast and one slow tape available
Numbers: Whole group or a smaller group

Activity:

Offer a big balloon as a prop for working in a pair. Suggest that the balloon can be held between two bodies and rolled around. It stimulates very particular kinds of moving, often bringing children's attention to their centre, and a particular attention to the cooperation required to keep the ball between you. Offer fast or slow music. As always, give the movers three or four minutes in the centre and then ask for feedback.

In the early days of working with this prop you might choose to offer slow music only, to aid focus. As they become more familiar with it, faster music may be very challenging and exciting for those children who enjoy taking risks.

As balloons frighten some people, always check before bringing one to the session.

Small balloons don't work as well as the bigger ones. Ordinary strength pop too easily - helium strength balloons, or a squashy ball of the type you can blow up with a straw, are best.

Movement Play Activities
Circle Time
Sticks and straws

Age: CHILDREN
Aims: To support learning about relationships; to give strong visual feedback
of the relationship
Props: Four short pieces of chunky dowell or four thick drinking straws
Music: Have one fast and one slow tape available
Numbers: Whole group or a smaller group

Activity:
Offer Sticks or Straws as a focus for two people to dance in the centre. Each child
places one end of each stick against the palms of their hands, holding the sticks
between them. Then they move as they wish keeping the two sticks in place. Offer fast
or slow music - slow music is easier in the early days. As usual, allow three or four
minutes for moving in the centre and then ask for feedback.

It takes time to get used to the Sticks and early trials can be accompanied by the merry
clatter of falling sticks. Don't worry. Let the children know this might happen in advance
so that it won't be a problem.

If there are members of your group who present challenging behaviour and might feel
the urge to poke or prod with the Sticks, use drinking straws instead. Whichever you
use, always talk about safety issues before using them.

Movement Play Activities
Circle Time
Small elastics

Age: CHILDREN
Aims: To support learning about relationships
Props: 1 small elastic ring
Music: Have one fast and one slow tape available
Numbers: Whole group or a smaller group

Activity:
Offer a small elastic as a focus for two people to move in the centre. Two children hold the elastic with one or both hands and see how they want to move with it, and each other. Offer fast or slow music. As usual, allow three or four minutes for moving in the centre and then ask for feedback.

Some children will gain increased confidence from the prop and will want to explore leaning and balancing. If this is an issue for your group, you may need to be ready to go into the centre to give support to a child, or pair, who are experimenting in this way. Such experimentation can underpin the development of trust in self and in relationships with others. If a child can give their weight, they can trust.

Talk about safety when you first introduce this prop. It can twang and hurt. Check the elastic regularly to make sure that it is well stitched and not frayed.

A small elastic can also be used in a threesome as the children become more sophisticated in their negotiation of relationships.

Movement Play Activities
Circle Time
Small lycra square

Age: CHILDREN
Aims: To support learning about relationships
Props: 1 small lycra square
Music: Have one fast and one slow tape available
Numbers: Whole group or a smaller group

Activity:

Offer a small lycra square as a focus for moving with another person in the centre of the circle. Two children start by hold the lycra between them. They explore the possibilities suggested by the stretchy fabric. As usual, allow three or four minutes for moving in the centre and then ask for feedback.

Some children may use the lycra to pull on and to practice giving and taking weight. If you have group members who like taking risks, you may need to go into the centre to give added support.

Some children might like to disappear underneath the lycra - playing with being seen and not being seen.

Some children might like to use the lycra to give a firm body boundary, pulling it around their bodies. Used in this way it gives strong sensory feedback.

Movement Play Activities
Circle Time
Two in ... one out

Age: CHILDREN - five and up
Aims: To work in a fluid way within the group; to support spontaneous
            responses
Props: None
Music: Have one fast and one slow tape available
Numbers: Whole group or a smaller group

Activity:

This is a structure for a whole group to use in circle time, to be used when children are used to working in pairs and comfortable with moving in front of each other. Two children start in the centre. They move together as they choose. When one of the watchers sees something that they would like to try, they move into the circle, gently touch the child whose movement they want to do, and start to move. The 'tagged' mover returns to the circle of watchers.

Children can move in and out as they wish, as many times as they wish. Encourage children to let movers have a little time to settle before they are 'tagged'.

At any time, there should only be two movers in the centre. You may have to stop and sort this out from time to time, if enthusiasm gets the better of order.

17
Activities
Focusing On Image

These activities help children to become aware of, and make use of,

their ACTIVE IMAGINATION.

Hopping Home Backwards

Movement Play Activities
Watching and drawing

Age: CHILDREN
Aims: To enable children to externalise images through drawing
Props: Paper and crayons
Music: None
Numbers: Whole group or a smaller group

Activity:
Give each of the watchers a piece of paper and invite them to choose two crayons. Invite them to draw or doodle something about the moving as they watch it. This might be a pattern showing the movements the child in the centre makes, or it might be a doodle that captures the feel of the movement, or a picture that sums up what the watcher imagines as they watch, or simply lines and squiggles that seem, to the watcher, to match the mood of the dance. Invite a mover to choose a prop, music and maybe a partner, and let them dance for three to four minutes. Afterwards, look at the range of different kinds of drawing the watchers have done. Invite any of them to talk about what they have drawn.

If the watchers become restless with 'just' watching, this is a good way of giving them an active involvement. They may not want to talk about the drawings very much. Some may not even want to show them to the group. Pastel crayons give the liveliest textures and colours, but they do make a mess of carpets or clothes if they shed small pieces. If this is a worry, try sitting the children on sheets or lengths of brown paper (which are a bit noisy so it may be worth exploring their musical potential first).

Movement Play Activities

Talking about pictures in the mind's eye

Age: CHILDREN
Aims: To enable children to externalise images through talking
Props: None
Music: None
Numbers: Whole group or a smaller group

Activity:

Invite children to talk about their inner experience following Movement Play. Help them to focus on what have seen in their mind's eye - colours, pictures, personal 'videos' of things that have happened to them before, fantasies ...

Let children use their own language for this, rather than feeling they must find find the 'right' words. Often, their own words are more descriptive than plain action words. Sometimes, the children's words become familiar to the whole group, creating a kind of group language. If necessary, provide a glossary for visitors who are unfamiliar with these words.

Movement Play Activities

Word poems

Age: CHILDREN
Aims: To enable children to externalise images through writing
Props: Paper and pencil
Music: None
Numbers: Whole group or a smaller group

Activity:
Invite children to write down words that have occurred to them as they watch. They can write these words down in any way, and then see how they want to order them.

Invite them to read out their words to the mover who inspired them, and to the rest of the group.

They can draw alongside their words - creating fabulous material for wall displays.

18
Endings

Movement Play Activities
Endings
Passing a rub

Age: CHILDREN
Aims: To acknowledge each person, in movement and sensation, at the end
Props: None
Music: Optional. Very quiet
Numbers: Whole group or a smaller group

Activity:
With the children in a circle, their arms around each others' backs, invite one child to start off by gently rubbing the back of a child to one side of them. When this child feels the rub, they pass it on to the next person. Gradually, the rub is passed around each child until it gets back to the start.

It can be hard for young children to rub just one back, in which case they accidently pass the rub off in two directions at once. This might need some practice first.

Movement Play Activities

Endings
Circle close

Age: CHILDREN
Aims: To focus on the ending and parting
Props: None
Music: None
Numbers: Whole group or a smaller group

Activity:

With the children holding hands in a circle, invite everyone to look around at each other, then - very slowly - to bring the circle into the smallest space possible. This mirrors how close the group might have felt as they played together. When you are in a huddle in the centre, touching rather than seeing each other, you can speak of anything important that has come up in the session. Then, gradually let the circle open out, looking ahead to whatever comes next in the day. Finally, if there is room, stretch the circle so that the children can only just reach each other ... finally slipping apart and away.

Good Luck!

Hopping Home Backwards

BILIOGRAPHY

J. Amighi, S. Loman, P. Lewis, K.M. Sossin; *The meaning of movement: developmental and clinical perspectives of the Kestenberg Movement Profile* Gordon and Breach Publishers 1999

T. Bruce; *Early Childhood Education* Hodder & Stoughton 1997

S. Horton Fraleigh; *Dance and the Lived Body: A descriptive aesthetics* University of Pittsburgh Press 1987

J. Fisher; *Starting from the Child?* Open University Press 1996

H. Gardner; *Frames of mind. The theory of multiple intelligences* Fontana Press 1993

D. Juhan; *Job's Body - A handbook for bodyworkers* Station Hill Press 1987

C.G. Jung; *Jung on Active Imagination.* Key readings selected by Joan Chodorow Routledge 1997

E.B. Le Winn; *Human Neurological Organisation* Charles C Thomas Publishers 1969

A. Montagu; *Touching. The Human Significance of Skin* Harper and Row 1971

A. Olsen; *BodyStories. A guide to experiential anatomy* Station Hill Openings Barrytown Ltd 1998

P. Pallaro (Ed); *Authentic Movement. Essays by Mary Starks Whitehouse, Janet Adler and Joan Chodorow* Jessica Kingsley Publishers 1999

J. Panksepp; *Affective Neuroscience. The foundations of animal emotions* Oxford University Press 1998

B. Russell; *The ABC of Relativity* Harper Brothers 1925

S.B. Shapiro; *Dance, Power and Difference* Human Kinetics Publishers Inc. 1998

D.W. Winnicott; *The Child, The Family and The Outside World* Penguin 1964

D. Wood; *How children think and learn. The social contexts of cognitive development* Blackwell 1988

L. Wood and J. Attfield; *Play, Learning and the Early Childhood Curriculum* Paul Chapman Publishing 1996

Reports, Papers and Articles

B. Bainbridge Cohen; *The Alphabet of Movement Primitive reflexes, righting reactions and equilibrium responses Part 1* Contact Quarterly Sping - Summer 1989   Part 2 Contact Quarterly Fall 1989

B. Bainbridge Cohen; *Perceiving in An interview on the Developmental Process underlying perceptual-motor integration* Contact Quarterly Sping - Summer 1984

B. Bainbridge Cohen; *The training problems of the dancer* Contact Quarterly Spring - Summer 1982

Department for Education and Employment; *Curriculum guidance for the foundation stage* QCA 2000

B. Lamont; *Children who need help* Seattle Developmental Movement Centre

B. Lamont; *Early trauma and psychological health* Seattle Developmental Movement Centre

B. Lamont; *The Learning Process and Developmental Movement* Seattle Developmental Movement Centre

A. Mindell; *Moving the Dreambody. movement work in process oriented psychology* Contact Quarterly Volume 20 Winter - Spring 1995

National Advisory Committee on Creative and Cultural Education; *All Our Futures: Creativity, Culture and Education* May 1999

S. Scott; *But what is it that you do?* The Northwest Neurodevelopmental Training Centre Newsletter May 1997 Volume 8 Issue 4

M. Sontag; *Attention Deficit Disorder and Developmental Movement Therapy* Seattle Developmental Movement Centre

Contact Quarterly

Attributions

Howard Gardner - extract from *Frames of mind - the theory of multiple intelligences* reproduced with permission from Chatto and Windus.

Amy Mindell - extract from *Moving the dreambody* reproduced with permission from Amy Mindell.

Department of Education and Employment - extracts from *Curriculum guidance for the foundation stage 2000* reproduced with permission from QCA Enterprises Ltd.

Mary Starks Whitehouse - extract from *Creative expression in movement is language without words* reproduced with permission from Feather King.

D Winnicot - extract from *The child, the family and the outside world* reproduced with permission from Mark Paterson Associates.

Several other quotations have been used in this book. Every effort has been made to trace the copyright holders and obtain their permission for the use of copyright material. The author and publishers will gladly receive information enabling them to rectify any omission in subsequent editions.

Photographs

Penny Greenland and Phil Vaughan.

Other titles from JABADAO Publishing

What dancers do that other health workers don't ...
Miranda Tufnell, Penny Greenland, Sandy Crichton, Katy Dymoke, Richard Coaten
Ed Penny Greenland

Movement Play - a regular newsletter for early years workers
Ed Penny Greenland, Phil Vaughan

JABADAO Elderly Papers
Sandy Crichton, Penny Greenland, Tessa Perrin

Dancing down the Century
Ed John Eno Daynes, Penny Greenland

Bags of Ideas
JABADAO